F

I hope that this inspires some new ideas and insights into effective Sales management.

Keep ringing the bell!

Cmdr Pettes

Don't Fire Them,

▼

Fire Them Up

▼

Motivate Yourself and Your Team

FRANK PACETTA

with Roger Gittines

A Fireside Book
Published by Simon & Schuster
New York   London   Toronto   Sydney   Tokyo

FIRESIDE
Rockefeller Center
1230 Avenue of the Americas
New York, NY 10020

First Fireside Edition 1995

FIRESIDE and colophon are registered trademarks
of Simon & Schuster Inc.

Designed by Barbara Marks

Manufactured in the United States of America

13 15 17 19 20 18 16 14 12

Library of Congress Cataloging-in-Publication Data
Pacetta, Frank.
Don't fire them. fire them up : a maverick's guide to
motivating yourself and your team /
Frank Pacetta with Roger Gittines.
p. cm.
1. Success in business—Ohio—Cleveland—Case studies.
2. Employee motivation—Ohio—Cleveland—Case studies.
3. Work groups—Ohio—Cleveland—Case studies.
4. Xerox Corporation—Case studies.
I. Gittines, Roger. II. Title.
HF5386.P134   1994
658.3'14—dc20   93–34734   CIP

ISBN 0-671-86949-3
0-684-80050-0 (Pbk.)

ACKNOWLEDGMENTS

The best acknowledgment is a simple thank you. It's a good thing because I wouldn't know what else to say that would come any closer to expressing my gratitude for the support and encouragement I have received throughout this project. When I started, I had no idea that writing a book is a team effort. The job couldn't get done without the closest coordination, cooperation, and orchestration, involving dozens of skilled publishing professionals.

Having said that—and meant it—I want to add an important caveat: I am totally to blame for this enterprise. The buck stops with me. Ultimately, I never would have been asked to write a book if I hadn't been lucky enough to go to work for Xerox more than seventeen years ago. But Xerox is an innocent bystander. The views and opinions expressed herein are mine alone. My superiors have been kind enough not to object to references to Xerox policies, personalities, and procedures, but there is no implied or actual corporate imprimatur, endorsement, or authorization. The same goes for the men and women who supported me with such enthusiasm and devotion in Cleveland, Columbus, and other Xerox operations. What a great group of people! They deserve the praise for a job well done, and I'll accept any and all complaints.

I'm going to resist the temptation to start naming the names of those who did the impossible—transforming a copier salesman into an author. Well, maybe I'll succumb a little: Margret McBride, my literary agent; Bob Bender, my editor at Simon & Schuster; Julie Pacetta, my wife; and Roger Gittines, who hammered the rough ideas and the raw words into the finished product that you now hold in your hands. Those four easily qualify for the all-star list. There are many others, but I'll just salute one fine "winning" team with two words from the heart —thank you!

—F.P.

To Julie, my wife, for her unwavering support, love, and
  encouragement.
To my children, Frankie and Alle, who make every day a joy.
To my dad, the best role model you can have.
To Mom, who taught me about courage, love, and the
  importance of family.
To Carm, my sister, and #1 fan.
To Sam and Meg who have treated me as their own.
To Jane, Mary, Pat.
And to my brother, Joey—this one's for you.

CONTENTS

THE FIRST RULE

OF WAR AND BUSINESS

This isn't just a book, it's life—real life. Actually, real lives; those of approximately eighty men and women who were my colleagues at the Xerox district sales office in Cleveland, Ohio, from January of 1988 until the fall of 1992. Their lives during that period and the story that I have fashioned from the raw material of dreams and disappointments, successes and failures, amount to a report from the front lines of American business.

Yes—front lines. It's a war. And on one battlefield, at least, we fought and won after nearly being crushed by our adversaries.

You're going to be reading all about a business turnaround and a comeback. Good news for a change. Dramatic, romantic, maybe even inspiring stuff. But my purpose couldn't be more basic and practical: to demonstrate how we did it; how, in one year, Xerox's northeast Ohio district went from nearly dead last, in terms of sales and revenue, to first in the region and fourth nationally; and, most importantly, how it can be done in cities and towns all over America no matter what the industry or product line—despite the odds, despite ferocious domestic and international competition.

How really is the operative word. In every sense, this book is pure "how-to": how to rebuild from the ground up; how to lead and energize a demoralized organization; and how to create a winning team, put it back on top, and keep it there year after year. I'm going to share literally hundreds of tips and techniques that you can use immediately to supercharge your business organization, no matter whether you're riding the crest of a boom or wallowing in the trough of a bust. It's stuff that works.

A KID WITH AN ATTITUDE

The Cleveland district was a disaster area when I was promoted to sales manager, even though Xerox as a corporation under the innovative leadership of David T. Kearns had largely stopped the hemorrhaging and regained much of the strength lost in the 1970s and early 1980s. My bosses, therefore, weren't taking much of a risk by appointing a relatively untested 33-year-old, fresh from Minnesota (by way of Brooklyn and Queens), to run the show. If I screwed up, I wasn't going to do much damage.

Their faith in me probably rested squarely on the knowledge that the leader of a cleanup squad should know what it's like to make a mess. My early years at Xerox weren't pretty! I was the classic kid with a lot of potential who, although he pulled off a fair share of sizable business deals, was just going through the motions and relying on native talent. If I had been my boss, I would have fired me at several points along the way.

Fortunately, I hung on and matured. The occasional near-death experience taught me important lessons about management and leadership. I knew firsthand what it was like to goof off, to be poorly managed and motivated, and to conduct business without an adequate plan and follow-through. I knew vividly how *not* to manage. But I had also been lucky enough to undergo hundreds of hours of superb Xerox training and to be exposed to solid guidance from a few savvy mentors and superiors.

When I got to Cleveland I was ready. I knew all about failure. We were going to show the world that Cleveland was no hopeless backwater and that we could compete with anyone. I wasn't going to fail and neither was my new team.

HARD CORE

If I were a conventional narrator, I'd move along to a scene that opens with Frank Pacetta getting off the airplane from Minneapolis under a gray, midwestern winter sky. Instead, the scene is a small kitchen in a two-story, wood-frame white house with a big wraparound porch in Far Rockaway, a section of the borough of Queens in New York City. It's summer. I'm sixteen years old and embarrassed.

My dad, who was born in that house and still lives there today, has taped the final report card of the spring semester to the refrigerator door for all the world to see. He is announcing with this gesture that he's disappointed with his son. Very disappointed. There are C's on the report card, not the A's and B's I promised to deliver in return for permission to attend a Jesuit prep school in Brooklyn.

I had made a deal with him and then broken it. He was teaching me a lesson that I have never forgotten. It came down to four words that I'll use throughout this book: accountability, communication, expectation, and consequence. There it was, right on the door of that big Frigidaire—all summer long!

And so *this* is the opening scene of a book on marketing and sales, management and leadership? Indeed it is.

The core values that must drive successful businesses and businesspeople for the remainder of the decade and into the twenty-first century were as much a part of that kitchen as the pots and pans.

Everything we accomplished in Cleveland was a direct result of what I learned, not in kindergarten—with apologies to Robert Fulghum—but from my mother and father.

Hold on before you dismiss this as a lot of cornball nonsense. Today's hottest business theories acknowledge that people are a corporation's most precious asset. What's the linchpin of a service economy? You've got it—people. Furthermore, only people generate intellectual property: the ideas, the applications, the innovations that will be the lifeblood of future business success. Everything else is merely a commodity that can be purchased by anyone—including your competition—thereby destroying any temporary advantage gained by a technological edge or an ingenious process. Yet, we continue to manage these assets as though they were in fact the commodities: easy come, easy go. As of 1992, American companies spent a miserly 1½ percent of total payroll on employee training and education. Meanwhile, the process, the product, and the mechanics of the organization itself are given paramount importance. And they are important—but not as important as the right people in the right places, with the right skills, attitudes, motivation, and dedication.

Unless we begin to rediscover the practices and methodology of our best leaders and managers—including caring, responsible, loving parents—our vital business enterprises will continue to founder.

Don't get me wrong. I can kick backsides with the best of the Attila the Hun managers. We've all got businesses to run. But it takes more than brute force. The real challenge is to nurture people to bring them to their full potential as human beings and as business assets. There's nothing warm and fuzzy or touchy-feely about it. I'm talking about the difference between winning and losing! You win with people if you cherish them, develop them, and show them that you sincerely care about their success.

We either build trust, create loyalty, and generate enthusiasm, excitement, and teamwork, or step to the sidelines and watch history and the competition pass us by.

The worst-case scenarios don't have to happen, though. Not if we're bold enough to come out of hiding and cut down all the undergrowth that we've allowed to get in the way of essential interpersonal relationships in the name of "effective management." And I mean *all* of it: the selfish, thoughtless, mean-spirited, ego-driven, lazy, by-the-book nonsense that passes for management in many businesses today.

I've read the books and lived with their consequences, and I keep coming back to the gut feeling that there is a similar dynamic at work in successful businesses and happy families. Parents put themselves on the line for their children. They take risks, make themselves vulnerable, suffer disappointments. Hands-on, up close, they guide and they coach, they scold and they punish. The objective is to help the child be everything that he or she can be.

That's what this book is all a...
land I was determined to make all ...
They didn't deserve to be losers. I se...
they wanted to be. Along the way, we ...
place with the force of a gigantic magne...
work in the morning—who'd want to be an...
be a place where the atmosphere was electri...

We did it—I knew from the very first day ...
show you how to do it too. But first I want to w...
easy. You'll have to take risks and make mistakes,
ample temptation to slack off, to give orders inste...
to succumb to the do-as-I-say-not-as-I-do approach.

Being a leader is hard work; that's why there are s...
easier to hunker down behind a desk and be a second-gu...
an absentee landlord who allows his property to fall into ...
while blaming it on the tenants, the termites, or the tax ma...
anybody but his own negligence.

I'm going to show you exactly how demanding it is to be a
leader. Maybe I will scare some of my readers away from pursu-
ing a career in management. And if I do that, the long hours of
effort it took to write this book will be justified. I'm a very patient guy, but I have no patience for people who want to run
things just for the prestige and the big paycheck. They do a lot
of damage to other people's lives, not to mention crippling a
business organization.

I also want to show you the rewards. There's nothing quite
so satisfying as knowing that you've made a positive contribu-
tion to another person's career and the well-being of his or her
family. I made a difference to eighty-one men and women in
Cleveland. At times, I was overbearing and testy, but I can look
anyone in the eye and say I always tried to do what was fair and
what was right. I helped them grow, provide for their families,
have some fun. None of them will ever be satisfied with being
second-best. They'll always be intolerant of mediocre management. They'll be a solid asset to any team they join.

Stop. Go back to the last paragraph. Look at the third word
from the end of the last sentence. T-E-A-M. It's a fighting word,

16

papers than from business
onto a football field eve
out to motivate you
team-building ski
cans love to wa
ticipating in
team play
erator a
ing o

here's nothing like going out
and having your brains beat
leadership, management, and
thing is, though, while Ameri-
they're allergic to actually par-
put it bluntly, most of us are lousy
the lone wolf, the independent op-
dels. And we wonder why we're hav-
en days a week.

er Bowl, not coaches or quarterbacks.
sson taken hold? It's not as if people
on. The largest TV audience in history
'93. The picture, however, was deceptive
s only that one game, not the hundreds of
ng effort on the practice field, the endless
the coaches—part tyrant, part shrink, part
ioning a bunch of big, strong, talented guys
onger, more talented organization.

hat about the man with the golden twenty-mil-
m? What about the 49ers in 1987? Joe Montana on
25-yard line, with two seconds left to play and a six-
deficit, guns it to Jerry Rice in the end zone to win the
game.

What about it? It's time to grow up. The cowboy culture gives Americans a lot of pleasure, but it's a myth. Maybe you can sell cigarettes to teenagers with it; for copiers, jet airplanes, microchips, biotechnology—you name the product—we're going to need reality, not mythology. And reality is teamwork.

If that's what you want, you've come to the right place. If not, take this book back where you got it and maybe they'll refund your money. I'm going to be teaching and preaching teamwork. Seriously. I've got to be completely up-front; otherwise I'm wasting my time and yours.

I want to bury the notion that teamwork means a few free-wheeling superstars setting records, on the one hand, and a bunch of weak, mediocre, uncoordinated, demoralized drones shuffling papers, on the other; sort of the "go-getters" and the "no-getters." That's not a team; that's an accident waiting to happen—and it will happen sooner or later.

Seeing the world down the barrel of the cowboy's Colt .45

six-shooter is a foolish and self-defeating habit. The genesis of this book, as a matter of fact, confirms it. In September of 1991, *The Wall Street Journal* published a front-page feature reporting on the turnaround in Xerox's Cleveland district sales office. The article opened with a quick summary of the problems that had developed: poor morale, a shrinking customer base, inroads made by the Japanese. Some employees were described as wondering aloud whether anyone would take the top sales manager's job.

Trouble in Dodge City. But wait! Who's that astride a white horse, wearing a white hat, ready to kill or be killed? It's high noon and Frank Pacetta has ridden into town.

I was described as a "can-do whiz kid," a "maverick manager," a "taskmaster who evokes both love and fear in his employees." Incredible! I got a stack of mail a couple of feet high thanks to that bit of creative writing. Many of my well-wishers read between the lines and realized what had really happened in Cleveland. Others drew the wrong conclusion. They decided I was a gunslinger. One of my Xerox colleagues, who had never met me or worked with me or checked with people who had, wrote to corporate headquarters to say that she felt that I was an embarrassment to her and the company.

The experience taught me a valuable lesson. For one thing, I now know that success does not speak for itself. Even *The Wall Street Journal*'s well-intentioned effort to report on our turnaround ended up missing the point. Why? I think it goes right back to the tendency to put success and failure in an exclusive context of individual effort. In either case, we round up the usual suspects: the good guy who works miracles, the bad guy who wrecked everything.

The *Journal* writer decided I was ten feet tall and, while I didn't walk on water, I walked over people to get the job done. He was wrong. I'm not and I don't.

Jobs never get done, or at least stay done, at the expense of people. What happened in Cleveland proves it. The district had lost focus and intensity. Expectations were low; there was no one to pick up a rep when he or she was down, or to give a jolt to those who needed it. There was an absence of leadership. Leaders coach and motivate. It simply wasn't happening.

When I got there, I found men and women who had come

to terms with being losers. They accepted it. In their view, Cleveland amounted to a deep hole, a mass grave; they were stuck at the bottom and there was nothing to be done about it. I didn't have to be miracle worker. I just jumped in there and let everyone know that we were going to climb out together as a team and fill in that hole one shovelful at a time—then we were going to build a mountain.

THE MANAGER AND THE MANAGED

In the pages ahead I will guide you through the process I used. There will be chapters on leadership, communications, motivation, building teamwork, and the other nuts-and-bolts aspects of managing and selling, interwoven with incidents and episodes from our success story in Cleveland. I'm going to give you a front-row seat. You'll be there for our high-powered product launches; the monthly outlook sessions; the done deals that suddenly go sour and have to be saved with snap decisions, improvisation, and guts. You'll see the importance of empowerment, of ruthlessly examining every assumption, of destroying all the hiding places, and of demanding total accountability.

In designing the book, I decided that business readers fall into two basic types: those who want a no-fooling-around "repair manual," and those who are interested in case histories and a story line within which ideas are presented and developed. The last chapter is pure repair manual. If you're out for a quick hit of tips and techniques, that's where you want to go right away. When something strikes your fancy, turn to the appropriate chapter for elaboration. On the other hand, there's much to be gained by starting at the beginning and reading to the end. It will be helpful to see how these leadership and management concepts worked in real-world situations.

Despite the sales and management decor, this is a book for anybody who works for a living. I don't care in what occupation or industry, there's something for the manager and something else for the managed. I'm particularly interested in reaching salespeople, but you don't need to be directly involved in sales. I agree with the old-time religion that all of us, whether we know it or not, are salespeople. Whether you put a foot in the door or your feet on the desk, about the only qualification needed to get the most out of this book is the ability to recognize that success depends on how well you satisfy the customer. And don't kid yourself, we've *all* got them. If you're a parent, tiptoe in and kiss your little customer goodnight. If you're an R&D engineer, shake hands with your customer the service rep. If you're a teacher getting sassed by a student, your customer is talking to you.

Customers. If we take good care of them, they take good care of us.

A License to Steal

I'd hate to think that I had written a book I wouldn't read myself. The fastest way to turn me off as a reader is to show me a pie chart or bar graph. I hate baselines unless they run between third base and home plate. So there will be none of that. The emphasis is on usable information; cash-and-carry, take-away stuff. I hope that at the end of each paragraph you'll put the book down and go do it. Rip the pages out and post them on the bulletin board. Send them anonymously through the interoffice mail to a boss who needs reminding that leaders lead from the front, not the rear. Please, steal my ideas. They usually work.

I say "usually" because I'm deeply suspicious of perfection. Books go right back onto the shelf the moment I see idiotproof concepts being presented. There's no such thing. I'll tell you what doesn't work and the mistakes that I've made. My feeling is that if I haven't made a mistake today, I'm not taking any risks; if I'm not taking risks, I'm not taking myself to the next highest level of the game. Therefore, I have included incidents and episodes that prove conclusively I'm no genius.

You've probably also figured out by now that I'm not afraid of being considered an oddball or of being regarded as compulsive about some things. If hating to lose is odd, I guess I'm guilty as charged. I loathe it. But I actually don't think I'm odd at all. Thriving on competition, struggling to achieve one's full potential, setting tough goals and achieving them, are bedrock human characteristics.

If you've come to this book without the will to win—if it's genuinely absent—you're the oddball, not me. Chances are the will to win is still flickering even in the most jaded person, re-gardless of all the disappointments, defeats, and the not-so-help-ful advice "to keep things in perspective."

In fact, what I did in Cleveland (and will do in this book) was to put winning in perspective. And, for that matter, why wait? Perspective coming right up! It's all about winning. You'll see that phrase again and again in the pages ahead. Winning is the ultimate driving force, as ancient as Cain and Abel, as rele-vant as General George Patton's first rule of war: kill the other guy before the other guy kills you.

For me, it's not much of a stretch to paraphrase Patton: beat the other guy to the sale before the other guy beats you.

Why?

It feels great! Come on. I'll show you what I mean.

1

▼

MAKING A STATEMENT:

THE LAST SHALL BE FIRST

Cleveland gets a bad rap. As a city, it's the butt of snide jokes and gibes. But having spent four years in Dayton, Ohio, as an undergraduate at the University of Dayton and another ten working for Xerox in the Columbus area, I knew there was more to Cleveland than a river that used to catch fire and a baseball team that wouldn't.

Unlike some of my colleagues, who refused to consider a promotion and a transfer to Cleveland to run the district sales office, I jumped at the chance. Their reluctance stemmed in part from a misperception that they'd have to undergo a sacrifice of lifestyle to move to the "rust belt"; and they were wary of taking on a job that was widely regarded around Xerox as Mission Impossible. It wasn't that I was bolder or more visionary. The fact was, I would have gone *anywhere* for a chance to run my own show. I was prepared, confident, and determined to succeed.

Having said that, let me add that I had no idea what I was getting into. First, I agreed to leave my position as a district sales manager in Minneapolis (the number two position at that time) and only then did I thoroughly investigate the situation in Cleveland. Talk about leaping before you look.

Even so, had I done hours of research in advance, I still would have eagerly accepted the assignment. Theoretically, the Cleveland office should have been able to run neck-and-neck with any other Xerox operation in a comparable metropolitan area. It was doing about $56 million in revenue. With a central city population on the order of 500,000 people, and responsibility for much of northeastern Ohio as well, we should have been at least keeping abreast of places like Columbus and Cincinnati. Theoretically.

At that moment, though, of the eleven sales districts in Ohio, and sixty-five nationwide, Cleveland was dragging along near the bottom. I later learned that its reputation had sunk so low that in the mid-1980s when Xerox began pushing "Leadership Through Quality," the formula that brought the corporation back from the brink of death, major customers in Cleveland thought it was a big joke. Looking back, one of them acidly commented that our marketing strategy was to "sell by confusion."

When I got a look at the data, all the indices that I checked showed that the district richly deserved its infamy as a basket case.* Even so, I spent my last days in Minneapolis planning ways to create a game plan and a mind-set that would put Cleveland back on top in the midwestern region and into national competition with bigger districts like Chicago, Atlanta, Boston, and Denver. Raising the bar—my favorite expression—had begun, and I hadn't even set foot in the office yet!

MAKE CHANGES IMMEDIATELY

I believe in the power of personal example. You can rant and rave and threaten, but the most effective way to get results is to show someone what you want done. On my first day in Cleveland it was clear that I had to reestablish the work ethic. I had reps and managers camped out in the coffee shop on the ground floor of our building at ten or eleven o'clock in the morning. I imme-

---

* I'm referring here to the sales operation. I have nothing but praise for my two management partners, Tom Bill and Tom Haywood, who respectively ran administration and service with dedication and skill. They deserve equal shares of the credit for nursing Cleveland back to health.

diately put the place off limits. Not by posting a "Keep Out!" sign, but by making it perfectly clear that a long, leisurely breakfast was a thing of the past.

I was at my desk the first day—and every day—by 7:00 A.M. The management staff didn't have to be charter members of Mensa, the society of geniuses, to know that it made sense for them to roll in at about the same time. The reps who reported to them quickly got the picture, too. The office was up and running by 7:30 A.M. Anyone lingering in the coffee shop had to be afflicted with suicidal tendencies.

And that's an important point that must be made right here. The new manager doesn't need to arrive on the scene with a sharp ax and a chopping block. No matter how shaky the operation, the first order of business is to start *doing business* again. A reign of terror, an immediate housecleaning, is only going to get in the way of that objective. Set a blistering pace at the outset and there will be no confusion as to what each person needs to do to keep his or her job. When there is no ambiguity— and no alternative—people usually either get with the program or select themselves out. The house cleans itself.

Here's tip number one, so get out your highlighter pen: Come in and make a statement. Put a stake in the ground with a can-do attitude that has no gray area whatsoever. The cavalry used to arrive with flags flying and bugles blowing. *You* are the cavalry.

It's a matter of leadership. My working assumption is that everyone wants to succeed. It makes sense, doesn't it? But why don't they succeed? There are three reasons: deficiency of skills, lack of desire, or poor leadership. Many times—probably most of the time—it's poor leadership. That's why on a sports team, when there's a losing streak, the coach gets fired, not the players. The players have the skills and the desire, otherwise they wouldn't have made the cut; what's missing is the direction, the coordination, the motivation that can only be provided by a leader. Making a statement early—and I'm talking about an actions-speak-louder-than-words statement—puts everyone on notice that the leadership vacuum has been filled. In itself, that's powerful and reassuring news. Even more important, though, is the central message of this truism—if you don't know where you're going, you'll never get there. Troubled organizations don't have the faintest idea where they're going, and the uncertainty is corrosive.

Whether you see yourself as a coach or the cavalry, tell 'em where they're headed! That's job one.

A CHOICE AND A CHANCE

By getting off to a fast start in Cleveland, I was providing leadership and a basic level of motivation, which amounted to "The train is leaving the station. Get on board or get left behind; the choice is up to you."

This can't be a bluff or flashy and meaningless rhetoric, because the skeptics will opt to wait and see whether you're serious. The train can't leave tomorrow or next week; it's got to begin pulling out the moment you set foot on board.

Those who have climbed aboard will immediately be demonstrating whether or not their skills are up to the task. The longer the startup is delayed, the longer it will be before you as a manager and leader really have a complete understanding of the resources at your disposal.

If I've inherited the gang that couldn't shoot straight, the first thing I'm going to do is hold a little target practice. I want to know what I have to work with, and I want to know immediately! Training, guidance, extra supervision can all be applied— that's what a leader is there for—but not if I'm just guessing about who can hack it and who can't.

I can't stress it enough. Get a fast start.

BACK TO THE FUTURE

On day one in Cleveland, I scheduled a meeting of the entire sales operation. We had a small auditorium set up like an amphitheater in the lower level of our building that suited the purpose exactly. I wanted everyone to get the same message at the same time.

It was great to be back in Ohio again. I was so pumped up I couldn't sleep the night before. If nothing else, I wanted the group to leave the room feeling the same way. And I wanted them focused on these key points:

- Change was already happening.
- Expectations were set.
- Nonsense was out.
- The work ethic and the customer were in.
- People were going to enjoy working in Cleveland.
- We would be tough but fair.

There were forty-four people on hand, the entire sales and sales support operation; all the seats were full. The sales management team stood together against one wall, looking like the receiving end of a firing squad or a police lineup. The imagery was unfortunate since they were the sales managers who would be running the seven individual teams of account and sales reps; in effect, my combat platoon leaders.

Aside from brief one-on-one conversations with the managers, I had avoided holding separate meetings that excluded the troops. At that stage, it would have been a mistake to work within any sort of hierarchy. Trickle-down communications guarantee confusion and misunderstanding. Don't use intermediaries; keep the lines of communication short and simple.

Going into the meeting, the atmosphere was definitely tense and apprehensive. Even those who had been performing up to par were worried. Those who hadn't were having a very bad morning indeed. The whole group knew why I was there. Or at least, they thought they did.

The first order of business was to recognize the heroes. It is *always* the number one item on the agenda when I open a meeting. What's the point of breaking your butt if nobody notices? Twelve reps out of thirty-four had achieved their sales goals the previous year. Overall, it was a rotten record, but those twelve deserved to be commended. Ignoring their success would have been a major blunder. Praise doesn't cost anything and it yields big dividends. A paycheck, no matter how large, isn't enough.

If you're a manager and haven't thanked one of your people for doing a good job today, you either have a seriously ill organization on your hands—one that doesn't merit any kind of praise, which I doubt—or you're cheating those people, ripping off assets that they've worked hard to acquire. So put the book down and go out into the office, or pick up the phone if you're home or on the road, and tell someone that he or she did a good job and that you appreciate the effort.

Don't be surprised if they're surprised. My people certainly were. They weren't expecting those few minutes of recognition at the meeting. The culture of failure was so well established that even the winners saw themselves in a negative light. I asked for a round of applause. I wanted everyone to get a taste of how good it feels to win. When the applause died down, I stood there for a moment in silence. Then, without a podium or notes, I began to run through the statistics to establish that the Cleveland district sales office's performance had been poor for the better part of three years.

The figures were grim. One set in particular spoke volumes. It showed that the average order rate per rep was the lowest in the region, even though Cleveland was nowhere near the smallest district. The ranking was close to the bottom nationwide, as well. I'd gone back and benchmarked several districts to track how well they were doing in other categories and products. In each case, these comparisons revealed that Cleveland lagged far behind.

Then I told them, "That's history. That was yesterday." I wanted to establish two things: first, those people who had worked hard and done a good job, despite the overall showing, were not going to be lumped in with those who had done poorly; and second, I needed to demonstrate that redemption was not only a religious doctrine. Each of them had a second chance. All they had to do was reach out and take it.

"I expect each of you to pay the rent every month," I said. They knew what I was talking about. Xerox top management sets a minimum level of business—we call it a plan—that they anticipate from the seven regions and the roughly eight or nine districts that comprise each of them. Most regions, I should note, are geographic entities—northeast, southwest, midwest, etc.— although, in some cases, special regions that have nothing to do with location are set up to allow for test marketing or special projects. In either case, allocation of the plan is based on the district's performance over the previous three years, but the regional vice president is permitted to do a little fine-tuning to account for a district's unique circumstances. Once that happens, the plan is apportioned among the various management teams based on the number of existing accounts and likely prospects for new business. The plan is the basis for the reps' compensation. If they beat it, there are bonuses commensurate with the percentage of the extra margin. If they fall short, IOUs come due and the draws that have been paid out must be reimbursed depending on the size of the deficit. When the system works right, with all involved participating in drafting a fair plan, it accurately reflects a district's potential sales, rather than imposing an artificial quota.

By referring to achieving the plan as "paying the rent," I was signaling that from then on, just as every family has a budget that must be met each month to put food on the table and keep a roof overhead, there would be no room for reps and managers who didn't cover their share of the budget.

I announced that each manager would sign a binding contract with me committing him or her to a specific bottom-line figure and a course of action to achieve it in the next year. Then the reps would work with the managers to develop contracts of their own to insure that each team would make good on its promises.

Achieving the plan is like paying a cover charge at a fancy nightclub. You get in the front door, but to buy a few drinks and a steak dinner takes additional cash. The shrimp cocktail, the noisemakers, and the funny hats are all extra. Just making plan isn't enough. The object is to beat the plan to advance beyond a meager subsistence existence.

The system won't work, however, if management panics and imposes unrealistic expectations on a district. A classic error is to rely on past performance. Conditions in today's marketplace change rapidly. Booms can flatten out and bust within a matter of weeks. If you're not paying attention, or living in a dream world, the wake-up call comes in the form of hardworking managers and reps who are wildly undershooting their plans through no fault of their own. Since compensation is based on achieving the plan, and exceeding it, the salespeople end up being deeply frustrated and demoralized.

Conversely, writing off a seemingly lackluster territory as a perennial loser doesn't take into account long-dormant business conditions that may be on the verge of blossoming again. To escape both of these traps, I've learned to be a statistical sponge. I want to know everything about the area in which I'm doing business; raw data, anecdotal evidence, analysis, gossip, even educated guesswork by the right people.

That's how, as I stood in front of the group, I knew that I was not asking the impossible. One look at the record told me that my new reps were not keeping pace with their peers in other districts in terms of the number of customer calls. They weren't getting out in front of the decision makers, and consequently, they weren't writing the business.

My rule is that if it is being done elsewhere, we can do it too and do it better. Cleveland's poor performance didn't have anything to do with inflated expectations. The opposite was true. Nobody was saying to the operation, "Just go do it! Just go do what they're doing in your sister districts!"

Salespeople are glib. That's why they've been hired. They can come up with a million reasons to explain why the deals aren't happening. Listen to them. Listen hard. Then look around at what other people are actually *doing*. Call a major account and ask when was the last time he or she heard from one of the competition's reps. Last week? Was your person in there last week? No. How long has it been? My feeling is that if the competition can work the block, so can we.

Xerox has a corrective-action program that I'll talk about later. It's very effective as a tool for catching and correcting substandard performance before the roof falls in. Yet, there were several people in Cleveland who had failed to make their plan for two or three years without being put into the corrective-action process. When I got there only one guy was on corrective action. One!

Does that tell you something? It told me that whatever the level of expectation—inflated or deflated—there were no consequences for failure. As a result, missing the plan was no big deal. If the boss doesn't care, why should they?

THE DEADLY BLAME GAME

What surprised me was that by January of 1988, when I arrived in Cleveland, the Leadership Through Quality (LTQ) Movement had really begun to take hold elsewhere at Xerox. It was no joke. In many ways Cleveland's performance was atypical, almost a throwback to the bad old days. The Japanese were gobbling up the business at the low end by offering cheap, reasonably reliable copiers that robbed us of significant portions of our market share. At the high end, Eastman Kodak was hammering away at an immensely profitable product line that until just a few years before had been our exclusive preserve. Cleveland's customers, large and small, were bailing out. They were sick of the erratic service and the headaches.

In turn, the account and marketing reps were mired in despair. There were a few stars, but most were running on autopilot and the plane was losing altitude fast.

Why? In a word, excuses.

Failure was somebody else's fault. The people in the Cleveland office saw themselves as victims of circumstances beyond their control. The workers blamed management; management blamed the workers. Together they faulted Xerox, the Japanese, the economy, even the city of Cleveland itself (not to mention Akron and Youngstown and Lorain).

Meanwhile, however, other districts were doing just fine. One difference was that aspects of LTQ were actually being implemented. Starting in 1982, when our CEO, David Kearns, decided that Xerox was headed for oblivion unless it reinvented itself, there had been a dramatic internal revolution. Gone was the poisonous attitude that a copier was a cranky, complicated piece of equipment that was prone to breaking down, costing a lot of money, and causing aggravation—and the customer would just have to learn to live with it.

Kearns was heavily influenced by the ideas of management gurus W. Edwards Deming, Joseph Juran, and Philip B. Crosby. He pushed, pulled, and prodded Xerox until a new definition of quality emerged that emphasized customer expectations and requirements as driving forces. To put it plainly, if customers had a choice of suppliers—and with the arrival of the Japanese on the scene that certainly was the case—the business would go to those who accurately identified and delivered what it was that really motivated the customer to purchase a particular product. Was it convenience? A low price? Cutting-edge technology? None of the above? All of the above?

This ongoing multiple-choice quiz challenges existing management practices by decreeing that those who get a passing grade today may well flunk out tomorrow if they do not continually monitor and satisfy customer requirements—requirements that are constantly evolving in reaction to emerging technology and the changing marketplace.

Sounds simple. Yet LTQ and the generic quality movement as a whole are ruthless toward those who are uncomfortable living outside the status quo. It's one thing to talk about the need for constant change, improvement, and responsiveness to the customer—and there was a lot of talk in Cleveland and in other parts of Xerox—but another thing to actually live that way day after day. To many managers, LTQ was the equivalent of being a high-flying circus trapeze artist doing triple somersaults without a safety net.

My job in Cleveland was first to take down the net. Second was to reintroduce the triple somersault to their repertory through personal example. Third was to kick them off the perch.

REVERSING THE DOWNWARD SPIRAL

In some ways, Xerox handles marketing the way a wise combat commander conducts a firefight. If your troopers can't hold the ground, pull back to a defensible perimeter where you can reorganize and launch a counterattack. Cleveland's plan had been adjusted downward to provide achievable goals. And still the targets were being missed.

The same competent combat commander, the one who is willing to beat a strategic retreat, knows he'll soon have his back to the wall if he can't demand and enforce a minimum level of performance, like keeping weapons clean to avoid misfires. Before falling back again, he orders his NCOs to start inspecting. He inspects weapons himself.

What I'm doing when studying the statistics or contacting

a major account is the equivalent of a weapons check. It's one thing if you're fighting like hell and still getting whacked; another if you don't even bother to load and lock. As a leader and manager you've got to find out what's going on and let everyone know exactly what has to be done to get back in the fight.

But that could take weeks, right?

No. I had a good sense of what needed to be done before I hit Cleveland. Working for Xerox helped, because the corporation keeps good records and believes in the value of statistical analysis, which is one of the key principles of Deming's version of the quality movement. If your company doesn't adhere to this practice, then in order to avoid the hazards of flying blind get on the phone and start asking this question: "What's wrong and how can you and I fix it?"

You'll get an earful from your customers. They know what's wrong. Outside suppliers of goods and services to your operation can also be helpful. Some of them have studied its strengths and weaknesses for years. Most will gladly share the information because your success is their success.

Start doing this homework before you take charge, otherwise you'll be sitting in the office studying your navel. When I walked in there, I knew the Achilles' heel of the district and had a good knowledge of each rep's performance. I wanted to show the importance of preparation no matter what the event. Sales is basically a three-step process. First, you have to identify the prospective customer; second, develop and convincingly present a proposal that will meet the customer's needs; and third, ask for the business. It all starts with preparation.

Here's what I did. I announced at the meeting that starting immediately, everyone, with the exception of analysts and other support staff, would turn in a weekly calendar to my assistant, Renée Smith, showing four sales calls a day. Everyone—including Frank Pacetta.

I didn't demand four orders; the requirement was four calls a day. There were a few people who could do four calls in their sleep. But for the majority it was a different story. Coming up with four new names on Monday wouldn't be a real problem. Tuesday was probably going to be okay. Wednesday would be harder. By Thursday and Friday there'd be considerable stress and strain. I wanted to jump-start productivity. What they had been doing up until that point wasn't working. I needed to get the achievers onto their tiptoes, and prod the others to at least stand up and fight.

This was not merely an academic exercise. Here's tip number two: Never assume anything. I had a hunch that the basic day-to-day sales calls were not taking place. It was time to dig in. I was literally beginning at the beginning by challenging the most basic assumption of all. The requirement forced the managers and reps to get organized and start planning. As I said, of the three basic elements of sales, the first is to identify the prospective customer. To do that, reps would need to take a hard look at their territories instead of simply reacting opportunistically to whatever happened to come along. The low order and demonstration rates suggested that the crop failure was caused by not putting enough seed in the ground. Maybe that wasn't Cleveland's problem, and if it wasn't, I would see immediately that the hitch was occurring later in the cycle. At the rate of four calls a day—twenty a week times forty-four salespeople—we'd soon be up to our eyeballs in prospective customers. And everybody in the room knew it.

DUMB QUESTIONS, SMART ANSWERS

I told them that I was going to look at their calendars and that I'd be around to ask each of them how the calls had gone. Pigpen, the disheveled character in the comic strip "Peanuts," lives under a perpetual cloud of dust. I have a swarm of question marks buzzing around me at all times, as my new district was beginning to discover. "How'd the customer react to the new product?" "Did you ask them in for a demonstration?" "How long until you crack the account?"

Questions, questions, questions. I'm reminded of the axiom "Ask me no questions and I'll tell you no lies." I can reverse it: Answer my questions and I'll tell you the truth. Don't be afraid to ask questions. Sure, some people won't level with you. But the more you ask, the more you're able to evaluate the veracity of what you're hearing. Some executives believe that if they ask questions their subordinates will assume that they are not on top of the job. It intimidates them into silence—and ignorance. There's only one stupid question, and it's the one you needed to ask and didn't.

Historians report that Napoleon would arrive at a meeting or to inspect one of his units as the dumbest man there. He would proceed to ask questions by the dozens. He was never afraid to show lack of knowledge. When the meeting was over and Napoleon departed, he departed the smartest man on the scene, having absorbed everyone else's expertise.

I use questions, not only for their information value, but as a means to impose consequences. Remember, if there are no consequences for failing to achieve minimum standards, then those standards will not be met. In the case of the calendars, the question and consequence sequence goes like this:

"Why didn't you turn in your calendar yesterday?"

"Sorry, Frank, I got busy real early and didn't get around to it."

"Busy with what?"

"Uh, the Masterson Company account is starting to show signs of life."

"Great! In what way?"

"I got in to see one of the key guys unexpectedly."

"Who was that?

"Gerald Tyce."

"Is he interested?"

"Sort of, but he's not ready to go for anything yet."

"Set up a meeting for next week and I'll ride down there with you and see if I can help out."

Checkmate. Perhaps I was being told the truth to begin with. Perhaps not. In either case, being a pest with all those questions put me in a position, one, to know the truth about my rep, and two, to offer my support to develop and close a potential deal.

There was a consequence for the rep. He hadn't turned in his calendar and had to undergo a grilling from me. That was probably bad enough. If he was telling the truth, he realized immediately that in the future he'd be better off turning in the calendar rather than undergoing another third degree. If he wasn't, the charade put him perilously far out on a limb. Before

I sawed it off, he would need to goose the Masterson account or generate some other piece of business. What's more, next week's calendar was more than likely to be on my desk right on time.

I expect and I inspect. A manager who doesn't is headed for trouble. The purpose of my first meeting in Cleveland was to lay out in the clearest, most straightforward fashion exactly what I expected. I don't want my people guessing. They'll get it wrong and it's not fair to them. In turn, my managers realized what I was doing and adopted the expect-inspect technique themselves. By cascading these lessons downward, you get everyone moving in the same direction.

I told the group that based on the record, they had lost the work ethic. We were going to rediscover it.

The time for doing business was 9:00 A.M. to 5:00 P.M. By that I meant doing business with the customer face-to-face. We were going to be out of the office during those hours. Preparation time, paperwork, team meetings, were all to be slotted before 8:30 A.M. or after 5:00 P.M.

All too often support functions get in the way of business. The job is to sell copiers, printing systems, and other products. Anything that interferes should be eliminated.

Like the calendars, that expectation was a way to jump-start the process. As a district manager, an office full of efficient bureaucrats is useless to me. Catching up on paperwork is an all-purpose excuse that takes salespeople out of the field. Even the best reps welcome the opportunity to burrow in and hide out. Sales can be grueling work. Nobody likes being told "... sorry," "... come back later," "... try next month"; the words vary, but it's still rejection, and you hear it day after day. Pretty soon a pile of paperwork begins to look good.

By restricting administrative and prep-work to the early morning or evening hours, I was also combating Parkinson's Law, which dictates that the work expands to fit the time available. If I'm going to have to use my personal time to fill out forms or prepare reports, you can bet I'm going to be a model of efficiency and speed.

STRAIGHT TALK

As I spoke, I had been clutching a black knitted ski cap in my left hand. I held it up so they could see the logo of a popular New York State resort. "This is where we're headed next year," I said. "I want all of you to join me there to celebrate. We're going to have one tremendous blowout. And you're going to deserve it because we're going to be back on top, where we belong." The ski cap was a symbol of the vision—Cleveland the number one district—and I carried that damned cap to every meeting that year.

Find some symbols and use them. When I brought that cap out, people knew what it meant without my having to say a word. And that cap was a little reminder of the way I work as a leader: those who give shall receive.

It's a lesson I will drive home in dozens of different ways throughout this book. I really do believe in asking "What have you done for me lately?" A rep or a manager could have been an outstanding performer last week or last month. But if it isn't happening today, it isn't happening. By the same token, he or she has a right to hold me to the identical standard. The ski cap symbolized that two-way commitment. Every time it appeared, it confirmed that I hadn't forgotten my promise or my expectations.

The trip to the ski resort was to be a payoff for what I knew was going to be several months of hard work. I made certain the staff understood what was coming—good and bad. Changes were going to be made. The pace would be blistering. I couldn't guarantee that all of them would make it. I promised to work with them, train them, support them in every way. There would be a relentless pursuit of excellence.

The group didn't realize at the time—it does now!—that the ski trip was a window into my soul. I love to party, play air guitar, and sing the words to "American Pie." Although I was over thirty years old at the time, I was, and still am, a rock-and-roll rebel at heart. I got my MBA from Springsteen U.

As teenagers, my friends and I hung out in the summer at the Jersey shore rock joints where Bruce Springsteen played and was still our personal secret before the world caught on. His lyrics always struck me as a personal anthem calling me out from behind a desk and into the street where things were happening—exciting, vibrant things, demanding to be tasted, felt, and lived. If the people in Cleveland heard it once, they heard it a hundred times—"No retreat, baby, no surrender." In due course, it came to mean the same to them as it does to me: don't let anything stop you from reaching your goals.

BE WHO YOU SAY YOU ARE

Honesty. Openness. Empowerment. Teamwork. I hammered hard on each theme for the rest of the meeting. I encouraged the reps to tell me and their managers what they liked and what they didn't like—and to expect the same from us. Cynicism, backbiting, finger pointing would not be tolerated.

"Anybody who's any good who tries to quit and walk out of this place is going to be tackled by me before they hit the door," I vowed. And for those who couldn't hack it, I promised to tell them straight that they had gone as far as they were going to go, and to work with them to find other alternatives.

"You don't know me, so you're going to have to trust me on this," I said. "I insist that as a business organization we will be who we say we are. If we say that we will satisfy the customer— that's what we're going to do. The same thing works for individuals. I am who I say I am. And that's what I expect from you."

I was connecting. I could see it in the body language around me. In each row of seats there were several men and women leaning forward, their eyes glistening. They'd nod as I made my points. I could also see the disconnects—just a few—arms folded across their chests, chins lifted slightly as if to say "Yeah, I'll believe it when I see it."

Sadly, cynics never "see it" even when it's staring them in the face. And what I did that day was to deliberately lay out what was going to happen and what wasn't. A leader must give his people a vision that will motivate them to give their very best.

I told them flat out that in time Cleveland was going to be the number one district in the region. Number one. I predicted that our success would be so spectacular that one day books would be written about it.

Later, I heard that my vision had come as such a shock that many people figured I had lost my mind, or as one of them told *The Wall Street Journal*, "We thought he was on drugs or something."

Less than six months went by and the first prediction had come true. A year and a half later, reporter and author David Dorsey was working on a book about us that he entitled *The Force*.

2

▼

START HERE:

THE WILL TO WIN

I made plenty of mistakes in Cleveland. But holding that initial meeting was definitely not one of them. It immediately changed the atmosphere.

Most of the people in the amphitheater had forgotten what it was like to have a sense of purpose and direction. Nothing fancy or complicated: we were going to sell more copiers, printing systems, and other Xerox products than any district in the region. I told them the goal was achievable—in fact, a done deal —and I was there to help them do it in any and every way that I could.

Luckily, my confidence rested on more than just rock-and-roll nostalgia. In the eighteen months that I had been in my previous assignment in Minneapolis, my teams smashed all the sales records for the office. In 1987, I had been the number one district sales manager in the United States.

Minnesota is a fabulous marketplace. The Minneapolis–St. Paul area offers abundant opportunities; the competition is aggressive and stimulating, and the quality of the work force is extremely high. It's a major-league area. By playing there and winning, I was confident that I could handle the challenge in Cleveland. In some ways, it had been a dress rehearsal. The district sales manager's job, as it was then constituted, has since been dropped. At the time, the DSM reported to the district manager who directly supervised the major account teams and ran the overall show. The extra layer of management had pluses and minuses; in the end, though, Xerox apparently decided it was too cumbersome and combined the two positions.

In my case, and I suspect for many relatively inexperienced executives, having the backup there was important. It gave me a chance to get comfortable with all the elements of the district manager's job, but if I ran into trouble there was somebody to turn to for help.

After about six months, Tom Stuart joined us as district manager. I consider Tom to be one of my most important mentors. He gave me encouragement and recognized that I had potential. Tom took a major risk by recommending me for the promotion to Cleveland. Although I had done well in Minnesota, other managers who had studied my file before I got there could well have concluded that the record-breaking run had been a fluke.

Back in Columbus, where I started for Xerox, I had been passed over three times for management jobs. The company has a panel-based interview process for screening and evaluating potential managers. Each time I was interviewed the verdict came back negative. The worst thing was that the judgment of the three managers on the panel was always unanimous—I couldn't even get a single vote. Finally, after the third rejection, one member of the promotion panel took me aside for a heart-to-heart chat. He told me some people just weren't cut out for management, and that I was one of them.

I was angered by the assessment. My reaction was to mope around for several days. Finally, though, I did the smart thing: I called my father for advice.

He listened to my story and asked a few questions. The committees were unanimous? Yes. Each time? Yes. What had I done differently to improve my chances after being rejected to prepare for the next interview? Nothing.

Nothing? I explained that I had been honest and was satisfied with my answers. I wasn't going to just tell them what they wanted to hear. That would be hypocritical.

Dad had spent more than forty years as an executive with Chase Manhattan. He told me that corporations have a right to insist on certain proven procedures, policies, values, and methods of operation. The string of rejections suggested to him that I had set myself at odds with the panel's legitimate expectations for an aspiring manager. It wasn't a matter of hypocrisy or even of competence, but rather a question of determining whether my approach was ultimately compatible with Xerox's. If not, the committee was right, and I should go elsewhere if I really wanted to be a manager.

I can hear him to this day, and I often paraphrase his wisdom when I'm dealing with unhappy, frustrated employees: "If things are so bad, if we're so unreasonable, so inflexible—there are plenty of other places to work. Maybe you'll be happier and more successful somewhere else."

As usual, he was correct. I had become a pretty good salesman, but I was still immature. What the panel was looking for, more than specific answers to specific questions, was a thought process. I was too quick to jump to conclusions. I shot from the hip. There were too many, "I feel . . ." answers, rather than thought-out, reasoned responses. The insight allowed me to look behind the questions I was being asked and realize that I was telling the panel—without realizing it—that I was impatient, impetuous, and a loner. In the crunch, if my sales team faltered, my impulse would be to blow them out and do the job myself. The brashness of my style and approach would have caused Xerox untold problems.

I could have remained impatient, impetuous, and a loner. I could have gone somewhere else. But I wanted to work at Xerox.

Dad suggested that I go out and ask my boss and other Xerox executives how they handled particular situations. He urged me to cast around for a variety of opinions and tactics. I took his advice and learned a lot. Just before I was interviewed for the fourth and last time, I got together with another rep who ran me through about twenty different question sequences to sharpen up my responses. The preparation paid off. The panel reversed itself and endorsed me for a management position.

Looking back on the experience, I think it validated the promotion process. I hadn't been ready to be a manager and those earlier panels were right to reject me. Many people give up after being turned down the first or second time, but I really wanted to be a manager. Just "wanting" wasn't enough, though. The panels forced me to grow up.

OUTCOACHING THE COACH

This isn't a memoir. I don't want to get bogged down in my personal background. However, there's another element that bears directly on my success in Minnesota and Cleveland. When I moved into my first slot as manager in Columbus, I reported to Neil Lamey (in fact, he was the one who decided to give me the job despite my checkered career). Neil was by far the best boss I've ever had. I owe him a lot.

Why? Neil was the ultimate coach. He made his managers feel they could do the impossible. He built phenomenal management teams by using his personal warmth and charisma. It was a blast just to come to work every day. You wanted to sell and lead your reps to hell and back just to please him.

He taught me that I could do the same thing, and I figured that I could raise the bar a few notches by using his techniques combined with a tight, well-executed process that extended down to the level of the sales reps.

And that's exactly what I set out to do when I got to Minneapolis. Tom Stuart liked what he saw, but instead of hanging on to me, as many managers would have done—why lose your top performer?—he decided I was ready to move.

Like Neil Lamey, he taught me a valuable lesson: Don't hold your people back. Promote them, move them, make them successful as fast as you can.

The logic is simple. The more people you put on the fast track, the more fast-track talent will be attracted to your operation. It's tempting to get a death grip on good people, to make the most of them as long as you can. However, in the end you're betraying them—and they know it. Tom Stuart's example made a real impression on me. I vowed to do it his way in Cleveland no matter how much it might temporarily hurt to have good people move up the ladder.

MENTORSHIP

I've mentioned three mentors: my father, Neil Lamey, and Tom Stuart. Mentors are absolutely essential. Find one. Find a dozen. Use them as role models and sounding boards. No matter how talented you are, it is essential to have backup, support, and a second opinion.

In Cleveland, my objective was to mentor each of my managers directly. In turn, I wanted them to serve as mentors to the reps. At the end of the first meeting, I turned to the managers and told them they had my full support. "Come to me, lean on me. But it's up to you to make it happen."

I'm convinced that our success in Cleveland started right there in the amphitheater a few minutes after I set foot in the building for the first time. I hadn't even seen my private office yet. The timing alone sent a message. When I was asked when to schedule the meeting, I said I wanted everybody there at 7:30 A.M. And that came as a shock. Meetings usually got under way later in the morning, at a more civilized hour. What I was saying was this: We're in trouble. We're going to need an extra hour or so to dig out. This operation is going to be up and running while the competition is still in bed.

At last! The magic word—competition. I used it repeatedly that morning. I believe in competition and thrive on it. When I was in Columbus, working for Neil Lamey, the aggressive young reps would put photographs of their principal competitors up on the bathroom mirror. We'd get up in the morning and look at the face of the IBM guy and say, "You've had it today, buddy!"

Juvenile? Probably. Effective? Definitely. Every sale that I lost, I blamed on him. Not on the market. Not on bad luck. Not on a lousy machine. He took money from my pocket and it bugged the hell out of me.

After I married Julie and we bought our first house, I looked at my depleted bank account with a little over a thousand dollars left in it, wondering how our finances would fare after the arrival of our first child—and got steamed at IBM, Kodak, and Xerox's other rivals.

When the competition placed a copier, it was one less for me to sell. When that happened, it suggested to me that someone else out there had been smarter, faster, and harder-working than I was. And when it happened, there was no sense agonizing over my failure. They beat me fair and square. Yesterday, they were smarter, faster, and harder-working. But today, it's my turn!

If that sounds strange to you, we've got a problem. By "we," I mean author and reader. Unfortunately, I can't look around the room as I did that first morning in Cleveland and spot the ones who were saying to themselves, "Sure, Frank . . . sure." I tell my managers to accept the fact that there will always be some cynics, but not to be intimidated by them into silence and to keep talking to the good ones.

That's what I'm doing here—talking to the good ones. I'm not going to be of any help to you, nor is this book, if your reaction is "Sure, Frank . . . sure." If you don't mind being beaten by the competition (I think you're kidding yourself, actually), then you'd better get used to losing.

We are in for an era of vicious competition, both as individuals and as a nation. For the United States, the first real taste of it came in the 1970s and 1980s. We were challenged head-on by foreign competitors using techniques and technology that had just a few years before been almost exclusively ours. The assault seemed to come from every direction.

Transportation and communications have torn the walls down, smashed the gates open, and drained the moat. There's no place to hide. None of us has a right to a job, a product line, or market share. It's too bad, but that's the way things are.

What's to be done? We can blame it on the market, bad luck, a lousy machine—just as it would have been so easy to do back when I was a young rep in Columbus. We can blame it on the so-called "shrinking pie," the agglomeration of resources and assets that is also always being divided into smaller and smaller pieces in *USA Today* and other publications. We can blame it on our wasteful lifestyle and learn to make do with less.

Or we can blame it on the competition; paste a picture on the bathroom mirror and go out and fight for the business, for our jobs, for our families, for ourselves.

That doesn't mean being anti-Japanese, anti-German, anti-Mexican. Just the opposite. They have my respect. It means learning what they're doing right, and going out and doing it better.

PERNICIOUS AMNESIA

Until fairly recently, the United States was on a long winning streak. So long, we started to take winning for granted. Like Woody Allen's line that "eighty percent of success is showing up," our leaders, executives, and workers just started showing up. We kept winning; therefore, it must have been enough.

I found that attitude in Cleveland. Like businesses all across the United States, Britain and parts of Europe, they had literally forgotten how to compete. I think that particular form of amnesia starts with forgetting how great it is to win.

I'm no anthropologist, but it seems to me that humankind's survival depends on two instinctive highs: sex and winning. Sex, for obvious reasons. Winning because the thrill of it ensures that we keep moving, keep hunting, keep foraging, fighting, farming, inventing (and selling copiers).

If I forget how good sex feels, I'm probably not going to get excited about Valentine's Day. If I forget how good winning feels, I'm going to call in sick tomorrow so that I can watch TV soap operas.

What I did in Cleveland—and what I'm trying to do in these pages—is remind everyone how good it feels to win.

And you know what? It can be a damned hard sell. When was the last time you won and felt great about it? A lot of people have to think long and hard before they come up with something. Keep trying. It'll pop. Isolate that moment in your memory and savor the pleasure.

Go ahead—smile.

In fact, go ahead and gloat. It's not good manners—Mom was right—but it has therapeutic results.

HABIT FORMING: THE TASTE OF SUCCESS

Here's a technique for rediscovering the thrill of winning that I often use to open meetings. I've put together a videotape of final, exciting moments in football games; a collage of action shots and excitement: players racing across the goal line and flinging down the football, clenched fists and high fives, the crowd going wild. I play the tape with the sound track cranked up full blast. When it's over, I ask the people in the room to stand up and celebrate. "You've just gone over the top. You're the number one district in the United States. Enjoy!"

It's amazing. Dignified, grown-up, oh-so-professional people go nuts. They stomp, they cheer, they hug each other. I love it! And so do they.

The group gets a blast of what it's like to win. It feels pretty good. In fact, I used this technique at the kickoff meeting when I moved from Cleveland to the Columbus district in 1993. Within six months, an operation that had been bumping along near the bottom of the overall sales and revenue rankings zoomed up to number two in the entire nation.

Try it. But let me warn you that the first few times you'll be absolutely terrified that the group will stand there looking around, wondering if you've lost your marbles. It hasn't happened to me yet. The response has always been enthusiastic. But if there is a moment of hesitation, wade in and grab the nearest hand and hoist it high! That will break the ice.

PERMISSION TO WIN

I don't buy the notion that the desire to compete and to win is a primitive instinct that needs to be suppressed in modern men and women. I believe that the opposite is true. Nonetheless, I'm bucking decades of conditioning that starts at an early age. Many parents, teachers, and employers find it easier to smother the competitive instinct in the interest of decorum and orderly behavior. A thick, fuzzy blanket is thrown on top of conflict, emotion, and turmoil. It's not "nice" to exult in being the smartest kid in the class, the fastest runner, the best tuba player.

What I do as a manager is give my people permission to compete, to win—to exult when they're the best. And to despair when they're not.

WILL VERSUS WANT

I could have subtitled this book "The Management Practices of My Father." I recall one of the first times he gave me permission to compete and to win. I was a small boy, probably six years old, playing with a friend who lived down the block. We got into a tussle and he ended up chasing me home. I was sobbing as I ran. My father heard the commotion and walked out of the house onto the front porch. I called to him for help as I got closer. All he said was, "Stop. Turn around and hit him."

I look for the same attitude in the managers I hire. They're the team leaders I expect to mentor and coach the people working under them. There will be bad days when all a rep can do is take a beating and run. What I want to hear is the echo of my father's voice: "Stop. Turn around and hit them."

I call this attitude "the will to win." Not the "want" to win. Everybody wants to win. Even the laziest, most unmotivated, most passive person wants to succeed but won't do what's necessary to insure that it happens. Winning is hard, risky work. And it entails losing from time to time.

Particularly in sales. Sales is an occupation that resembles a porcupine. The job is filled with quills, each one a rejection, a major or minor defeat, constantly jabbing you while you try to roll the creature over onto its back. If you don't have a well-developed will to win, the loss of blood is a killer.

THE WILL TO WIN: A CHECKUP

When you take over a new, troubled business organization it is safe to assume that the will to win is either absent or badly depleted. The series of questions below will help determine the extent of the problem.

- Do your people arrive late for work?
- Do they leave early?
- Is the activity level erratic or low in volume?
- Do they talk mostly about problems, disappointments, difficulties?
- Can they tell you what the competition is doing in detail?
- Are the same mistakes being made repeatedly?
- Are you hearing praise from the customer? Complaints? Nothing at all?

Let's take them one at a time. Consistently showing up late for work indicates the individual is losing his or her enthusiasm for the job. Sure, things can go wrong unexpectedly at home, or there's a traffic jam on the way to work. But when it happens regularly, once a week or more, I read it as a sign that the person isn't willing to take the necessary steps to reorganize the family's morning routine, leave a few minutes earlier, or resolve whatever situation is creating the problem.

As I said, the will to win takes hard work. All of us have problems. We have to work to solve them, otherwise they become excuses for failure: "If I didn't have three kids, I could get to work on time"; "The traffic around this town is murder."

Leaving work early is similar. If it happens frequently, I would conclude that the person would rather be somewhere else, or, again, is letting demands outside of the job take precedence.

We'll go into this in depth later, but I want to touch on an important point here. As a manager and leader, when I ask the question "Do they leave early or show up late?" and the answer is yes, I don't stop there. I ask why. I'll direct the question to the employee, but I'll also put it to myself: Is this operation the problem? Is it so boring and such a drag that my people can't wait to get out of here and go home? Is it my fault that I haven't made this office vibrant, electric, and fun? If you believe, as I do, that winning is a thrill that more than compensates for the extra effort of getting the kids rousted out of bed and off to school in plenty of time, or leaving early to beat the traffic, then maybe you are not doing what needs to be done to build a winning team.

Or have you simply failed to state your minimum level of expectations? In Minnesota, one of my managers quit the second week that I was on the job. She had become accustomed to leaving every day at 4:30 P.M. I told her she wouldn't be successful as a manager if she didn't put the hours in—and she hadn't been particularly successful up to that point. If I had just let her continue leaving early, as if it didn't matter, I would have been encouraging her to go on losing. In the process, I'd be contributing to the failure of all of the people under her.

STIR IT UP

The activity level tells me a lot. It amounts to asking "What's happening?" People who are discouraged and frustrated tend to pull back and lick their wounds. The winners are so excited by winning that they're out looking for action anywhere and everywhere. Customer contact is the lifeblood of sales. If you're an executive in another line or work—and this is not just a book exclusively for salespeople—ask yourself what it is that drives your business. Once you've identified it, you'll know what has to be done every day, day in and day out, to keep the doors open.

As a rule of thumb for boosting the activity level, take the percentage of where you are and where you should be—the financial and sales targets that were set but not achieved—and double it for good measure. If business was off by 10 percent, you'll need a minimum of 10 percent more activity to make your goals. However, go for the full 20 percent for good measure and the extra margin.

Does that sound unreasonable? If I'm making ten customer calls a week, two more won't kill me. Spread across the organization, the extra activity level will have a major impact.

Less is not—not, not, not—more! More is more. The more a sales force gets out in front of the customer, the more things happen: leads begin to materialize; the rep's familiarity with the territory grows; he or she learns to present the product more effectively; and success starts breeding success.

This is not voodoo. It's common sense.

Go one step further. Ask your best people, the strongest performers, to do more. Instead of two additional calls, make it three or four. They've already demonstrated that they can do the job. Let them get a kick out of knowing that you are relying upon them for that extra, over-the-top push. And *tell them* how much you appreciate the extra effort.

As for an erratic activity level, it's a sign that your people are working like duck hunters who sit there in the blind, shivering in the cold, waiting for the next flock to fly by. They've got to be out in the marketplace on the move. Otherwise boom-and-bust cycles will wreak havoc with your business.

Erratic activities can also stem from an overreliance on periodic incentive programs that get reps cracking to win a fat bonus or make midyear goals, only to have them start coasting afterward. A minimum activity level has got be set without regard to incentives. If the level of activity spikes suddenly because there's extra money on the table and then drops back, you might consider notching it upward to a more realistic level.

DUGOUT CHATTER

Listen closely to the shop talk around you. What are the managers and reps talking about? If I start hearing a lot of complaints about the customers, I get worried. When a sales rep is having trouble, a favorite rationale goes something like this: "They love their Ricohs . . . They love their Canons." What's being said between the lines is "I can't figure out a way to crack the account, and I give up." It usually has little or nothing to do with whether the customer is truly satisfied with the competition's products.

Those with a well-developed will to win aren't talking about problems, they're talking about opportunities. If I'm having trouble knocking out Canon or Ricoh, I want to strategize with my fellow managers and reps. "Do you think this idea will work?" "How about . . . ?" "I'm going to go back in there every week until that Ricoh blows up."

Just as in sports, where a silent, sullen locker room or dugout portends trouble, an office that wallows in its problems is in deep trouble. It's up to you as a manager and leader to switch off the can't-do talk and turn it into can-do. The quickest fix is to start with yourself and make sure that you're totally focused on making success happen. It doesn't mean firing Mr. Gloom and Doom, it means firing him up. When you hear the equivalent of "He loves his Ricohs," come back with, "Let's go over right now and ask him why. Then we'll know what we're up against."

THEM

Nobody can sell in a vacuum. In a competitive marketplace, you must keep track of the competition. If a rep doesn't know and doesn't care what the competition is doing, he doesn't know and doesn't care that it's being done to him.

If you suspect that your people are not well acquainted with the competition's product, maybe you should wonder whether they are getting adequate exposure to the marketplace. The products are out there. In the copier business, particularly in the 1980s, even the laziest rep was bumping into the competition's machines all the time. It was an excellent educational opportunity.

Reps who can't tell me as much about the competition's product as they can tell me about our own machines have probably concluded that "what you don't know can't hurt you." They suspect the competition has produced a superior product and that's the reason business is bad. Preserving that illusion is a form of self-protection. Don't let them do it. One thing I do is hold periodic pop quizzes for the reps, to test them on their knowledge of the competition. I'll end a meeting by handing out a six-question multiple-choice quiz. I'm not looking to grade anybody and make a big deal of it, but if the knowledge level is slipping I'll let the group know that it's time to start boning up on the competition.

WHOOPS!

Mistakes. Don't be afraid to make them—once. When the same errors are repeated over and over again, it's confirmation that something other than winning has assumed primary importance in an organization.

We are trial-and-error creatures. We learn our most vivid lessons via our failures. It hurts to fail. But if the lessons aren't sinking in, failure doesn't hurt enough. In fact, we may have contrived to create a system that rewards failure.

Your top performers will occasionally reach too far. Don't discourage the instinct. But require them to transform that setback into the basis for the next success.

THE D-WORD

No news is good news. Right? Wrong!

If I'm not hearing from the customer, something is very wrong. For starters, it may be that the reps are not building the kind of relationships with the customers that generate honest feedback.

If I don't like a sales rep, his product, or his organization, I may just write them all off. Who cares? On the next buying cycle, I'm going elsewhere.

As a salesperson, I want to delight the customer. And that's a word I use constantly—delight.

A silent customer is not a delighted customer. Delighted customers show it. You hear from them constantly, and it may be criticism rather than praise. Their expectation levels can be raised so high that the slightest glitch comes as a major disappointment.

No news is bad news.

HORSE SENSE

Okay. You've run through the checklist and concluded that the will to win is in short supply. What's next?

Run a check on yourself.

Business organizations may seem to be made up of gray flannel suits and white collars, but those enterprises are more horse than haberdasher. The horse knows when the rider is nervous or uncertain. If you don't have the will to win, your horses are going to sense it. Whips, spurs, and two-by-fours won't help.

Fear, intimidation, and the threat of firing may achieve short-term results. But the gunslinger eventually shoots himself in the foot. Oddly enough, though, I'm the beneficiary of a gunslinger's reputation. The people in Cleveland had heard what a bad hombre I was, and they expected the worst. But I wasn't there to fire people. By deliberately not making precipitate personnel changes, I wanted to see if I could devise a process that would succeed with the existing work force—a work force that had failed under the previous administration.

If I could—and I did—I'd know that the problem wasn't the people. The problem was the process.

My assumption was that these same people could win if they were given the right process and the right leadership. It was my job to provide both, not to conduct a reign of terror. Be careful, though. My father always says that a new manager must "find Judas." By that he means there is always at least one person who isn't dealing straight with you. Judas will tell you what he thinks you want to hear; he'll seem to be an enthusiastic supporter and then work behind your back to undermine your position. The only reliable way to find Judas is to evaluate people by their actions, not just their words.

FAST FORWARD

At the end of our first meeting, I turned to my managers and said, "I hope everybody has a full day planned. I know I do." I told them that when the meeting adjourned, all of us were going to hit the street. All of us—myself included. I wasn't going upstairs to wade through papers and hold meetings. I was going to spend the rest of the day traveling with the reps as they made calls.

From that moment on, the motto was: "Just Go Do It."

3

▼

LEADERSHIP:

PASSION AND PREMEDITATION

Are you a manager or a leader? There's a difference, a big difference.

In this chapter, I'm going to show you what I mean. Along the way, I hope to prove a favorite contention of mine: Most businesses are overmanaged and underled. That's why they get into trouble.

There's got to be a balance. Right now, in most places, leaders aren't particularly welcome. They're looked on as flaky and unpredictable.

I'm not knocking managers by praising leaders. You've got to combine the best of both roles to be really successful. Every organization needs a process, and that process doesn't get executed by itself. It takes planning, decision making, supervision, and follow-up. But I believe that an effective leader can pick up a good manager's process and wring another 10 or 20 percent out of it in terms of overall performance. And the right leader can needle a mediocre process into producing 50 to 100 percent gains.

The hang-up is that leadership seems to be more art than

craft. It's hard to define, hard to teach, hard to accomplish. Management is a safer bet.

Right? Well, not really.

By conventional standards, my immediate predecessors in Cleveland were good managers. They did what their superiors expected. Paper flowed through the proper channels; budgets were prepared on time; corporate policies were implemented according to guidelines laid down by headquarters in Rochester. But . . . the district was sinking like a rock.

I suppose it's human nature. If we take an aspirin for a headache, but the headache doesn't go away, the next step is to take two aspirins. In business, the managerial aspirin is doubled and tripled and quadrupled until the patient responds. We have faith in the cure. Besides, what else are we going to do?

Unfortunately, the cure can be worse than the disease. The life-support systems proliferate and grow cumbersome, draining off what little energy there is for day-to-day business. The people who are supposed to be minding the store don't have time to do their jobs. The crisis means additional paperwork, meetings, conference calls, and trips to the home office for consultation. After a while, the investment of time and effort from so many different management quarters completely tangles lines of authority in knots. At that point, if you ask, "Who's in charge here?" you get a lot of blank looks in response. The reaction then is to either give up by scaling back on expectations—and that's usually what happens for several months or years—or to send in someone with a sharp knife to do some knot cutting.

I was supposed to be the knot cutter in Cleveland. It's a very dangerous specialty. Some top managers don't really like knot cutters and use them only as a last resort. The breed tends to lack a feel for managerial niceties. In other words, we make trouble.

After all, each knot was tied by a conscientious manager who was only trying to do his or her job. Every one that's cut amounts to a reproach. You make enemies in high places real fast. That's why many knot cutters go bad. They become nut cutters.

Slashing away at people is a favorite short-term expedient. It can actually scare an operation into action, but not for long.

However, the quick fix is often enough to allow the nut cutter to get in and get out without damaging his or her career.

RESPECT FOR PEOPLE

I don't work that way, though. One of the main reasons is my retarded older brother, Joey. He and I were best friends. We roomed together until I left home for college. My sister and I never thought Joey had a problem; he was Joey: a big, happy, friendly kid who was just . . . different. Over the years, without trying, or even being aware of it, I developed the feeling that I was supposed to help Joey and be what he couldn't be.

To this day, when I encounter people who are ill, infirm, or just struggling to make it through life, it really hits me in the gut. Empathy is not the right word. It goes way beyond empathy.

So you can see why I'm no nut cutter. My people in Cleveland were in a lot of trouble and I wanted to help them dig out of it.

I also wanted to make more money, gain responsibility, and climb the corporate ladder. Charity begins at home. To succeed in a turnaround situation, as I did, you don't need a retarded brother or an old-fashioned Italian-American family. What you need—and I don't care where it comes from—is respect for people. If it's not there, please do something else with your career. Forget management.

Leadership starts and ends with people. You don't have to be a saint to be an effective leader. Leadership can actually stem from seemingly selfish roots. Whatever the reason, I'm extremely competitive—to the point that I come close to being physically ill when I lose. Therefore, I've got very personal reasons for wanting to be an effective leader: I want to win.

When I arrived in Cleveland, I could see myself standing in every pair of shoes in the room. Many of the people, particularly the managers, had been extremely successful at various times. They had been up—way up. Now they were down. It was embarrassing and terrifying. I knew what it was like. At any point in my previous Xerox career, I could have been a victim of the nut-cutting approach to problem solving. And it was a miracle that I wasn't.

In twelve years, the managers I worked for taught me many invaluable lessons about what to do and what not to do. There were good managers—great ones—but I'd be kidding you if I didn't acknowledge that I endured my share of bad managers as well. As a result, my career developed in a very erratic way. Without adequate coaching and counseling, I'd run hot and cold as a sales rep. My discipline was poor. When I needed a pat on the back or a kick in the tail, I usually didn't receive either.

Finally, I got lucky. I had a boss in Columbus who hated my guts. One day, after I had written a major order and was hanging around the office feeling smug, he called me in. Instead of offering congratulations, he told me that if he could get away with it politically, he would fire me. He made it clear that the second my performance went sour, I'd be a goner. I got a scathing lecture on my bad attitude and other shortcomings, but I was also informed that my great failing was that I was squandering my talent. He told me I could run circles around anybody in the office but I was too arrogant and lazy to get off my butt and do it.

The praise came as a greater shock than the scolding. I knew the man didn't like me, and the positive comments about my ability, coming from him, had real impact. I went home that night and thought hard about what he had said.

Years later, I am still trying to do for others what he did for me. The tongue-lashing was one of his finest moments as a manager. It pulled me back from the edge. I've used the same technique to the same ends since then: I'll sit on the edge of my desk and look into the eyes of a cocky young man or woman and say what needs to be said. I never pull any punches; I do just what my dad used to do when I was goofing off. He gave it to me straight and hard. I call it hardball with a heart.

I can see the shock, just as I was shocked. And most of the time I can also see the light beginning to dawn. Want another example?

I'll change his name because I don't want to embarrass him. Steve will do. Steve was a top performer in an operation that was going nowhere fast. I had been in the district manager's job a few months when I finally encountered him in the office. Until that moment he had deliberately kept a low profile. Steve was feeling awkward and he tried to turn the tables on me. "How come you've been ignoring me, Frank?" he asked.

"That's not the way it works, Steve. You've got my phone number; you know where my office is. Have you once stopped by to ask how my move went, if my family is all right, how things are going? No, because you're not a team player. You're Mr. Macho star. The heck with all these other underachievers. I'm ignoring you? You couldn't care less!"

"But . . ." he tried to interrupt.

"No 'buts,' Steve. Right now you're doing fine. It won't last forever, though. And the moment your performance slips, you're on your own, and I'm coming for you."

Tough stuff. Steve's jaw dropped. He went home that night and did some serious thinking. He had to get the message and get it straight: a lone wolf doesn't succeed. The team succeeds.

That's not management. That's leadership.

Some managers would leave Steve alone because he was delivering strong numbers. But Steve is poison. He is a negative role model. Whenever I hire or promote, I ask "Can Fred, or Sharon, or George serve as a role model that will encourage the team to do what has to be done?"

If I promote Steve, or even seem to tolerate him, everybody in the organizations sees that being an outsider is a benefit. Before long, I'll have to contend with three or four other Steve clones.

So who cares if a rep is standoffish as long as he or she is selling copiers? I care. I need forty people selling copiers, not just a handful of hotshots. If one person doesn't make his or her budget, the whole district will be dragged down. I want the strongest performers to help energize the not-so-strong.

Take a close look at your organization. I bet you've got a few people like Steve. Talk to them right now. Don't put it off; it only reinforces the negative behavior. If you don't—if you take the easy way out—you're sabotaging your own team. Be a leader.

HIT THE ROAD

Before I set foot in Cleveland, I knew the names of my new managers and reps. I had reviewed their business backgrounds and acquainted myself with important aspects of their personal lives—spouses, kids, hobbies. Believe me, it isn't hard to do. Just dig into the personnel files and have a look.

But there are more important things to tackle!

No, there aren't. Start with the people.

By hitting the road with the reps immediately after the first meeting, I did two things: one, I let them know I was going to be a hands-on manager—a leader—who gets out in front of the customer, and two, that I intended to stay in close personal contact with the reps and managers.

Now I had already *told* them that during the meeting. But a leader has got to walk like he talks. Don't just tell them, show them.

Write that down: Walk like you talk. Words aren't enough. Action. Action that implements the words.

Both have got to be absolutely clear and unmistakable. You don't have to be Knute Rockne and deliver a dramatic locker-room pep talk when you first walk in the door, but at a minimum, a leader has got to show the troops the route of the march and the destination.

Here's a sample overhead projection slide that does the job:

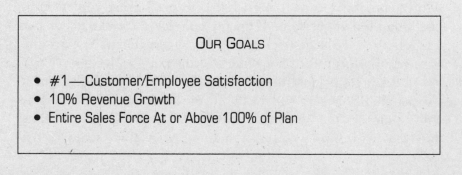

OUR GOALS

- #1—Customer/Employee Satisfaction
- 10% Revenue Growth
- Entire Sales Force At or Above 100% of Plan

If I had shown that slide and then gone back to my office to answer phone messages or process forms, the message would have been totally lost. It would have been business as usual with three unattainable goals tossed in on top.

What a leader must establish is that the unusual is now usual. At the end of the first meeting, I chose two reps, basically at random, and spent half a day with each one, calling on customers.

There was no opportunity for them to pad the schedule or dress it up to impress the boss. They had to go with what was on the books. If the proposals they were presenting to the customers that day were sloppy or inadequate, I would see them with all their warts and get a quick read on what was happening in the field.

Would I rip into them for demonstrating poor preparation ability?

No way. At the end of the call, I'd probably tell the rep I thought he could do a much better job of preparation. I'd give a few specifics for next time. But when next time rolled around, I would have already gotten back to the rep's manager to alert him or her to the problem. The manager would know, in no uncertain terms, that the reps were going to have to be given a refresher on preparation techniques and inspected before they went out on calls. Furthermore, my conversation with the manager would tell me whether he or she possessed the necessary preparation skills to pass along to the team. If not, and if I failed to step up to that particular problem, it would not be the reps' fault that their preparation was faulty—it would be my fault.

DON'T COUNT ON THE TOOTH FAIRY

I hope you're beginning to see how important it is to get out of the office to gather firsthand information. If you saw the movie *Dirty Harry*, you probably remember this line: "I never give much credence to advice from people whose ass is the same shape as their chairs." That just about says it all. Many times, you'll have to rely on secondary sources. You can't be everywhere. But frequent trips into the field serve as invaluable reality checks. Take a break from the book right now and hit the road. You won't offend me. In fact, for maximum value you should be a hit-and-run reader. This is action-oriented, interactive stuff. Dip into these pages, find something that makes sense, and, just as we did in Cleveland, go do it! Don't expect me to do all the work.

As soon as you break out of jail—I mean the office—I think you'll find, as I did, that the troops will notice and appreciate your presence in the field. In addition to gathering first-hand information, my purpose on the initial run in Cleveland was to give the two reps I traveled with a chance to see me in action and spread the word back to their colleagues that "Frank walks the way he talks." Salespeople tend to measure their superiors by a simple criterion: Can I take this person on a customer call? Will he or she be a help or a hindrance?

At the very least, the boss should do no harm. Even so, some managers can't even meet that meager standard. They second-guess, they showboat, they send conflicting signals to the customer. If you're not a supersalesman, don't worry. You're not out there to close a deal or prove that the sales rep is a novice. You're out there to show them that the boss—the leader—is a resource to be tapped. You didn't get the job because your superiors were playing spin the bottle. You got it because they perceived in you a particular constellation of skills, talent, and potential. Those are the resources the leader has at his or her disposal.

I had just raised the bar on the Cleveland office by announcing that everyone was going to make or exceed plan. How was that going to happen if I didn't bring additional resources to the table as a leader? It wouldn't have happened.

The tooth fairy doesn't deliver 10 percent revenue growth under our pillows at night. And 100 percent customer/employee satisfaction doesn't just happen in a district with a reputation as a black hole of bad feelings. My presence in the field that first day, however, even though I did more listening than talking, was a giant step toward attaining the goal. The reps were shown they'd get backup and support from me—and from their managers, who would take the cue from the top. The customers, long used to being kept on the outside of the Xerox organization, suddenly had another friend and ally on the inside. I still needed to earn their trust, but it was a start.

FINGER-POINT

So, the most effective management strategy is to start at the bottom and work upward, right? Not exactly. You have to be able to do two things (or more) at once. I wanted to be out in the field where the action was, but simultaneously I was engaged in trickle-down management as well. If the district sales manager tries to run each of his sales teams personally, why does he bother hiring team leaders? Those seven people—eventually there were eight—had to be given running room. Otherwise, the team structure would have been meaningless. Teams give a district immense flexibility by grouping together reps who have similar experience, accounts, and territories. The managers aren't forced to juggle widely different portfolios, and the reps have a sense of camaraderie to counteract what can be a lonely —"nobody appreciates what I'm going through"—occupation.

By traveling with the reps, I was not only evaluating the team's strengths and weaknesses but also showing the managers how I expected them to manage from then on. I'm no autocrat— you won't hear "It's my way or the highway" from me—but I do believe that managers must be engaged, right beside the troops, in the hand-to-hand combat of their businesses. Delegating responsibility is fine. Xerox insists on it. However, there's one responsibility that doesn't get delegated, as far as I'm concerned —the responsibility for success or failure.

I never want to hear "We lost the deal because Joe blew it." My comeback is "Why wasn't Joe being backed up? Why wasn't Joe supervised? Why wasn't Joe better trained?" And the answers must start at the top, with me. That's why I was in the field on day number one. If Joe is in trouble, I want to know about it; and I want my managers to know about it and do their damnedest to fix the problem. If Joe chokes, it's not just his fault. We weren't doing our jobs. Paul MacKinnon, who joined the Cleveland district as marketing manager in 1989, likes to interrupt when the blame game starts being played. He holds out his right hand with the fist balled up and the index finger extended in the typical accusatory way. Then, without saying anything, he slowly bends the finger inward and back at himself.

PLAN TO WIN

Let me stop and give you a list of things to look for when you go out in the field with your reps for the first time:

TEN QUESTIONS FOR EVALUATING YOUR SALES REPS

1. Is the rep well prepared for the call?
2. Is he or she fully acquainted with the customer and the customer's needs?
3. What's the purpose of the visit?
4. Is a proposal being made to the customer?
5. Do the customer and the rep have a personal rapport?
6. Is this a sales call and nothing but a sales call?
7. Can the rep pinpoint where the customer is in the sales cycle?
8. Was the call scheduled in advance or on the spur of the moment?
9. Were you kept waiting? How long? And did the rep make positive use of the time?
10. Was the rep able to evaluate the success of the call afterward and determine the next step?

If you look closely at those questions, my underlying assumptions will probably float to the surface. Got any ideas? If your answer is "Frank's antsy about poor planning, poor preparation, and poor discipline," go to the head of the class.

If you don't plan to win, you plan to lose. The very best salespeople and the very worst do the same thing—they improvise. The best, because they don't think they have to plan: "I've got this customer just where I want him." The worst, because they don't think planning will make a difference: "I'll just go in there and give it a shot; nothing ventured, nothing gained."

By requiring four calls a day, as I did initially in Cleveland, I was forcing the reps to shake the apple trees. By going out with them selectively on calls, I was able to observe how they did it.

Were they working the wrong orchard? Were they pounding their heads against the trunk of the tree? Or going after the lowest branches with the smallest fruit?

As leader, you've got to see for yourself. Go back to the first question. A rep who treats an established customer like a cold call is probably wasting the customer's time. What are the chances of hitting a target if you're firing a pistol in a dark room? A million to one? It tells me the rep hasn't taken the time and the trouble to figure out what it is that Xerox should be doing for the account.

And that leads to the second question, about the customer's needs. Another way to put it is, "What does this customer do for a living?" If you don't know, how are you going to sell him products?

By asking and answering these questions during and after a call, you have a chance to begin coaching and counseling your people. The questions themselves become resources that were previously unavailable to the rep. How many times have we heard: "I hadn't quite looked at it that way"? That's what you're after.

The questions are a means to a new perspective. The two reps I accompanied that first day hadn't looked at it that way before, and when they did, they started to see the possibility of winning again.

THE VALUE OF A STRONG PROPOSAL

I want to see proposals. It's not enough to say "Please buy my copier. It works great." Success in sales is really a pretty simple proposition. As I said in Chapter 1, there are only three elements: identify the customer, make sure your product fulfills the customer's requirements, and ask for the sale.

An effective proposal nails down the first two ingredients. I compare the process to the one I used when I asked Julie to marry me. When I saw her the first time, I said to one of my buddies, "I'm going to marry that girl." I identified the customer: she was single, she was smart, she was pretty, she was right for me. But she wanted nothing to do with me, as I quickly discovered. It took months of persistence to get a date. I would pop into where she worked to say hi and ask if she was ready, and I'd get the same cold shoulder. I kept trying. Eventually, she agreed to go out with me. By refusing to take no for an answer, I was demonstrating something—and that something was sincerity and commitment. I really wanted the date. Like a salesperson, I was identifying Julie's requirements one by one, and slowly showing her that I would meet them. She wanted sincerity, she wanted commitment—and she got them.

That's what an effective proposal does. It forces the salesperson to figure out what it is the customer wants—bottom line —and what he can to do to fulfill those requirements.

The third step—asking for the sale—is a major problem. I'll go into it in a big way later in the book, but in passing, let me say that more salespeople have trouble with this than any other thing. It's one reason I push my people to get over the hurdle early so that it won't loom as a seemingly insurmountable obstacle later down the road. I call it preclosing or preselling.

If I had tried to preclose Julie it might have gone like this:

Julie: "I don't like the way you dress, I don't think you make enough money, and you drive like a maniac."

Frank: "If I let you pick out my suits, if I double my income, and if I promise never to exceed the posted speed limits—will you marry me then?"

By preclosing you're establishing exactly where the process is headed. But to do it effectively, the salesperson must know the customer's minimum requirements, and that's where the proposal comes in.

CIRCLES AND CYCLES

Question 5—Do the customer and the rep have a personal rapport?—is one that can tell you a lot. All you have to do is sit there and listen. I don't expect the reps to be best buddies with the customer, but there should be an easy two-way flow of information that comes from repeated contact and familiarity.

If the rep and the customer are still warily circling each other, it suggests, if nothing else, that the account has not moved past the early stages of the sales cycle. If the rep is forecasting (or outlooking, the term we use at Xerox) a high level of business with the customer, you should know right there that he or she is being overly optimistic.

Some reps and customers never hit it off, no matter how many calls have been made. The personal chemistry may be wrong. If that's the case, it's easy enough to put a different rep on the account, but not so easy if you haven't been out in the field and detected the problem.

NO SALE

I've found that a common customer complaint is "I never see this person unless she's trying to sell me something." If the contact with the customer is nothing but sales calls, I conclude the reps are really only living for today. You've got to water the garden and weed it if it's to remain productive. The rep should be there not just as an order taker but as a resource for the customer. I like to think I'm going into business with my customers, that we're partners. Tipping them off to a new, creative application I've learned about is a real service. Or I can warn them about problems that have developed with a particular product at another account.

You soon wear out your welcome by only saying "Gimme, gimme."

A GOOD PAIR OF EARS

A rep who can't pinpoint where the customer stands in the sales cycle is prone to overestimating his or her chances for securing the business. Such reps will trash your planning process. Usually they're not listening to the customer or asking the right questions. And that's one of the reasons I'm such a pest with all of my questions. I want to teach the reps to do it my way: questions, questions, questions.

It's so simple. Ask the customer, "Where do we stand?" "How long does it take the purchasing committee to grant approval?" "What can I do to speed up the process?"

Most reps, particularly younger ones, are optimists. They're eager and want the business. The assumption is it will happen sooner rather than later. Experience, however, proves the opposite. Later rather than sooner tends to be the business norm.

You've got to watch out for the pessimists as well. They're the ones who protect themselves from rejection by getting bogged down in preliminaries. They're reluctant to push a deal along because it might go sour. The best approach in that case is to press the rep for a specific assessment: "When is it going to happen? And what are you doing to get it to that point? Can I help? What's your manager doing to back you up?"

WAIT WATCHING

Cold calls are to sales as KP is to the army. It's dirty work, but somebody has to do it. However, a steady diet of spur-of-the-moment calls indicates a sales rep is not exploiting his territory intelligently. "Just dropping in" to see a potential customer seems like good prospecting, but it's more productive to lay the groundwork in advance. There'll be less time spent waiting in an outer office or getting caught in the routine of: "I'm squeezing you in between appointments—you've got two minutes, so make it fast."

Some reps call on customers unannounced when they have a guilty conscience. The account has been neglected and they want to show the flag. Here's a question to ask the rep: "When was the last time you saw this customer?" You may find out that it's been several weeks because there was a problem or a complaint that wasn't handled properly. And another question: "Why didn't you take the time to set it up in advance?" The usual answer is something to the effect that the customer is too busy and can't be pinned down. It may mean that the customer doesn't like dealing with the rep and that the sneak attack is being used to catch him off guard.

WAIT LIFTING

Being kept waiting is not unusual. I've found, though, that my best customers tend to be the most punctual. They want to see me because I'm good for business. A good rep, who plans his or her day intelligently, knows which accounts are prone to getting bogged down or caught up in a crisis. A string of "Sorry, she's running late(s)," indicates the rep has not studied the dynamics of the territory, the personalities involved, or the characteristics of the industries he or she is doing business with.

If I know I always have to wait for Bernie, Sally, Carl, and Monica, I won't schedule them in back-to-back sequences. But if those four executives are strangers to me, I'm going to end up wasting huge chunks of my time.

Unavoidable delays occur. I want to see the use the rep makes of the down time. Does he or she ask to see someone else? There may be executives in other departments who are key players in the purchasing process. It's always good to contact employees who actually use the product. They provide feedback about performance and problems. Some customers don't like reps wandering around their buildings; others don't mind at all. In the latter case, the rep can gain a lot of information by exploring. He or she can stand in the background while the product is put through its paces. This kind of intelligence gathering can help explain an unusually high breakdown rate or confirm that the customer is pushing its applications too hard and needs a higher-volume machine.

Knowing a customer "in depth" means having more than one contact. If Sally cancels out or is delayed, how about Fred? Flexibility is a valuable attribute, and it indicates the rep knows the customer well enough to make some quick changes and salvage a call.

MEAN TIME

It's easy to spot the inability to evaluate a call after the fact. Just ask this question: "What did you accomplish?" You'll hear some amazing answers, most of them vague and imprecise. Many people are terrible listeners. They're too busy worrying about other things: "Did he like my sales pitch?" "I hope she hurries—I'm going to be late." "I hope he doesn't ask me about. . . ." All this extraneous stuff gets in the way of important information. When that happens, the rep starts jumping to conclusions—the wrong conclusions.

When I'm traveling with a rep who I think isn't listening to the customer, I'll wait until after the call and then ask for an evaluation.

"Where do we stand?"

"He's ninety percent there."

"I think it's more like five percent."

"Frank, you don't know the guy."

"I know that he hadn't read your proposal."

"He didn't?"

"No, because all the questions he asked were addressed in your executive summary at the beginning of the proposal. [More on this in Chapter 9.] If he had so much as picked up the sheet of paper and glanced at it, he wouldn't have bothered to ask those questions."

Listen to the customers. They will tell you exactly what's going on.

ARTS AND CRAFTS

When I got back from the calls, my personal data base was overflowing with information. It would take a manager who stayed in the office weeks to gather the same amount. I'm too impatient for that. Here's a tip: Learn the art of impatience. Keep pushing for action and answers now. Keep asking "What have we done today to advance toward our objectives? Have we done everything we can to make it happen?"

And another tip: Learn the art of patience. Keep trying, pushing, probing. Never give up. Quick results always make me wonder if the objectives were too cautious and easily obtainable.

These seemingly contradictory commandments—patience versus impatience—can only be cultivated by leaders who touch and taste and feel the reality of the marketplace. The art of leadership is mastered by those who get their hands dirty practicing the craft of leadership.

During my early days in Cleveland, reps would say to me, "I can't believe you spent the whole day with me in the field." My answer usually was, "What else would I be doing if I wasn't in the field with you or another rep?"

In a very premeditated way, I was showing them that there

wasn't anything more important than standing in front of the customer and selling. Two words come to mind to describe effective leaders: passion and premeditation.

But sometimes I wonder if we shouldn't stop using the term leaders and leadership. A lot of baggage comes with the terms. The worst of it is the image of the leader saying "Jump!" And the classic response from the followers: "How high?"

Leadership is not the process of superimposing one big ego on a lot of little egos.

When I try to define it, I keep coming back to what an associate justice of the U.S. Supreme Court once observed about pornography. Potter Stewart said he really couldn't define it but "I know it when I see it." I feel the same way about leadership. Most people do.

And that may provide the best working definition of leadership. If we know it when we see it, what are we seeing? Several distinct characteristics:

- High energy
- Vision
- A relentless pursuit of goals
- Careful planning
- Risk taking
- Highly focused
- Effective listening ability
- Compassion
- Perceptiveness
- Coaching and motivational skills
- Adaptability
- Creativity
- Fairness
- Toughness
- Loyalty
- Honesty
- Articulateness
- Decisiveness

Wow! It reads like the Boy Scout oath. I'm all over the lot. But so what? I'll add a few more. A leader is:

- Willing to share power and responsibility,
- Ready to recognize the contributions of others,
- Willing to give feedback, quickly and explicitly,
- Able to serve as a positive role model.

It's a mouthful. But as I consider the leader/manager role, I recall all the mentors, sports coaches, and military and political leaders whom I've been drawn to over the years, not to mention the good and bad managers who enhanced or blighted my business career, and I'm convinced that it takes *all* of the above characteristics to be a consistently good leader day-in and day-out.

Sounds impossible, doesn't it? That's why we're told that leaders are born, not made. Certain personality traits are essential. Run through the list up above and see how you stack up. Are there gaps? Do some characteristics fit and not others? Before you decide that leadership isn't your thing, ask whether those missing traits are really there in the background, dormant, but need to be developed.

I'm living proof that leadership skills—skills as opposed to the bone structure of one's personality—can be developed. Is it possible to read a book or attend a class to become a leader? No way. But books and classes can help you cultivate inherent leadership potential. Years ago I read Jerry Kramer's *Instant Replay* and I was amazed by the energy, discipline, and vision that Vince Lombardi brought to bear on the Green Bay Packers. Coach Lombardi was the guy who said, "Winning isn't everything, it's the only thing." When I read that, there was an immediate click. I could hear the button being pushed. I didn't rush right out and become a leader by any means. But I had permission from then on to use my own energy, discipline, and vision, characteristics that probably would have gone underutilized without Vince Lombardi's example.

And I probably didn't even realize the effect he had had on me. I was the quarterback of an intramural football team at the University of Dayton. One spring, I got a call from one of the university's assistant deans who organized the league, and he wanted to know if my team would be taking part in the program. I was so damned cocky! I told him that they better start painting the lines on the field where the playoffs were held because we were going to be there.

My team won the championship (not that year, though), and I was a quarterback with a lousy arm and not all that fast on my feet. Years later, one of my former teammates reminded me of my athletic shortcomings and said, "But you were a great quarterback because you worked so hard at it and surrounded yourself with the very best players."

Vince Lombardi taught me that. Just as the good managers I worked for at Xerox taught me through their example how to get the job done. Just as the bad managers taught me how not to lead. In both cases, I started taking notes and wondering what I would do if I were in charge. I looked and listened and collected a catalog of what people liked and disliked about management. One day, along came Neil Lamey, my boss in Columbus, who said to his management team, "Here's what we're going to do," and made us believe we could do it. From that moment on, I was ready.

Are you ready? You've got to take stock and honestly answer the question. It requires huge amounts of time and effort. Not everyone is willing to make the commitment and the sacrifices. But if the desire to be a leader doesn't hit you like a Mack truck—if you can take it or leave it—leave it! If there are doubts, leadership simply isn't worth the endless effort and the agony. You can't fake leadership.

I'm still studying to be an effective leader, and it's a course I'll be enrolled in for the rest of my life. Just when I think I know it all, I discover I know nothing.

Even so, I wouldn't want anything else, and it's a course I wish more people would enroll in. There's nothing like it for sheer satisfaction. I get high watching my people succeed, going to their first President's Club to be honored by Xerox for having a great year, and just feeling good about themselves. That's the thrill of leadership. I wish I knew a few more powerful adjectives to make my point. But in the end, you really can't adequately describe the feeling. Words are only the shadows of the real thing. I can tell you this from personal experience, though— you'll know it when you live it.

4
▼

BREAKTHROUGH:

HIGH FIVES IN SIX MONTHS

One of the things I like best about Xerox's Leadership Through Quality is the emphasis on the customer. It helps keep our heads screwed on straight about the number one priority.

If you're reading this book because your business is in trouble—or you're trying to stay out of trouble—rediscover the customer pronto!

In the last chapter, I related how I spent several hours on day one traveling with two of my reps. Not only did I want to see how they were doing business, my purpose was also to establish contact systematically with the district's customers.

Question: When was the last time you met with a customer? Be honest. And nobody gets a free pass on this one. I don't care if you're a CEO pulling down ten million bucks a year. Was it last week? Last month? Last year?

No matter what the answer was, I want you to put the book down right now and contact one of your customers. And don't stop at one. My objective in Cleveland in the first few weeks was to get in touch with my top ten customers. Ten's a nice round number. Try it yourself. Let me toss in a warning, though. You could end up like the politician who goes out on a busy street corner and asks "How am I doing?" And the answer comes back like a boomerang—"Awful!!!!!!"

It's happened to me. I've contacted customers and gotten such an earful of negative comments from every one of them that, in despair, I've asked my people, "Doesn't anybody like us?"

It's frustrating in a big way. Once a major account is botched up it can take anywhere from three to five years to get things back on track. All the previous effort goes down the tubes and you have to start all over again.

Here's a sampling of what you might hear if your operation's engine is only firing on a couple of cylinders:

- "We're not treated like a major account."
- "Your own team doesn't talk to each other."
- "I didn't appreciate the way your rep went over my head."
- "I don't trust the proposal that has been delivered."
- "You're just trying to jam products in. . . . We've been over-sold."
- "You're inflexible."
- "You didn't understand my requirements."
- "You were sore losers when we chose another vendor."
- "I didn't know you offered that product."
- "I haven't seen anyone from senior management in ten years."
- "I don't feel that I'm important to you."

If you're hearing similar comments, consider yourself lucky —at least the customers are still talking to you. It's like the old line that a mild heart attack is nature's way of telling you to slow down. Those comments told me that my district was having a heart attack, and that I'd better speed up.

The truth hurts and it heals. The tongue-lashings confirmed that the process was faulty and that I had better put the strongest reps and managers on those major accounts PDQ—pretty damned quick. Sometimes, though, the damage is hard to repair. To this day in Cleveland, after more than five years of success, there are still customers—ex-customers—who won't let Xerox back in the door because of what happened in the mid-1980s. Should they be written off? Absolutely not. We just have to keep trying to show them that it's a different corporation and a different culture.

TRUTH SERUM

Don't create a fool's paradise by isolating yourself from the customer. It's so easy to make that mistake. You'll get rosy second-hand reports from the field because nobody wants to bring the boss bad news. You'll have to go out and find it out yourself. Once you do, there's an instant readout on the accuracy of the information you've been receiving. You'll know who's been blowing smoke and who hasn't. Right away, honesty will be established as the best policy.

Keep a list of must-do chores, and put this one on it: Tell everyone that a surefire way *not* to win points with the boss is to withhold unpleasant information. I want to know everything, good and bad. It doesn't mean that I'm unwilling to delegate responsibility or to empower my people. Just keep me informed. I hate surprises. One of the surest ways of getting on my bad side is to spring something on me. By establishing that fact early on in Cleveland, I guaranteed the purity of the information flow that was reaching me and made certain that I was always in the loop.

"Don't tell Frank" is the same as saying, "Here's a gun—go shoot yourself in the foot."

PHONE ETIQUETTE

This next one is another technique that works, and I recommend you try it right away: No matter what you're doing, drop everything when a customer calls. I have a standing order that I'm to be interrupted during any meeting if a customer wants to speak to me. I don't care if I'm having a conversation with Paul Allaire, Xerox's chairman and CEO (which doesn't happen very often). If I'm in the office, I take the call.

What's amazing is the attitude among many managers as they rise through the corporate ranks, that one of the perks is not having to deal with the customer. Here's a tip: Lean back and look up the ladder. You'll see your boss on the next rung and his boss just above him and the boss's boss's boss up a little higher. Do them all a favor. At the earliest opportunity, arrange to either have them join you on a customer call or bring the customer in to visit them.

Want to break glass? Shake up the bureaucrats? That's how to do it. I have found that senior management will say no, no, no to me or my managers, but when I pry some of those "Doctor No's" out of the office and take them in to see a customer, the words often become yes, yes, yes.

I have had some of our top executives go out on customer calls, and afterward change—I mean substantially change—Xerox's process and policies to meet the customer's requirements.

Another warning: I've made enemies at Xerox this way. To dynamite a logjam, I have been known to go over the heads of my superiors with an invitation to the next level to come meet an important customer. Once, I was getting nowhere with a request to provide financing for a small chain of copy centers I believed was destined for big things. A decision kept getting sidetracked until I went shopping for a more senior executive who would travel to Cleveland to see the potential himself. I found the right person; he came, he listened, and he approved the request for somewhat risky, unconventional financing. The customer turned out to be a tremendous success.

The customers appreciate it when you don't take no for an answer and they take note of your sincerity in getting things done for them. It helps build a strong bond and a sense of loyalty. Also, your people are turned on by a leader who has enough courage to buck the system to get the job done. You don't have to set yourself on fire every day of the week. What it takes is an unrelenting commitment to customer and employee satisfaction.

When Xerox made that the number one corporate priority in 1987, some people in high places scoffed—and they still do. I believed in it 100 percent—and I still do.

IT TOLLS FOR THEE

I had a ship-captain's bell installed just past the reception area near the bull pen where the reps had their desks. Whenever anyone got an order, they were supposed to ring that sucker good and loud.

Think about it logically: winning isn't much fun if nobody knows about it. By making each deal a public event, I was giving the successful reps a little instant recognition and gratification. I was also increasing the pressure on the reps who weren't ringing the bell. They'd look up from their desks all smiles and offering congratulations, but saying to themselves, "I can do that and I better get on the stick."

I knew we were going to make our plan in February when the bell started clanging with greater frequency. The place wasn't sounding like a firehouse during an arsonists' convention, the way it would toward the end of the second quarter, but the sounds of silence weren't as deafening as they had been. The noise would start just after 4:30 P.M., when the reps returned from their calls. There'd be a cheer from the troops and the managers would rush out of their offices to see if it was one of their people doing the honors. And I always responded with a handshake and a pat on the back. I wanted the rep to know that, if nothing else, I appreciated his or her hard work.

A bell is one of the oldest tricks in the book for motivating salespeople. Simple—some would say simpleminded—but effective. Everyone got a kick out of the bell and it is still rung with gusto to this day.

As in most Xerox districts, I also prominently posted photographs of the sales leaders in various categories for each month. We called it the wall of fame. There'd be immediate complaints if I was slow about getting the pictures up.

PROGRESS

I started every month with a business meeting. Attendance was mandatory. The purpose was to lay out the objectives for the next thirty days, do some training, and spread the gospel. At the outset, without fail, I recognized the accomplishments of the preceding month. If a rep or an entire team made plan, I always noted it and thanked them. Even if an individual fell short but was still trying, I noted the effort.

The meeting in March was special, although I didn't treat it that way. Cleveland, as a district, had made the plan for February—as I had predicted. I hadn't made major changes, and I told the group it proved they could be successful without a wholesale housecleaning. I made it clear we still had a long way to go. The chip was still on my shoulder: they had to prove themselves; I had to prove myself.

I should stop at this point to add that I had been forced to fire one rep my third day on the job for a violation of ethics that occurred before I took over. It is easier to get into Xerox than it is to get out. There are very strict procedures governing the steps that lead up to a dismissal, but an individual goes onto the fast track for the exit when business ethics are involved. Even though I've piqued your curiosity, I'm not going to provide more details on the case simply because it wouldn't be fair to the person involved. Later in the book, I'll go over ethics in a general way. There's no reason why an operation can't be superaggressive and nevertheless always play by the rules.

The second change was to pull a young guy by the name of Larry Tyler off his assignment handling a product that was dead in the water as far as I was concerned. It was a desktop work station that took too much effort to sell and support. I had found out the hard way in Minneapolis that persistence is fine as long as there is a payback commensurate with the effort. The work stations were losers, and by the end of the year Xerox recognized the error and dropped the product.

The quick decision to redeploy Tyler was well received. We weren't going to be spinning our wheels. The way the ethics violation was handled also made the point that I expected my people to play it straight. When in doubt, bring the issue to me. I had told them that on the very first day, and I meant it.

At the March business meeting, I put another important stake in the ground. In the past, there had been racial tension in the district office, and it was going to stop. Although I had heard about the problem in the first few days, I deliberately moved slowly to give myself a chance to gather information. What I

discovered was that there were no villains or culprits to be sin-
gled out, but I told everyone gathered in the amphitheater that
they worked in a color-blind district. Period. If they didn't like
it, couldn't live with it, they could get another job. Everyone was
entitled to the same shot at success; everyone would be held to
the same standards of excellence. At an earlier meeting with the
managers, I gave them the word and said mankind had wrestled
with the problem for hundreds of years and obviously I wasn't
going to solve it. "But let me tell you this," I said, "I don't care
what goes on in the outside world, in here there's no bigotry, no
insensitivity, no racial disrespect. I won't tolerate it for a second.
If you're a racist, I want you out of here!"

I repeated the same message to the whole group. Nobody
stirred while I spoke. For months afterward, I kept my ear to the
ground for any indication that minorities weren't getting a fair
shake. What I heard was the sound of gears meshing throughout
the organization, not the clanking and grinding you get when
the sand of hatred is poured into the machinery.

THE NATURE OF THE MODERN WORKPLACE

Morale and performance were definitely ticking upward. One
reason was that I was smart enough to change my mind. Every
year at Xerox, the districts have a large recognition dinner to
celebrate the previous year's successes. These can be pretty lavish (later on I'll tell you about some of them) depending on just
how well a district performed. I had made up my mind that
since Cleveland had done poorly, there would be a bare-bones
recognition event.

However, one of my managers, George Urban, bribed me.
He knew I was a Bruce Springsteen fan and that the rock star
would be appearing in Cleveland that February. He came up
with two tickets, which I guess he figured would soften me up.
George definitely had his foot in the door. He went on to tell me
that the district needed what he called "a road trip"—à la the
movie *Animal House,* to get charged up. I was adamantly opposed to rewarding failure. As far as I was concerned, a road trip
would have to wait until the following year, when I would make
good on my promise to take everybody on a ski weekend.

George argued with me. He said if we jump-started enthusiasm there would be a quick payback. I really was a jerk about it. The district hadn't paid the rent in 1987, and I wasn't going to pay for a party. I thought the road trip would interfere with my 'tude—the attitude—that I was trying to project to get Cleveland cranked up again.

But George Urban was right. Having gone through the worst of times, he knew the group desperately needed a small taste of the best of times. My locker-room pep talks, process, high level of expectation and accountability, and personal example were going to do the job eventually. But our goals would be reached faster if I relented and let the good times roll, if even for just a few hours.

The lesson I drew is this: listen to advice and keep an open mind. My no-road-trip decision was wrong. Flat out. If George hadn't told me I was wrong—crouched for protection behind those bulletproof Springsteen tickets—I would have ended up violating one of my own commandments of leadership: Make it fun!

Write that down. Please. Make it fun. Millions of dollars are spent trying to figure out what ails business these days. Keep the money and ask a simple question: "Do you enjoy coming to work?"

An honest answer will explain almost everything. It will tell you why productivity is down and absenteeism is up, why quality is poor and customer satisfaction so abysmal, and will explain the reason for high employee turnover, low stock prices, and angry shareholders.

Why? It's not fun to come to work.

Ask yourself the question, without hiding behind the rationalization that "work isn't much fun, but that's the nature of the modern workplace."

Nonsense. We were selling copiers in Cleveland, for Pete's sake, and it was fun. Copy machines are not exactly what is traditionally considered to be a glamorous, wild, and crazy business. I'm proud of my career, but I don't expect my eight-year-old son, Frankie, to say "Daddy, I want grow up to be an astronaut or a copier salesman."

It's one of the reasons that I emphasize competition and winning. By plugging into that human instinct, I'm drawing enough power to overcome all that's boring, mundane, and un-pleasant about the job—any job.

The same goes for trying to create a familylike atmosphere. Some people didn't have happy families when they were children. I did. We had a ball. We cared for each other, cried for each other, kept trying for each other. As a leader, I want to come as close as I can to capturing that same spirit.

Not having fun on the job has nothing to do with the nature of the modern workplace and has everything to do with the nature of the modern manager. Instead of creating the right atmosphere, it's easier to hide behind the numbers.

PASS/FAIL: A REPORT CARD

While I was researching and writing this book, there was a get-together of reps and managers one Saturday afternoon at the home of Paul MacKinnon, my invaluable right-hand man in Cleveland (since he is always cool and steady in a crisis, a fount of wisdom, we nicknamed him "Padre"). Padre served up lots of beer, pasta, Italian sausage, and war stories. I was struck that the group kept reminding me about how much fun those five years had been. And these were men and women who had really worked their tails off.

One rep said he used to get into arguments with his wife when their baby woke up early and threw his morning routine behind schedule. He wasn't worried about being chewed out for being late; he was worried about missing the fun.

He felt that way because I was doing my job. "It was hard not to get caught up in it," a manager recalled. "There's Frank driving into the parking lot at 7:00 A.M., windows down, radio blaring hard rock, slapping the steering wheel, jiving to the beat of music. He was ready to go."

That was no act. I can't wait to get to work in the morning. I've always been that way. In college, I hated to go to bed at night because there was so much else I wanted to be doing.

Maybe I'm a little hyper. But you don't have to be. Just keep asking the question—is this a fun place to work? And then another question—why not? And another—what can I do to change it?

What I did to change it was listen to George Urban. We got some buses and loaded up the whole crew before dawn one Saturday morning in late February or early March. The road trip wasn't as wild as in *Animal House*, but there was some roaring. We spent the day on the slopes of Peak 'n Peak in New York State. It snowed. We came back to the lodge for chili and pizza. After dinner, the reps did satirical skits about the managers, scoring with a lot of barbs and getting plenty of laughs. There was a disc jockey and rock and roll—of course. We didn't get back to Cleveland until ten-thirty or eleven o'clock that night.

Keep in mind that those same revelers had been sitting in the amphitheater a few weeks before wondering whose head was going to be the first to be lopped off.

What had changed in the meantime?

Pardon me if I sound too poetic, but let me count the ways:

1. Vision
2. Expectation
3. Accountability
4. Consequences (for failure and success)
5. Commitment
6. Atmosphere

Use those six items as a report card. Grade yourself on a scale of one to ten. By the time we got back from Peak 'n Peak, I'd say Cleveland merited sevens for vision and expectation; and that may be a little high. Six for atmosphere. Fours for everything else.

All failing grades. It's got to be ten straight across. Never be satisfied with anything less. And when the tens appear, go for eleven.

OF CARROTS AND STICKS, BONDING AND BLUE JEANS

There is much to be said for giving people a preview of coming attractions. I've done it for my readers a couple of times by promising to talk about customer proposals, Xerox's ethics and remedial-action programs, and our recognition dinners. And I will keep the promise—but not right now.

I want to make a final few comments about the road trip, since it really was a preview of coming attractions. Peak 'n Peak became a district tradition. We went up there three or four times to celebrate our successes. You could probably make too much of the importance of that first trip. After all, we put in an enormous amount of hard work between March and July of 1988, and some of the people who partied that Saturday didn't make the cut. Despite that, the outing accomplished several beneficial purposes. First, a factionalized, demoralized, bickering organization had a chance to do some bonding. The term is overused these days, but don't knock bonding. It's very important. Second, as a leader I was able to show them that the future was not going to be all stick and no carrot. I gave them a taste of the carrot; just a nibble. Third, they got a chance to see me *au naturel*. No, I didn't take my clothes off. Just getting out of the suit and into jeans and a sweater helped. You won't hear me advocate dressing down for success. But I do think letting your people see you in a casual setting makes it easier to forge a strong working relationship.

CAUGHT IN THE MIDDLE

I won't pretend that it's easy to be a friend and a leader. In fact, it can't be done. Leader and friend—okay. The role of leader always comes first. Just as being a father or mother—a firm, responsible, loving parent—takes precedence over being a friend to one's children.

Probably this is an area that I shouldn't go anywhere near because I don't have easy answers about how to reconcile two roles that in many ways are so contradictory. It's one of the things that humans don't do very well. Not all of us are good parents. It's hard to be firm, to say no, and to stick to it. On the job, we make good friends, we love them and care about them, but when the time comes for being tough and delivering bad news, we choke. A leader must step up to this responsibility even if it means erecting a wall that inhibits friendship. It's one of the hazards of the job.

How do I do it? I was afraid you'd ask. Constant self-examination is one way. I'm always asking myself, "Am I letting my personal feelings get in the way of a sound business decision?" "Am I getting too close?" "Am I taking the easy way out by not telling this guy that he isn't doing the job?" If the answer is yes, it's quickly corrected by putting on my "game face" and going to work. But just asking the questions helps.

A leader mediates the interests of the group or organization against the interests of the individual. He or she must be an honest broker. And that's not an impossible task as long as you're fair and honest. A good mediator offers counsel and perspective, and poses alternatives when there is a conflict. It is rarely an all-or-nothing situation. As an executive, I'm always ready to tell my superiors that a mistake has been made or that a policy isn't serving Xerox's purposes. And Xerox listens; I wouldn't be working for the corporation if it didn't. I'll fight for my people when they're right, and when they're not, I'll tell them and work with them to find an acceptable accommodation.

The mediator's function is one of the things that make being a leader worthwhile. Without a mediator, there's nothing but a no-man's-land, a killing zone, between the company and its employees. It's characteristic of a leaderless organization. I don't mind being caught in the middle. Put me in the middle. I like it.

Example: Early on in Cleveland, my boss wanted to dismiss a young rep who had been too eager and too aggressive for his own good. But he wasn't all bad. The kid's sales numbers were steadily improving. At first, he hadn't been much of a team player, but his managers were slowly bringing him around by using the coaching and accountability techniques that I had introduced to the district. I thought he had terrific potential. I told my superior we couldn't afford to lose that much raw talent and that I would work with him on discipline and procedure. It was not any easy sell, but I convinced him to give it a try.

Then I went to the rep and explained exactly what was going on. I said he was right on the verge of losing his job. He could sink or swim—it was all up to him. There was no varnish. I told him I had interceded on his behalf. I wanted him to know —and I told him flat out—that I was taking a big risk. As far as I was concerned, though, it was worth it: he had the right stuff. "You better not let me down," I said.

That was mediation. It was also pure premeditation. I knew the kid would probably get mad and quit if I just told him that Rochester wanted his scalp. Instead, I told him he owed me. I presented him with an IOU. A classic either/or: either he was going to be successful, or he would be breaking faith with me.

Today, the customers would kill for that guy. They love him. He's a solid performer and a role model for the other employees. He makes money for Xerox, for his managers, even for the executive who wanted him fired.

I played a similar mediator's role from the other direction on the very first day in Cleveland. After I met with my people and vowed to tackle any good reps or managers who tried to quit, my bluff was called immediately.

A manager grabbed me and said one of his reps, Brian Walsh, was so frustrated that he was planning to resign. He assured me the rep was worth saving. I told him to set up a meeting later in the week and I'd speak to Brian.

"You better do it right now," he said. "Otherwise Walsh is gone."

It wasn't what I had planned. I wanted to hit the road and see customers. But I spent half an hour with Brian. He was down in the dumps. His assessment of the district's problems was pretty accurate. I asked him to give me a chance to fix things. "I don't know you," I said, "but your manager tells me you're good, and I'm going to take his word for it. I need good people around here." He was in his early twenties at the time, and Xerox had been his first job out of college. "I know you're frustrated," I said. "So am I. But I've learned that nobody should quit when they're losing. You've been on a losing team. As good as you are —you're a loser. You haven't earned the right to quit until you start winning."

Brian stayed. Brian won.

SHOW AND TELL

I'm running out of space in this chapter to cram in all I need to tell you about the first six months in Cleveland.

I don't want to forget this: Tell your people explicitly what you are going to do for them. Don't weasel around.

Expectation is a two-way street. You've laid out exactly what you expect from them, haven't you?

If not, do it today. Do it within the hour. The next step is to print up a handout sheet or an overhead slide projection displaying what they can expect from you.

Here's one that I've used:

WHAT YOU CAN EXPECT FROM FRANK

- Five + Customer Contacts per Day (Travel/Phone)
- Two—three Executive Interviews per Week *
- Review Action Plans
- Involvement in Top 50 Accounts
- Involvement in Community
- Work Ethic
- Open Door
- Hold Manager Accountable for:
  —Development
  —Career Counseling
  —Customer Involvement
- Ethics
- Employee Input
- Push Hard on Rochester to Benefit Customer/Employee
- Openness and Trust
- Tight Inspection
- Visible—Available
- Relentless Pursuit of Excellence
- Turn Major Accounts
- Fun—Reward—Recognition

* These are one-on-one interviews that I conduct with each of the reps throughout the year.

This slide amounts to a contract that I committed myself to honor. You can modify it to fit your needs. Slice it, dice it any way you want—but make a commitment. Hand it out, post it on the bulletin board, and live by it.

I guarantee your people will respond positively. They'll hold you to the bargain. And the moment you back off—kiss your credibility good-bye. As a manager, once you let down someone on your team, you're done—or close to it!

Another bit of show and tell is this "eye chart" that goes up on the wall. Its purpose is to improve everyone's vision and vocabulary.

NEW EYE CHART

Out-Sell

~~No Prospects~~

Out-Prepare

~~I Can't~~

Out-Strategize

~~Recession~~

Out-Execute

~~Whining~~

Out-Work

~~Cynicism~~

Blame No One; Expect Nothing; Do Something

~~Bad Territory~~

EARLY WARNING

In late March, it was time out for President's Club, a Xerox institution for recognizing reps and managers who have exceeded their plans by anywhere from 20 to 50 percent. The company takes the winners to a world-class resort area, and a good time is had by all. In 1988, the location was Hawaii. I qualified for the club on the basis of my performance in Minneapolis and I was also going to be recognized for being the number one district sales manager nationally. Julie and I were looking forward to the trip in a big way.

Probably a dozen people from Cleveland also attended President's Club, but that was not a good showing, since fewer than a third of the district's sales personnel were eligible. The first day there, each district manager was introduced and asked to stand up in front of the crowd of several hundred people. The applause was polite but restrained. Bear in mind that after about two months, I was still pretty much a stranger to the people in Cleveland. In that setting, Julie and I felt a little awkward being among all the old Cleveland comrades who were having a good time. But when my name was announced, the Cleveland delegation just went nuts—cheering, whistling, stomping. None of the other managers got that kind of reception.

It was a shock. It stunned me and it stunned veteran Xerox hands to hear that kind of exuberance from a district that had been written off as Deadendsville. I read it as a vote of confidence.

I said to Julie, "I think we've got something going here."

And did we ever. Back home, the captain's bell was clanging away. By April, making the thirty-day plan was a piece of cake. The interlude in Hawaii had given me a chance to compare notes with other Xerox executives. I saw that business was slow around the country, which meant that if I could get Cleveland cooking right away, there was a chance of coming out on top or damn close.

I instituted what came to be known as Major Suspect List Reviews, MSLRs. If any one thing can be credited with the Cleveland turnaround, it was the MSLRs. But let me tell you, it was an incredible amount of work. I met with each rep and ran through his or her accounts in depth—every one of them—in thirty-, sixty-, and ninety-day slices. I'd hold an MSLR meeting in the morning, go on calls, and come back late in the afternoon for two or three more reviews.

Nervous managers would come to me in advance to say that

the reps were chewing their fingernails and wanted to know what they should be prepared to cover. "Everything," I said. "If it wiggles, I want to know about it."

I repeated this grueling process every quarter for the rest of the year. We literally took the wheels off and stripped the sales vehicle down to the chassis. Not only was I educating myself about the district's potential, my reps' abilities, and the skills of their managers, but I was plunging the group deep and hard into the vortex of its own business.

At the same time, I started nudging the district higher by offering mini-challenges, or blitzes, that were above and beyond the numbers called for in the plan. I'd set a goal of five or six orders to be written in the next ten days, with the prize for the winners to be an afternoon off and a lunch as my guests, rounded out with a few hours in a sports bar in front of a big screen TV watching NCAA playoff games. I restricted these events to winners only. If you didn't write the business, there was no reward. The first time out, we had twenty-five winners. More than half the reps in the shop were beating their own plans.

THE YELLOW BRICK ROAD

Midyear is make-or-break time at Xerox. If you're not steaming by the time June rolls around, the year overall will not be a good one. In 1988, June 30 fell just before the long Fourth of July weekend, which meant the final figures for the month and the second quarter wouldn't be available by the time the district broke for the holiday.

I had a hunch we'd be in the mood to celebrate, so I arranged a golf outing for the managers that weekend at a posh local country club. There was no way, however, I could show up on Saturday morning without knowing where we stood. The uncertainty would be a killer. I told everybody I expected us to do about $3.4 million worth of business, which was unheard of for Cleveland, even at the end of the year. They thought I was nuts, and I was beginning to wonder myself if I hadn't been a little overoptimistic. I was a nervous wreck.

Although the administrative staff was off until Monday, Glenn Hines, one of my managers, said he knew how to access

Rochester's computer, and I arranged to meet him at the office along with another manager, Bill Hookway, who lived near me. When we arrived, Glenn had stretched computer paper from the elevator down the hallway to my office like the Yellow Brick Road. Bill and I walked hunched over, reading the printout's figures. At the end of the road, there it was—bingo! Cleveland had jumped in front of Cincinnati and Columbus, two much larger districts, to lead the region, and we were in the top five nationwide.

We had made it! Bill, Glenn, and I jumped in the car and headed for the country club. It was some kind of ride. As we turned into the gate, I started madly honking the horn and blinking the lights, computer paper streaming from the windows, wild men leaning out of the car and waving. On both sides of the road, golfers cursed and shook their fists at us for messing up their games. We screeched to a stop at the practice green, and the waiting Xerox people let out a huge cheer when they saw our excitement and realized what it meant.

Hugs and high fives. Amazing that we didn't get thrown off the course. And if we had, it wouldn't have mattered a bit.

5

TEAM BUILDING:

ALL IN, ALL-OUT

I owe it all to Monty. Between April and June, before mid-year 1988, he made two or three appearances in Cleveland. What a star! Wearing a loud, ugly, black-and-white checked sports jacket with crumpled dollar bills stuffed into the pockets, Monty would burst into our amphitheater ready to "make a deal." He talked fast, talked glib, talked turkey.

Yes, I have no shame. If motivating the district meant doing a bad impersonation of TV's Monty Hall from time to time, I was willing to make the sacrifice. And it was a lot of fun. I'd have someone shill for me—my district marketing manager, Paul MacKinnon, got really good at it—by standing up and chanting "Monty, Monty, Monty" until the group joined in. I'd make a grand entrance and come down the center aisle wearing that ridiculous sports jacket, a loud tie, and a pair of wraparound shades.

Waving a five-dollar bill, Monty would proclaim, "Five dollars for the first rep who brings me a calendar with five confirmed calls on it." At first, there was puzzled silence until somebody decided to get into the spirit of the thing. A hand went up in the back row. "There we go! A calendar with five confirmed calls . . . come on down, sir, and play the game." I'd get the rep in front of the group, wave the microphone in front of his nose, and say, "You know how to play the game. Five dollars or—you can have what's in the box!" Monty would ham it up, strutting around with the mike, and making smart-alecky comments.

It was a cockamamie cross between "Let's Make a Deal" and "The Price Is Right." We'd have three or four boxes to choose from. There might be a travel alarm clock inside or a worthless gag gift like a set of refrigerator magnets or a tiny toy Corvette. The audience would start yelling, "Take the box," or, "Keep the money!"

But the major prizes—Sony Watchmans, boom boxes, four tickets to a Cleveland Browns game and such—were tied to specific sales targets that I wanted to hit. There was a drawing every time Monty made an appearance. Two weeks before the big day, we'd announce that in order to get their business cards into the fishbowl from which Monty selected the players, the reps would need to write an order (or orders) on a 1065, one of our mid-range products. On the next round, the requirement was that reps had to be their team's number one in installed revenue, equipment that was being sold and delivered by the end of the midyear period. Then, for Monty's final appearance of the cycle, I ratcheted up the value of the prizes and decreed that only reps with the highest number of total orders on each team would be eligible for the drawing.

I kept changing the mix so that anyone riding a wave in one area would be forced to diversify to stay in the game. By the time Monty arrived on the scene, my Major Suspect List Reviews had told me where I needed to really bear down.

Believe it or not, Monty was a hit. Grown men and women, many with salaries pushing six figures or more a year, really went out and hustled to qualify for the drawings. I pulled names out of the fishbowl and they played the game as if it were live network television, bantering with me, negotiating back and forth. "Here's my final offer," I'd say, shaking my head. "You get this nice crisp twenty-dollar bill and I get to keep what's behind the box . . . deal?" The group would scream "No!" or, "Go for it." We had a good time. After my daughter, Alexandra, was born, Monty started offering twenty dollars to anyone who could produce her picture. There were no takers the first time or the second. But when Monty made the request again a couple of months later, figuring that he had a good running gag, about forty people rushed forward with Alle's picture, demanding twenty dollars.

Monty, the meanie that he was, refused to pay on the grounds that he had been set up.

FIRST THE BASICS

You may not have the stomach for playing Monty Hall—sports jackets that ugly are hard to find—but I can't overemphasize the value of carefully timed incentives as a way to boost sales performance higher and higher. People love to be recognized; it's not the size of the prize that's important. The enjoyment comes from the fact that they're competitive, they have pride, and they want to win!

Monty is just one of several incentive techniques that I used. Before I share those with you, however, I want to make sure you understand that random, scattershot incentives are counterproductive. If your basic process is not in place and functioning smoothly, incentives can be a distraction. The purpose of incentives is to goose an effective process to the next level.

Before Monty made his first appearance, my Major Suspect List Reviews were well under way. "Let's make a deal," as Monty would say. First steal the MSLR idea from this book, implement it, and then you're welcome to Monty or my other incentives.

I know you probably already conduct account reviews. Most sales executives do. But not like these. I want to backtrack and take you through the Major Suspect List Review process that I summarized in Chapter 4 in the hopes that you'll see the importance of a "total immersion" account review.

I swiped the MSLR concept from Tom Stuart, my mentor in Minneapolis. I noticed a major improvement in performance by comparing my first year out there as district sales manager, which was only so-so, with the second, after Tom took over the district, when we really started moving. My variation on the MSLR was to do it more intensively and more frequently than Tom did.

Try at least one round; four times a year may be too much to ask. I imagine, though, that you'll find it so helpful that MSLRs will become annual or semiannual events. At first, your people won't like them. Mine didn't. After a while, the best managers and reps really take to the process. They see it as an opportunity to put together a comprehensive strategic package for all their accounts. And those who don't take to it . . . ? I don't want to seem brutal, but they won't survive. They'll be lapped and run right off the track by the others.

As I said, the account review divides into thirty-, sixty-, and ninety-day slices. Don't take any shortcuts on this. There's a temptation to focus on only the ripe deals coming in within the next thirty days and let the rest "develop." I work just the opposite by going even further down the road. I'll say to the rep, "You're projecting an income this year of eighty thousand dollars. How are you going to get there? Show me how each one of these accounts is going to contribute to that bottom line in the next thirty-, sixty-, and ninety-day periods." Xerox has an income-planning system that works well. It's based on the simple premise that the rep should be able to sit down and plan out annual income on the basis of how many machines he or she intends to sell to various accounts: four here, ten there, two around the corner.

The income plan is a very incriminating piece of evidence. I can take one look at it and say, "But that's not going to get you where you want to go. You're still way short." To block the shot, the reps tend to point to the deals coming up in the next thirty days. "What makes you think that the next thirty days will be any different from the last thirty days?"

My objective is to force him or her to take a cold, hard look at each customer, spread out over 365 days. Once you get a rep to name a specific figure for each account, the next question is simple: "What are you going to do to generate that level of business?"

I refuse to accept generalities. Generalities tell me the rep is winging it.

I'll make a prediction: You'll hear a lot of generalities. Step on them immediately.

"You've been in the assignment over a year now, and you say you're going to do this, that, and the other thing. . . . But if you add up those numbers today, you can't make it. You're not doing the activities, nor do you have the strategies that will make this thing happen."

I get really irked when I hear about a business process that requires people to fake it by just putting meaningless figures down on the page. What's the point? Don't bother to waste everybody's time. Go out and sell something instead.

I suppose cooking the books makes people feel good at the time it's happening. But in six months or a year, the imaginative chef has to start frying up another batch of fiction to explain why the four-star restaurant he promised to be running looks more like a soup kitchen.

Even worse is the charade of developing a business plan knowing full well that no one will be held accountable. I've had bosses—the bad ones—who did that. The outlook and planning documents went right into a bottom drawer. It's a rotten thing to do. The reps are left absolutely defenseless. They're out in the marketplace relying on luck and raw talent. No strategy, no tactical guidance, no priorities.

How long would a coach last in the NBA if his one and only principle was "Run hard, shoot often, and don't foul out"?

If you have a process or a procedure that's not being followed up on—get rid of it.

TAKING SNAPSHOTS OF THE BUSINESS

The MSLR forces the reps to put their accounts and assumptions under the microscope. They should be doing that as a matter of course—but they probably aren't. No one has ever asked them to. What I have to do as a leader—and what you have to do—is ask.

- Tell me what's going to happen ninety days from now.
- Show me what each account has and tell me this: What are you doing for each one?
- What's the organizational structure for each account?
- Who makes the decision?
- What's the competitive situation?
- What help do you need?
- What are you doing to knock Kodak out?

And remember—this is all happening in front of the rep's manager. He or she should have been asking those kinds of questions. Your involvement early on will tell you a lot about both the rep and the manager, and it's a teaching tool as well.

Now, I'm educating three people: myself, the rep, and the manager. We're getting a quick snapshot of the territory. All of us can see right away what's happening, what isn't happening, and what needs to happen.

It's amazing how people tend to live on wishful thinking and vague possibilities. The MSLR can come as a real jolt to someone who prides him- or herself on being practical and hard-headed. Every now and then we all need a reminder that sales is a cause-and-effect business. No cause, no effect. What I'm doing with the review is making the rep show me the linkage.

JUST SAY KNOW

What you'll see during a typical MSLR isn't pretty. I had one rep finish the two-hour presentation, get up from the conference table, and say gloomily, "I guess I've got a lot of work to do, don't I?" But I'd rather have that reaction than a false sense of confidence that comes from ignorance and overestimation.

If nothing else, the reps know what they don't know. But the question marks aren't going to last long. Each rep who's being reviewed walks away with an action plan that is very specific. "Okay, you need to find out the expiration dates of the competition's contracts within ten days. In thirty days, we want these six accounts in here for demonstrations." It's not just a slap on the wrist and then back to business as usual. I make sure I come back over the next ninety days with inspection and follow-up.

Don't bother doing the MSLR if you aren't going to follow up. It's like discovering a cure for cancer and then never using it.

In some cases the follow-up takes place almost immediately. On one occasion, a rep was so groggy from the pounding he was taking that the review turned into a career-counseling session. There were so many blank spots that the question came down to "Is this the right career for you?" He left there and gamely attempted to deal with the problems but soon realized that it was beyond his capabilities. He came back to me a few weeks later and said, "Frank, I'm trying but it's not working. I think I'm going to start looking for something else." I told him I thought his assessment was correct and that he should take thirty days and find something that was right for him.

As a manager and a leader, you are not doing your people a favor by shielding them from reality. The MSLR is a tremendous reality check. At the end, they all know where they stand. But sometimes knowing isn't enough.

A major account rep in Cleveland knew at the end of his review that his performance was falling far below what I felt was possible, given his major accounts. It was tough for him to swallow because he had been to President's Club a couple of times. He was exceeding his plan and making money.

The review showed me that he was sitting on a gold mine. Instead of tons of bullion, however, he was producing small change. We weren't getting the depth and development out of the accounts—many of them substantial national operations— that was obviously available. I told him what I thought, knowing that a guy who considered himself to be one of the top salespeople in the district wouldn't easily accept it.

If I hadn't done the MSLR, I would not have had the knowledge to make the judgment call. On paper, the numbers looked impressive. And that's the problem with paper. You run down a column of figures comparing last year with this year or one territory to another and jump to the wrong conclusion. Paper-dependent executives all run the same risk.

Like a surgeon, you've got to get into the patient's chest up to your elbows. Don't be squeamish. Ask the necessary questions even if it means putting a senior person on the spot.

"Why don't you know? It's been your account for months. Let's pick up the phone right now and ask them." Don't set out to embarrass the rep. The object is to get the accounts—and the rep—up to potential. I rarely raise my voice. It's much more effective to say, "You can do better than this," pointing out the fact-based reasons why. And implicitly—or explicitly—the next line is: "And I'm here to help you do it." If you don't have the background and the skills to assess the situation accurately and to help that individual, he or she should be the manager—not you.

But if the answer is "I can't do better" or "I don't want your help," then you as a manager know where you stand. Changes will have to be made.

In this case, I went into the field and talked to the rep's customers. Something was obviously going wrong considering the configuration of the territory. Was it too large? Was the mix of accounts wrong? Was I misreading the potential?

I found that at least three customers, one of them a big steel company, simply did not have confidence in the rep. They didn't like doing business with him, but not to the point that they wanted him fired, and they were reluctant to speak up. The accounts were large enough to allow him to survive comfortably despite the ongoing struggle with customer relations.

When I looked closely, I saw that the competition's machines were still in place after two or three years—they should have been long gone. And our own equipment wasn't being upgraded in a significant way.

Major accounts are the underpinning of an entire sales operation. They've got to be handled in an adroit and aggressive way. The person I'm discussing in this case was a major account rep on the major account team, which is the way Xerox differentiates its customer base to avoid mixing small and large customers in one portfolio. I wasn't about to walk away from doing everything possible to light a fire under those accounts.

Once I had investigated, I didn't see any choice other than to pull the rep off the accounts, seeing that the problem was a personality conflict with the customers. Dicey? You bet. He was a member of the President's Club, a rather endangered species in Cleveland at the time. But within about six months, I transferred him to a territory with smaller accounts, and I explained why.

He was not happy. He wrote Xerox CEO David Kearns a scathing twenty-seven-page letter complaining about me. But the decision stood and the territory began to prosper. Today, it does twice the business it did when I arrived in Cleveland.

A TOOL FOR SAVING TIME

The Major Suspect List Review is like a divining rod. Instead of discovering underground water, the way old-timers did, using forked willow sticks, the MSLR points out the business that's right there under your nose. And, even better, it finds the right people to put in the right places at the same time.

It would have taken me years of going out into the field with each one of my reps and managers to learn as much as I did in one month of conducting MSLRs. As I said earlier—and it still stands in capital letters: THERE'S NO SUBSTITUTE FOR GETTING OUT IN FRONT OF THE CUSTOMER. In fact, as I pointed out in Chapter 4, I continued my customer contacts throughout the review process. It's not one or the other. You've got to do both. But I probably still wouldn't have the same depth and breadth of knowledge today if I had relied solely on accompanying the reps while they made their calls.

You've got to get a look at the big picture, and get it fast. Meeting the customers gives you a sliver of real life—it's invaluable and irreplaceable—but it's only a sliver. The review is a crash course for you as the manager, and, to be candid, I didn't know just how powerful a tool it was until I brought it to bear in Cleveland.

Inside of four months, I was able to start shifting people around with confidence. The MSLRs showed me who had potential for mastering the process and who didn't.

Try an experiment. Do one MSLR with your strongest rep. Run the individual through his or her paces for two hours. Ask a lot of questions. Then hold another review with a rep who's in trouble. Do the sessions back-to-back for comparison. Probe deeply. Challenge assumptions.

What you're doing is benchmarking your own operation.* When it's over, you'll be amazed by the differences in the reviews. Or you should be. I can predict that you will find in the first review a depth of knowledge about the accounts that is lacking in the second rep's review. Recently, I conducted a review with a young woman who took me through her entire port-

---

* See Chapter 9 for more on benchmarking.

folio of accounts—and it was a thick one—tossing out names, backgrounds, company histories, individual quirks, without once referring to her notes. At every suggestion I made, she was either already two steps ahead of me, or wrote the idea down in her notebook for future reference and action. We ended up sitting there using the time to fine-tune her accounts and to tweak her strategy. It was an excellent session for both of us. She came away with a fresh approach to her job, and I was a smarter manager.

The comparison that I'm recommending will give you an instant profile of the kind of personal and professional qualities that are essential if an organization is to succeed. The first rep you are using as a standard may not be perfect, but right away you see why he or she is head and shoulders above the others. I've found that three common characteristics stand out:

1. Depth of knowledge
2. Confidence
3. High energy

Write this down. No, don't write it down. First, go do it. Go to your strongest person—the one with depth of knowledge, high energy, and confidence—and throw him or her smack-dab into the middle of the district's toughest assignment.

I really believe in the motto that's often quoted: "When the going gets tough, the tough get going." But it's your job to find the tough ones and give them the opportunity to show what they can do. Those are the people who will propel your entire organization. Give them visibility, rewards, and running room.

My father always said that you could beat a donkey all day long and the animal would just stand there. But tap a thoroughbred and it will run all day.

The ability to find those thoroughbreds makes the difference between a good manager and a great one.

Use the MSLRs to help you judge the quality of your horseflesh. Here's what I look for in addition to the three characteristics I've already mentioned:

- Discipline
- Competitiveness
- Pride
- Intensity
- Enthusiasm
- Work ethic
- Team spirit
- Creativity
- Selflessness
- Honesty
- Long-term thinking

The great thing about the reviews is that reps who have been having a hard time but nevertheless possess the right characteristics will start showing their stuff in the intense exchange that takes place. You can tell from the way they react to the questions, the coaching, the suggestions. They'll say to themselves: "He's right. Why don't I know that? I'm going to go find out right now!"

After one of my first rounds of customer calls in Cleveland, the rep I was riding with got out of the car and told me, "I want you to come out with me every day." I read it as a wonderful compliment. And I also saw that she was so eager to do her best that the downside of having the boss looking over her shoulder all day was worth it if I could give her a competitive edge.

You'll see that kind of attitude flare up during the MSLRs. I can tell within five minutes whether the rep has what it takes.

"Who are you talking to at this account?" I'll ask.

"Harriet Richardson."

"Who else?"

"She's it."

"Nobody else is involved in the decision? Nobody?"

"I don't know. I've got other accounts to work. I can't spend all my time on this one. Harriet's better than nothing."

Inexperienced or mediocre reps simply do not get beneath the surface of their business. The good ones do. They are deep-sea divers, and you can tell right away.

In the exchange above, there's also an element of defensiveness. "I've got other accounts to work" is a telltale sign of someone who's floundering. The best people know almost instinctively (and certainly by experience) that any question that is asked and can't be answered has to be addressed sooner rather than later. An unanswered or unanswerable question has to be taken as an indication that one's knowledge of the account is incomplete. And that's a situation a good rep wants to remedy right away.

HIGH RISK, HIGH REWARD

There's no team without team leaders. The Major Suspect List Review process will supply you with potential leaders—providing that you are willing to put those individuals where they belong. It's one of the riskiest things that managers are called on to do. Inevitably, the status quo is threatened, toes are stepped on, and egos are bruised.

Do it! And do it right away. The longer you wait, the more difficult it is to make changes. What kind of signal are you sending if you leave your major accounts in the hands of reps and managers who, while they may have seen better days, today lack depth of knowledge, confidence, and high energy? The bad example will ripple through the entire organization.

Conversely, a reorganization that emphasizes the right stuff —boy, did Tom Wolfe come up with the right phrase!—spreads those leadership qualities far and wide. You can't do it alone as a leader.

I've asked you to write things down periodically. Here's another item for the notebook: Get help! If you don't, the ship may stay afloat thanks to the skipper's seamanship, but it will never run with the wind. You've got to go on a talent hunt every day. Not only is it an important challenge, it's one of the most pleasurable aspects of the job. Wouldn't it be great to be a talent scout for a major-league team?

Well, you are.

REMEMBER THIS

A famous line from the movie *Casablanca* obviously inspired my Major Suspect List Reviews: "Round up the usual suspects." Don't forget, though, that you are a "usual suspect." If things are going poorly, the problem may start with you. Yes, you!

I've devised a test for managers to take with the purpose of double-checking their own management and leadership skills.

A MANAGEMENT TEST

1. Did you recognize someone today? How about a pat on the back or a thank-you? Yes or no.
2. Did you make an impact today? Yes or no. Specifically list what you did to move the business.
3. How many customer contacts did you have today? (None gets you an instant failing grade for the entire test.)
4. Did you teach, counsel, or motivate someone today to give him or her an edge? Yes or no.
5. Did you listen today? Yes or no. If yes, write down what you learned.
6. Did you think about your vision for the team? Yes or no.
7. Are your people focused? How do you know? A short essay required.
8. Did you act to insure that your process was up and running today? Yes or no. If yes, what was it?
9. What three leadership techniques did you use this month?
10. Driving home tonight—what is the thing you're going to do to make your team better tomorrow?
11. Is each member of your team meeting your expectations? Yes or no. If no, write an essay describing your efforts to improve each person's performance.
12. Did you provide a blast of energy, electricity, and excitement today? Yes or no.
13. Did you assume that everything is okay today? Yes or no. (Assume nothing. A yes earns you a D −.)

It's a tough test. I've yet to score 100 percent on a daily basis, but I keep trying. It's my job, your job—our jobs as leaders —to ace this test. We owe it to our people.

CRAZY LADY

The hardest, most rewarding thing a leader is called on to do is build a team. The flashiest rhetoric, slickest marketing strategy, and most sophisticated management techniques are useless without an effective team. The subtitle of this book could easily be "How to Build a Team and Take It to the Top." It's really what I've been talking about from the very first page.

Conceivably, a few excellent people can carry an entire organization. All I can say is bravo! How long will the virtuoso performance last, though? Six months, a year, two years? It won't last much longer than that. And then what? It could be a long while before the right combination of people and circumstances comes together again. In the meantime, the rent isn't paid. In today's business climate we can't afford the downtime.

A well-built, well-run team is a self-perpetuating organism. It's constantly renewing itself. When you finally put that team together you'll know it, not just from the improved business that results but because you'll feel the loyalty, the togetherness, and the we're-all-in-this-together attitude. As people come and go over the years the spirit will continue (if you or your successors don't drop the ball).

I remember when I first got the job in Cleveland, our regional marketing manager, Diane McGarry, told me it would take two years to turn the district around. I heard what she said and thought to myself, "Diane's crazy! I'm going to do it this year." Now I know she was right. I was able to implement an agenda, restore profitability, and shake the place up in a year, but building a genuinely effective team took much longer.

The turning point in Cleveland—and look for it in your own organization—came when the managers I was coaching finally "got it" and began coaching the people under them. One day, I started seeing many of the leadership and team-building techniques I'd been using on those managers being employed throughout the organization. And some of them were taking what I had and improving it 1000 percent. After having only one leader doing the hugging and the squeezing, setting expectations, and doing the inspecting, I suddenly had seven or eight leaders cascading it from the top to the bottom.

Think of the influence you can have by causing this flow of leadership and teamwork! You've set off a powerful chain reaction. I call it the T(eam)-bomb.

Sometimes, if my managers are slow to "get it" and I'm forced to do things for them that they should be doing themselves, I say, "If I've got to handle this stuff for you—who needs you?" The message usually takes. And, while I'm not looking for Frank Pacetta clones by any means, I'll know for sure when I pass an open door in the office and hear a manager tell his or her team, "If I've got to handle this stuff for you—who needs you?" Then I know it's time to fasten our seat belts, and, boy, are we going to fly!

PASS THE POWER, PLEASE

I saved empowerment for the end of this chapter. I wanted to make sure we dealt with first things first. Empowerment is important, but it isn't a "first thing." First you find good people—then you empower them.

The idea of empowering untrained, unmotivated, untested people is ridiculous. You're inviting disaster. It's bound to fail, and when it does, those who are skeptical about the whole notion of empowerment say, "See, it doesn't work."

It does work. I want my people to act as though they were independent entrepreneurs. Forget Xerox. If this was your business, if you'd invested your life savings in it, how would you operate?

Would you stay in close contact with your customer? You bet.

Would you delight the customer? Of course.

Would you track your competition, battle them head-on, work long hours, take risks? Yes, yes, yes, yes.

So go do it. And how can I help you?

That's empowerment.

As a corporation, Xerox is pretty good at this empowerment

drill. More and more decision-making authority has been transferred out into the field, where it belongs.

In turn, what I do is pass along as much of my power as possible to the managers under me, and they are expected to hand it down to the reps.

I'll give you an example involving Xerox pricing: Depending on the way a deal is structured—its size, duration, and other factors—substantial adjustments can be made. It's up to the district sales manager to sign off on the exact numbers and terms. However, I don't sign off on them. I've given that authorization in advance to the reps. I want them to use their best judgment to make the deal work.

Look around and determine how you can strip yourself of power. Give it to the people under you so they'll have the entrepreneurial flexibility they need to satisfy the customer.

Another example of empowerment: Should a deal hinge on the issue of a customer's right to return equipment for a refund within the first six months, the district sales manager is given the discretion to set the terms in a letter of authorization that accompanies the contract.

If a rep tells me he or she needs the letter, it is sent out without any questions being asked. The rep and the customer work it out. And that's no minor act of empowerment. Waves of returned equipment can be a catastrophe. An inexperienced or unscrupulous rep may have no business encouraging a customer to use certain kinds of machines. He or she may be looking for a quick killing. If the stuff comes back six months later, there will be major problems. But I'm willing to take the chance that it's not going to happen because I've done first things first. I've put the right people in the right places.

Does that mean that I walk away or turn a blind eye? Not unless I've gone soft in the head!

The process I'm presenting to you in this book is based squarely on *continuous* inspection. Anybody who would empower without inspecting would probably enjoy a nice little game of Russian roulette.

If the inspections reveal that execution is faulty, I don't withdraw empowerment. If you don't have the power to make mistakes, you don't have power. The manager's job is to teach and counsel so that the mistake becomes a learning experience.

DIFFERENT STROKES

Empowerment must not be used as a sneaky, back-door way to impose management conformity. I had seven sales managers in Cleveland leading seven teams of reps. Each one of the managers ran his or her business in uniquely different ways. I could have cared less. All I insisted on was paying the rent—that is, making the plan each month—satisfying the customer, and delivering on a few other requirements. The rest was up to them.

Rob Onorato was a sales rep when I got to Cleveland; today, he is one of the district's top sales managers. Rob received an early taste of empowerment he'll never forget. I was out of town when Rob and his team were wrestling with one of their first major deals. Midway through, he got nervous and tracked me down on the phone for advice. There was a sticking point and he wanted to know the best way to handle it. I told him, "Rob, I don't care how you do it . . . just don't come home without that deal." Then I hung up. Rob came home with the deal, as I knew he would, because he was ready to fly. All he needed was a push.

Another Cleveland manager, Fred Thomas, is a living, breathing advertisement for empowerment. He was in Cleveland for about six months before I arrived. Long enough to become demoralized, not long enough to be ruined.

At first Fred was worried about his job. I could tell. But I could also tell that I had inherited a good manager. We were walking down the hall one morning discussing the raft of problems we faced. Fred was down in the dumps, and I put my arm around his shoulder and told him, "Fred, you're going to be great."

Fred later said he figured I was just doing a number and trying to cheer him up. A year after our conversation, Fred was the number one sales manager in the country.

Empowerment. It works.

6

COMMUNICATIONS:

LISTEN UP

Most business organizations communicate badly.

Huh? What did you say?

I said . . . most families communicate badly. Home sweet home is probably where many of us pick up our communications skills—or lack thereof. My parents were superb communicators. Their favorite medium was the dinner table. We spent hours around it eating and talking. We'd be joined by my uncles and aunts and cousins, all of whom lived within a few blocks of our house in Far Rockaway. The talk would start early and go on late into the night.

I learned many things around that table: foremost was to keep my mouth shut and listen.

Effective listening is where effective communication starts.

Are you a good listener? I'll bet your answer is yes. And I'll also bet that you're wrong.

Take a blank sheet of paper and write down everything you heard yesterday. I'll get back to you in an hour.

WORD PROCESSING

Time's up. Chances are there's still an awful lot of white space on that sheet of paper (chances are many readers didn't even try). Count up the words—fifty or a hundred maybe. A whole day of listening amounts to thousands of words. Of course we edit out the trivial, unimportant stuff. But only fifty or a hundred important words were uttered in an entire day? I doubt it.

My colleagues accuse me of having total recall, the auditory equivalent of a photographic memory. I guess it would be called a CD-memory these days. But my listening skills are nowhere near perfect. Yet, as the saying goes, "In the land of the blind, the one-eyed man is King," and what I hear and others don't makes a crucial difference. Most people aren't deaf or hearing-impaired. Many are listening-impaired. The words aren't being processed.

I can't teach you how to listen and I won't even try. You have to teach yourself. My skills have been honed by years of practice that began with the need to listen to my customers. I'd leave a sales call and write down everything that I had heard and learned. I didn't wait a month or a quarter until the boss was screaming for a report and then try to make it up in a couple of hours of frantic scribbling.

If this kind of instant documentation becomes a habit, your listening ability will improve immensely. The brain is like a filing cabinet. What's immediately important is selected and put into the "hot file" up front; the rest is pushed toward the back into the subconscious. It's there but we just can't access it readily.

By forcing myself to write up my customer notes, I'm activating and expanding my mental hot files. I'm listening for what I need and pulling the material forward to a place where I can get at it.

The physiological explanation for what's going on is that we are "chunking" or making patterns of the incoming data in order to retain it in our active memory. The next time you find yourself staring off into space while somebody is talking, come back to earth and start chunking.

The way I chunk is to ask myself things like, "What does this mean? I wonder why that is? Is that the real reason?"

I force my managers to chunk at the end of our monthly outlook meetings by going around the table and asking them to give me instant feedback on the meeting. I want them to tell me what we accomplished, whether we wasted time, to prioritize decisions that have been made.

Try it yourself. Don't let anybody off the hook. Demand a specific assessment of the meeting. "What are you going to do about what we discussed today?" "Was Sharon right about what she said regarding that Cumberland Brake account?" "Where do we go from here?" "Did we accomplish anything?" "What can we do to improve the next one of these meetings?"

Listen, listen, listen. Chunk, chunk, chunk.

CRUISE CONTROL

I turn on my ears and cruise the office every day. Usually, I'm out there several times during the day just talking to the troops and listening to what they have to say. I do it so often that it is not a big deal; people aren't uptight about having the boss around. If you're not doing the same thing at least once a day, you'll never develop what's known as "mother's ear," the ability to pick up on and react to the faintest sounds of impending trouble.

As I cruise, I'm listening all the time: snatches of phone conversations, the banter that's being exchanged between reps, shop talk. An office is like a baseball dugout. The chatter is very revealing. There's a healthy hum—you know the sound when you hear it—and an unhealthy silence or rumbling.

These forays out into the office also give me time for quick mini-inspections. A few brief questions will tell me who's following through and who isn't. But when I stop at a rep's desk, I always begin by asking about his or her family. And I'm not just doing it for the sake of politeness. What I hear about the family tells me a lot about how that person is functioning on the job.

Digression time. Don't ask about their families if you don't care. If you don't care, find another job.

Dave Leedy, a wonderfully entertaining and profoundly moving inspirational speaker who is active in the Midwest, does a bit about the bad habit of asking "How you doing?" or "How's the family?" when you could care less. Leedy is a schoolteacher, and he tells the audience about passing his principal in the hall during a very bad day. The principal waved at Dave and said, "How you doing, Dave?" and immediately turned away. Dave took a few more steps, whirled around, rushed back to the man, and confronted him: "You don't care how I'm doing! You're not at all interested, are you? You're just asking for the sake of asking."

Leedy finishes the story by saying, "We've become a nation of insincere greeters." Hi, nice to see you. Isn't that a great tie. Glad you could come. The truth is: it isn't nice to see you, the tie is ugly, and the last person I wanted here today was you.

I'm digressing because Dave Leedy's story strikes me as a good illustration of why we don't listen very well. We've allowed our verbal forms of communication to be corrupted by insincerity and obfuscation. Our ears are closed because the assumption is that meaningful information is not being exchanged. Why? It might be painful, unpleasant, or require some effort on our part.

Dave Leedy's phrase "We've become a nation of insincere greeters" really hit me when I heard it. I apply the standard to myself when I cruise around the office and ask, "How's the family?" I want to know.

These seemingly casual questions that I ask as I roam provide me with important information. First of all, if I pick up the scent of family problems, and it comes as a surprise, I know that either my managers haven't been keeping me informed or they're not informed themselves.

I want to be the first to know of a birth, an illness, a divorce, or a death. Why? I want to be able to provide whatever assistance I can. It's the right thing to do.

As a manager, you cannot expect people to give 150 percent and to work long hours that might otherwise be spent with their families if you aren't going to be there when they need you. When your people know that, they will break down walls for you.

It's no cliché—what goes around comes around. A few years ago, as we approached the year end with a lot riding on the outcome, my father went into the hospital for open-heart surgery. I immediately returned home to New York. The Cleveland office rallied. What was shaping up as a great year became a fantastic year because those people were bound and determined not to let me down. "Let's get this one done for Frank" became the war cry. It was payback time. And I was a rich man indeed.

WIRED UP

I could probably write an entire book on communications alone. This book is all about communications.

You can have the most powerful vision and the greatest process, but without effective communication you're dead.

The problem is that business communication is carried out on so many different channels or circuits that it's easy to lose track of important information because you were literally listening in on the wrong line. You've got to "surf" through all the channels constantly. Just tuning in on your managers or the home office isn't enough.

Cruising the office is one way to cross-check what I'm hearing from other sources. Managers who limit themselves to a few channels of communication are always in danger of being fed misinformation—advertently or inadvertently. Some people are very good at wiring themselves into the manager's communications network and loading down the circuits with their own messages.

We all know by now that the squeaky wheel gets the grease. But often the whiners and complainers occupy a manager's time and attention to the exclusion of productive business. The squeaks and screeches become deafening. Sometime the whiners and complainers have a point, but you've got to verify what you're hearing. If I start to get a lot of negative vibes from the princes and princesses of darkness, I don't automatically discount it, but I do a little cruising to see if I hear the same stuff from those who tend to pull their oars without complaint no matter how rough the seas get.

One way I cross-check is to hold executive interviews with my people. Over the course of a year, I have two or three comprehensive sit-down meetings with each of my reps. This way, I get a thorough sampling of opinion, attitudes, and insights. I'm not being monopolized by any one faction or segment or personality type.

I believe the essence of leading or managing is *knowing* your people.

Do you understand what makes them tick, what drives and motivates them, and what worries and distracts them? How about their feelings toward the company, their careers, and their families? Do they want more recognition, more money, more fun and fulfillment?

Take the time to find out. You'll have to work at it, but the effort is rewarding. In his terrific book *Swim with the Sharks . . .* Harvey McKay lists all the questions that should be asked of the customer. There are dozens of them. It got me thinking about questions you should also be asking your troops. After all, the people who work for you are as much your "customer" as the person or organization buying the final product. If you don't know those "customers," how are you going to meet their requirements? And then how are you going to meet the requirements of the external customer? You're not.

They say "ignorance is bliss." Forget it! Ignorance is blinding.

I'll give you a list of questions I ask our reps and managers during executive interviews and other occasions. The answers have always given me more usable information than any personnel file, and have served me well in helping me know my people, how to motivate them and how to stretch them.

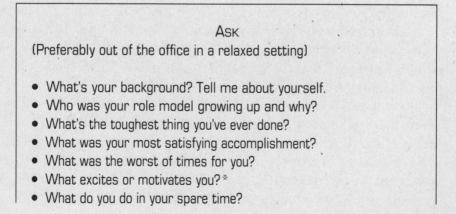

ASK
(Preferably out of the office in a relaxed setting)

- What's your background? Tell me about yourself.
- Who was your role model growing up and why?
- What's the toughest thing you've ever done?
- What was your most satisfying accomplishment?
- What was the worst of times for you?
- What excites or motivates you? *
- What do you do in your spare time?

- Tell me about the best manager, coach, or teacher you've ever had.
- What can I improve on as a manager and leader?
- What can the company improve on?
- How do you like being treated?

* Don't underestimate this one. By asking it, I found out that one of my guys was really turned on by the idea of having his own private office. I made sure he got one and he was unstoppable from then on.

Asking this set of questions will tell you a lot about an individual and provide key clues on how to motivate and work with him or her. It sounds simple, and it is. Remember, though, it takes time and a commitment to do something with the information that you've gathered. You can probably come up with far better questions than the ones I use. But here's one last question that I'll direct squarely at you: How much do you know about the people who work for you?

THE PRINCIPLE OF THE THING

If questions are the guts of the executive interview, the backbone is a personnel review and rating process that I am sold on. It's one area where effective communication is absolutely essential and where breakdowns frequently occur. The havoc that personnel reviews can create is brought on by your failure—the leader's failure—to articulate clearly day-to-day, month-to-month, year-to-year objectives. It doesn't have to happen.

Communicate.

I start by formulating a statement of district principles, a code we live by and work hard to attain. The principles are presented at the kickoff meeting each year. Before the rep ever hits my office for the executive interview, he or she has signed the statement and promised to uphold it. All up—all in. Take a look:

DISTRICT PRINCIPLES

- We will achieve the business plan.
- We will satisfy our customer requirements.
- We will treat everyone with honesty, equity, dignity, and respect.
- We will implement and practice the quality process.
- We will establish and maintain high expectations and recognize performance.
- We will lead by example.
- We will all practice teamwork.
- We will strive for open communication.
- We will adhere to Xerox business policies/ethics.
- We will encourage career development.
- We will strive to have representation of minorities in all facets of the business.
- We will all participate in keeping our work environment professional and maintain respect for company property.

Many of the items included in the statement were part of earlier presentations I made when I first arrived in Cleveland. I'm not afraid to repeat myself. Much of what we see and hear, as a matter of fact, doesn't stick the first time. The retention rates, depending on which communications theorist you read, may be as low as 20 percent. That means if you repeat yourself five times, you might get the message across to 100 percent of the audience.

A statement of principles is a handy guide and summary of where you intend to take your district. I distribute it to all my people, post it in prominent places, and periodically flash it up on the screen if I'm making a presentation with slides and overhead projections. Many reps and managers find a place on their cubicle or office walls for the statement of principles, and if that doesn't happen, your statement needs to be reworked; it's missing the mark.

A SOLID PLATFORM

I've something else to show you. It's a memo I write to my managers before they begin work on their yearly business plans.
Again, this happens *before* the executive interview process begins. If you're wondering, "What happened to the personnel reviews he just mentioned?" I'll get to it, but you cannot review
an employee's work without objective standards. An effective
business plan has to be the template against which your
managers and reps are judged. Don't start personnel reviews or
even executive interviews until one is in place and functioning. But don't wait. This memo is sent out just before Christmas so that managers will get their plans ready early in the new
year.

To: From:
The management staff   Frank Pacetta
                                         District Manager, Sales

Subject: 199__ Business Plan

To organize, plan, and execute a concrete Business Plan is essential. As a leader it is important to have a process that is tight,
repeatable, and has buy-in. I would like you to prepare your 199__
Business Plan using the following platform:

- Mission statement
- Customer satisfaction: How will your team delight the customer?
- Process: How are you going to run your business, i.e.:
  —Day-to-Day
  —Monthly
  —Quarterly
  —Activities
  —30/60/90-day forecasts
- Human resource management/Employee satisfaction
  —Action plan
  —Career counseling

▶

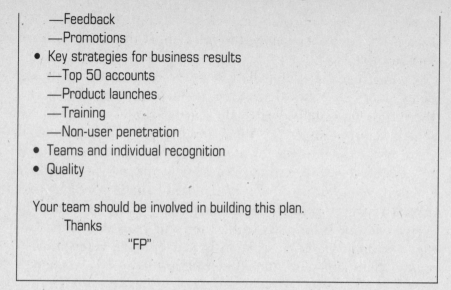

—Feedback
—Promotions
• Key strategies for business results
—Top 50 accounts
—Product launches
—Training
—Non-user penetration
• Teams and individual recognition
• Quality

Your team should be involved in building this plan.
    Thanks
                    "FP"

Some managers would read the memo and start writing a plan. Then they'd meet with their teams and divvy up the responsibilities for executing it. That works. But the best managers turn to their reps and say, "Okay, what are we going to tell Frank?" They hash out the plan as a team, and in doing that, they develop the ultimate standard by which they will be judged in their personnel reviews—the contract.

Don't complicate the concept of a business plan, simplify it. Think in terms of a quilt that is made of individual scraps of cloth sewn together. Each scrap represents what each rep is doing to execute the plan.

What I'm doing during the executive interview with the reps is deconstructing the quilt. I look at the individual contract —based on the district principles I've just shown you and the team's business plan—to see how the rep is functioning within the overall scheme of things. Now I have a standard for evaluation. Communication is possible.

NOT-SO-CRAZY QUILTS

The contract is a simple one- or two-page document that outlines what the *individual* will do to deliver the team's plan. And since just making the plan isn't enough, as far as I'm concerned, I want the contract to show the extra effort that will be necessary to truly excel.

See what I'm doing here? Power and responsibility are being shifted downward from me to the manager to the rep. It's the rep who actually writes the business plan. The manager merely coordinates, orchestrates, and fine-tunes. The manager is the seamstress who puts the quilt together.

The best way to do that is for each manager and rep to know exactly what's expected and buy into it—that's why I've been dwelling on the district statement of principles and the development of business plans by each team. Buy-in is essential. If you arbitrarily impose standards from the top—particularly when it's a question of going beyond minimal levels of expectation—it's difficult to get voluntary and enthusiastic compliance. The contract, on the other hand, promotes buy-in because the individual sets the terms to start with.

To promote teamwork, the standard contract must be developed jointly by each team. Essentially, the manager says, "Here's what we have to get saleswise. How are we going to do it? And how are we going to go even higher? You've read Frank's memo; I want us to clobber those six other teams."

If the team is writing its own contracts, every member must take his or her own capabilities into consideration. If the team commits to 100 percent participation in the President's Club, it means everyone must exceed the basic plan by 20 to 50 percent. What I want the members of the team to do is to ask questions like this: How are we going to do that? How am I going to do that? If three members of the team just barely achieved plan last year by making twenty calls a week, won't we want to stipulate that all of us are prepared to make thirty calls a week—a 50 percent increase? Also, since we did demonstrations about once a week last year, should we increase that to twice a week? Can everyone handle that? Yes or no?

What's happening here is that the team members are developing their own business plan as well as a personal scorecard. It's not a cookie cutter. Every plan reflects the unique perspective of the members. By writing it themselves, it's difficult for the reps to come back and say the expectations were unrealistic.

Yes, there's pressure to push oneself to a higher plane. There has to be. But the manager's job is to coach the reps honestly and realistically so they produce an achievable contract. President's Club may be totally beyond the capabilities of a brand-new rep. It's nice to have him or her shoot for the stars; however, the manager is going to be held accountable for the reps' failure to deliver on their contracts.

That's the kicker!

The manager is no longer an innocent bystander. He or she has to make sure that the rep's contract is doable to start with. Each one can be sure I'm going to look at the contracts and ask, "Why did your entire team contract to go to President's Club, and why did only two of them qualify?"

There's no place to hide. If the manager responds, "Their prospect bases were too small," my rejoinder is, "Why didn't you know that?"

The pressure is on the manager to prevent his people from treating the contract like a wish list. If you wish for it, you'd better work for it and make it come true.

KEEPING SCORE

I'm going to show you a sample contract, but first I want to provide a little more background. We review the contracts each month. Your business cycle may be different, but at Xerox I've got to deliver month by month. It makes sense, therefore, to review at the end of each thirty-day period.

The rep is scored on a basis of one to five. A string of threes tells me a rep is just about holding his own. Ones are a sign he's being swamped, and fives indicate a blowout is under way.

When I hold executive interviews with the reps, I make sure I have their current reviews (based on the contract) on my desk. It gives me a quick readout of where they stand. If low scores don't start to move upward from, say, January to March, I want to know why.

"Is your manager working with you on this?" I might ask.

"He says I need to familiarize myself with the products."

"Have you?"

"I want to, but I just don't have time."

"Have you let your manager know that?"

"Yeah, and he told me to make the time."

Now I know what the problem is and how to fix it. Time to talk to the manager:

"You can't allow this to drag on. He needs training on the equipment and he needs it now," I might say.

"I know, but he's barely keeping his head above water. If I take him off the street for training, he won't be making the calls."

"The calls aren't productive if he doesn't know the equipment. You better do something. You'll be bumping into midyear and he won't be up to speed."

Notice that I didn't tell the manager what to do. If that's necessary, I'm probably going to have to get a new manager. He or she should know enough to realize it's time to go into the field and determine why the rep is running so hard but only standing in place. The manager should be able to spend a couple of hours coaching the rep on making more efficient and productive calls. Once that happens, there will be enough slack to take the rep off the road one morning a week for training.

AN EARLY WARNING SYSTEM

Without the contracts, the executive interview lacks focus. I can tell at a glance how well the rep is handling his or her assignment. The contract also gives me a standard to use in evaluating the performance of my managers.

Let's look at a sample contract:

NORTHEAST OHIO DISTRICT
PERFORMANCE MEASUREMENT SYSTEM
EMPLOYEE CONTRACT

Rep:_____   **Month:**_____

OBJECTIVE	MEASUREMENT TARGET	SCORE 1-5	COMMENTS
BUSINESS RESULTS	100 Net Comp Revenue		
	100 ISR (sold revenue)		
	Order Standards —5 units/month —1 Centralized/mo. —2 mid-volume/mo. —3 color		
	Complete, timely, accurate paperwork		
	Forecast Accuracy		
	Activities: —appointments, 4/day —prospects, 5/wk, 20/mo —demos, 2/wk —proposals/mailers, 5/wk —30/60/90-day prospects		
	Expense Management		
EXTERNAL AND INTERNAL CUSTOMER SATISFACTION	100% Customer Satisfaction		
	Return phone calls within four hours		

	Utilization of Xerox Account Management Process: —accurate and complete files —relationship plan —account strategy		
	Order Quality, 95% accuracy		
	Field Time: 8:30 to 4:00		
	Timeliness and responsiveness to internal requests —meetings —paperwork —follow-up action items		
EMPLOYEE SATISFACTION AND DEVELOPMENT	Knowledge and improvement in: —products —pricing —selling skills		
	Career counseling		
	Developmental action plan		
	Ethical conduct		
	Professionalism		
LEADERSHIP THROUGH QUALITY	Effective use of quality tools		
	Participation in quality project		
	Sharing and adopting best practices		
	Team player		

The beauty of these contracts is that the need for a time-consuming annual review is eliminated. Each month, the manager scores and comments, filling in the boxes in longhand, preferably in front of the rep. There's an opportunity for a discussion. Best of all, the manager is looking the employee in the eye and explaining why he or she feels that a particular score is appropriate. The reps may not be able to negotiate the score upward, but they have a chance to point out extenuating circumstances that the manager might be unaware of.

What I like about using the contracts is that it removes the "I didn't know . . ." factor. There's nothing worse than an annual or semiannual review process that blindsides people with negative evaluations when it is too late to do anything about them. I don't want reps to think they're doing okay, only to find out halfway into the year or at the end of the year that their performance has been unsatisfactory. My assumption is that deficiencies can be corrected. We're not talking about brain surgery here. Most of what we do in sales or in business generally can be taught, learned, practiced, and mastered. But if there's no opportunity to learn and practice, the rep is doomed and the success of the whole team suffers.

In the event that a manager reacts quickly to signs of trouble but the rep is unable to improve, changes can be made early enough to keep the team from being dragged down. If midyear rolls around and the manager is just beginning to face up to an employee's weaknesses, he or she is so far behind the curve that the entire year will be lost. Add it up: six months go by before there's action, and after two or three months of remedial work, the employee might be up to the performance level that should have been on display in January—and it's now October; there are only three months left to salvage the year. The turnaround is going to have to be mighty spectacular.

Then there's the other possibility: three months of retraining doesn't do the trick. How long does it take to reassign or fire someone in your company? At Xerox, three months isn't unusual. By waiting so long to bite the bullet, the manager has blown the year, and that's not counting the time it takes to recruit and acclimate a replacement.

LIKES AND DISLIKES

If your personnel reviews sit in a file drawer gathering dust, don't waste your time.

If your personnel reviews are used as an instrument of terror and torture, don't waste your time.

If your personnel reviews are a headache and a burden, don't waste your time.

If your personnel reviews are subjective and unquantifiable, don't waste your time.

Corporations deserve absolute candor from their executives. Personnel reviews can be an excellent tool or a lethal Uzi submachine gun pointed at your head. Tell headquarters what you like about the reviews and what you don't like. Develop your own format, use mine—do something!

The sample can get you started, but it's not perfect. The fourth item from the bottom, for example—"effective use of quality tools"—is a clinker. I spotted it while writing the book. Actually, a young rep spotted it. During an executive interview, I asked her what she thought of her performance review, and she was generally upbeat about the process. But she pointed out there really wasn't any way for her manager to know how effective or ineffective she was in using quality tools (i.e., specific aspects of Leadership Through Quality like benchmarking). She was right, and that item needs to be worked on.

SHORT AND TO THE POINT

I'll run you through a few slices of the contract to give you the hang of filling one out:

OBJECTIVE	MEASUREMENT TARGET	SCORE 1–5	COMMENTS
BUSINESS RESULTS	100% Net Comp Revenue	1	Wrote $540 NCR... less than 10%
	100% ISR (sold revenue)	1	No ISR

Don't let the Xerox terminology confuse you. Basically, net comp revenue is the total dollar amount established in the rep's monthly sales plan. Other companies may call it a quota or budget. ISR tells us precisely how much of the rep's revenue was generated by actual sales booked and delivered that month.

Both of these are very easy to track. In fact, the manager doesn't even need to look up the orders. He or she can just ask the rep to bring the paperwork to the review.

	Order Standards —5 units/month —1 Centralized/mo. —2 mid-volume/mo. —3 color	1	One low/volume order written
	Complete, timely, accurate paperwork	3	Timeliness okay but some errors creep in
	Forecast Accuracy	1	Forecasted five units... did one
	Activities: —appointments, 4/day —prospects, 5/wk, 20/mo —demos, 2/wk —proposals/mailers 5/wk —30/60/90-day prospects	2	Appointments, 2/day. 5 prospects for the month; no demos; 2 proposals; excellent prospect base.

Again, the data is easy to document and is not subjective. The rep is getting a useful evaluation. In the above, the lowest rating in the "order standard" category, which sets sales targets for specific products, put him or her on notice that there is a serious deficiency in a key area. The rep is new on the job, so a bad first month is understandable—a veteran with that kind of discrepancy would be highly unusual and would really set off the alarm bells. Yet, the pressure is on. There it is in black and white. There's got to be an improvement the following month.

As for the activities, the rep doesn't even need to be told that he or she has to pick up the pace. The 2 rating could easily be bumped to a 3 just by meeting the standards set down in the contract (it would also impact positively on the order standards).

EXTERNAL AND INTERNAL CUSTOMER SATISFACTION	100% Customer Satisfaction as measured by CSMS target	5	*100% percent of CSMS... great!*
	Return phone calls within four hours	3	*Follow-up has been strong*
	Utilization of Xerox Account Management Process: —accurate and complete files —relationship plan —account strategy	3	*Good XAMP process. Not all accounts have XAMP documentation.*
	Order Quality, 95% accuracy	2	*This needs work... double-check after forms are filled out*
	Field Time: 8:30 to 4:00	4	*Good use of time*

Naturally, you'll rewrite the form to suit your purposes. When in doubt, keep it short. There are only four nonnegotiable categories on my reviews: business results, which hinge on net comp revenue and sold revenue; external and internal customer satisfaction as measured by the CSMS, Xerox's customer satisfaction management survey; and Leadership Through Quality. The reps and managers have leeway on all the rest. The product mix will vary according to the team's territories and accounts. Activities can be adjusted up or down to suit requirements. But I think you will find that one team's contract is similar to another's because of common training values, the corporate culture, and the emphasis that you as a leader put on various aspects of the business.

I hammer so hard on teamwork that it would surprise me to see contracts without that element included in some way. The same goes for the development of selling skills and ethical business conduct. Customer/employee satisfaction and quality are a way of life at Xerox, and a manager who forgot to give them more than a passing reference in a contract would have to be visiting from another galaxy (and I'd probably pack him off in his flying saucer for quality indoctrination at Xerox's Leesburg, Virginia, training center).

THE OPEN AGENDA

The sales advisory board is another communications tool I highly recommend. Each team selects a representative to sit on the board. I meet with them once a month and the agenda is wide open. It can be anything from the need for more copiers on the office floor (Xerox can be like the shoemaker whose children go barefoot), to concern that service response time is slipping. Anything that impacts on the business is open to discussion.

I ask for input and advice: What should we do for our next recognition event? Why didn't the last incentive blitz live up to expectation? How can we improve our product launches?

This isn't just a lot of talk. An action sheet is compiled for every meeting. I leave the session determined to take action on each item by the end of the day. Nothing is left hanging. I use Voicemail or notes to let the board members know what the final disposition is. When I run into a brick wall, or there is a policy that can't be changed for valid business reasons, I explain what's going on. I want my people to know they'll always get a fair hearing even if things don't break the way they would prefer.

The advisory board members are expected to go back to their teams and keep them fully informed. In turn, they've got to find out precisely what the team wants and thinks. I don't want them to guess or interpret. The board members have to hold meetings and conversations with their colleagues and fellow reps so that everyone is plugged into the communications matrix.

Let me give you a quick end-of-the-chapter review of all the various methods of communication that I use throughout the year:

EVENT	ATTENDEES
—Monthly Business Meetings	—The entire district
—One-on-ones	—Managers, every month
—Outlook Meetings	—Managers, every month

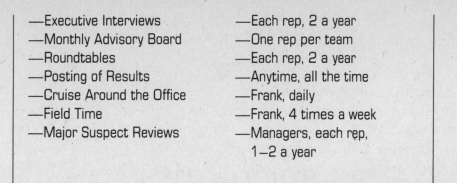

—Executive Interviews	—Each rep, 2 a year
—Monthly Advisory Board	—One rep per team
—Roundtables	—Each rep, 2 a year
—Posting of Results	—Anytime, all the time
—Cruise Around the Office	—Frank, daily
—Field Time	—Frank, 4 times a week
—Major Suspect Reviews	—Managers, each rep, 1–2 a year

If it all sounds like a lot of effort, you're right. You've really got to work at communication. There's no such thing as too much of it. Tell your troops how they're doing; tell them how the company is doing. Explain why things are being done! They may not like the answers or policies—and maybe they've got better ideas.

Here's my communication trinity:

1. Tell 'em.
2. Show 'em.
3. Ask 'em.

A leader doesn't have a choice when it comes to communication. You choose either communication or isolation. There's no alternative.

Top Ten Tips:

And Ten More

When I was profiled by *The Wall Street Journal* a few years ago, the newspaper's editors ran a box beside the story displaying my top ten tips. I'm still getting requests for copies of those tips, and I'm told they've been spotted on office bulletin boards around the country.

What's the big deal? The tips are nothing but common sense. But maybe that's the big deal. I'll run through them one at a time in this chapter, and then I'll toss in ten more for good measure.

1. Prepare customer proposals on weekends and evenings.

I'm a fanatic when it comes to adequate preparation. Selling is 90 percent preparation and 10 percent articulation. The days of the fast-talking salesperson are over. Most buyers are too sophisticated to rely solely on glib presentations and promises. They want facts, creative applications, and a genuine effort to fulfill their requirements.

Therefore, winning or losing a business deal depends on what happened long before the salesperson even gets in front of the customer for the final yes-or-no decision.

A rep doesn't need many weeks on the job before he or she realizes that a golden tongue isn't enough. At that point there's a tendency to pull back and spend a major portion of the day in the office prepping.

Soon the act of selling a product takes second place to the mechanics and logistics of selling. It's the equivalent of a well-drilled football team that never actually gets around to playing a real live game against real live opponents.

Rob Onorato, one of my best managers in Cleveland, re-members that during the first few weeks I was on the job I would pass his desk and ask, "How's life at Ernst and Whinney?" Rob, who was still a rep at the time, says he couldn't figure out what I meant. Day after day, he'd get the same question from me: "How's life at Ernst and Whinney?" Finally, it dawned on him. It was my oblique and teasing way of telling him to get his butt out of the office. If he wasn't working for Ernst and Whinney, the accounting firm, he was sure acting like it. Accountants work in the office; salespeople belong in the field.

Rob got the message and hit the road. One of the things he had been doing in the office was writing proposals. Fortunately, Rob didn't react by saying, "If I can't write them in the office, I won't write them." He did them at home and on the weekends. As a result, he became an outstanding performer.

Why? He got the most out of his workday by being in the field in front of the customer. He wasn't necessarily selling, in the sense of closing deals. Rob was out there listening and look-ing. When it came time to write the proposal, he knew what to put down on paper.

By forcing the reps to do this work on their own time, I'm breaking down the Berlin Wall between business and private life. There has to be integration. Excellence is impossible to achieve on a nine-to-five basis. You don't have to be a workaholic or neglect your family. You can interweave your two lives in ways that will enhance both. Two hours of proposal writing at night, as opposed to two hours of watching television, is not going to "make Jack a dull boy." It might also give the kids a role model and get them more interested in homework.

2. NEVER SAY NO TO A CUSTOMER—
EVERYTHING IS NEGOTIABLE.

It is too easy to say no. The word is a killer. It murders creativity, initiative, effort, and possibilities. This "can't do" attitude is probably a throwback to the days when we had so many customers that losing a few of them was no big deal.

Today, it should be a very big deal to lose a customer. As far as I'm concerned, aside from violating the law or ethics, messing up a customer is the number one hanging offense.

While most customers will push hard to protect their own interests, they'll conduct themselves honestly and fairly. I tell my reps and managers to level with our customers when we can't do it their way. Tell them why, rather than just slamming the door shut by saying no. The candor is usually appreciated and reciprocated.

Look for ways to accommodate both sides in a deal. The old win-win concept is the key to success. The two parties should each walk away with something of value.

I see myself as the middleman between the customer and the corporation. It's my job to get them together. I won't get paid otherwise.

When there's a deadlock, always remember the rule "It ain't over until it's over." Keep looking for a compromise. Use your creativity. The great thing about business as opposed to sports is that it ain't over even if it's over. A decision that goes against you can be reversed next month or next year. I don't write anything off. Done deals are great, but the dead deals that come back to life are even sweeter.

3. MAKE CUSTOMERS FEEL GOOD ABOUT *YOU*,
NOT JUST YOUR PRODUCT.

Sales is a people business, otherwise we could just rely on mail order. We call the customer a "customer" and lose sight of the fact that it's a human being, or a group of them, making the decisions.

Why is "being businesslike" misconstrued as projecting a

cold, indifferent, and distant attitude? As a young rep, the best salesperson I've ever known, Steve Urban, taught me to walk into a customer's office for the first time and look for a way to make a personal connection. What's hanging on the wall? Is it a picture from a fishing trip or a tennis trophy or a child's kindergarten watercolor? Steve could sit there for fifteen minutes chatting about fishing, his tennis elbow, or a purple cow with six legs and handlebars.

It's not just a sales technique for breaking the ice. What's happening is that you're selling yourself along with the product. Successful reps have been doing that since the days of Enzio's A-1 used chariot lot next to the Roman Colosseum. Enzio knew there were dozens of secondhand chariot dealers around Rome selling similar products, but there was only one Enzio. Today, business theorists and consultants tell us customers don't just buy a product, they purchase an "experience"—the package, the documentation, the service, the corporation's image, the design, etc. They purchase Enzio.

If your next-door neighbor received a promotion, you might send him a note of congratulations. He's just your neighbor. Why not do the same thing for your customer? Send out birthday and anniversary cards. Don't forget thank-you notes when a deal is completed. Take your customers to lunch, ball games, and other outings.

You know what? There's no law against making a customer into a friend.

4. MEET CUSTOMER REQUIREMENTS, EVEN IF IT MEANS FIGHTING YOUR OWN BUREAUCRACY.

If you don't fight for the customer, who will? Many bureaucrats think the customer is a pest. As one of my bosses used to say, "If the customers are a nuisance, try doing without them for thirty days."

Most salespeople don't need to be reminded that the customer pays their salaries and commissions, but the more removed you are from the firing line, the easier it becomes to forget the facts of life.

Don't be afraid to be the customer's advocate. Jobs may come and go, but if you're good at sticking up for customers you'll never go without business.

But I've got to admit that sometimes it is very frustrating and aggravating. After about four months into my assignment in Cleveland we had a customer ready to purchase sixty machines. One of their requirements was that they had to receive summary billing each month. In other words, they wanted Xerox to depart from its usual practice at the time of sending out an invoice for each machine—in this case, sixty different bills. The customer said, "I want one piece of paper."

No sweat, right? Hah! You'd have thought that the customer had asked for a seat on the board of directors. I was told Xerox just didn't do summary billing. There was no way we were going to lose that deal because of the format for a lousy invoice! I enlisted Al Byrd, who was the regional vice president, and we got some good people in administration to give us a hearing. It took three months of phone calls and memo writing until Xerox finally agreed to the customer's request. Today, the practice is routine, and it probably saves the corporation tens of thousands of dollars in administrative costs that would otherwise be chewed up by duplicative billing.

The absurdity still makes me chuckle. "No, we won't sell you sixty machines if it means sending out only one invoice each month. Sixty machines, sixty bills . . . take it or leave it!"

5. DO THINGS FOR CUSTOMERS THAT YOU DON'T GET PAID FOR.

Don't let yourself get compartmentalized. By that I mean there's a tendency in business to step back from situations and say, "Not my job."

Make it your job. The customer probably doesn't have a Rolodex filled with the names and telephone numbers of the various people in your company who are responsible for handling specialized problems. But he does have your name and number.

A leading Ohio bank executive once let it casually drop that one of his branches was about to run out of toner and that the manager had been told it would take ten days or two weeks for a shipment to arrive. The customer didn't ask me to intervene. The comment was almost an aside, sort of a "I'm glad this isn't happening to me" kind of thing. I went back to the office, made some calls, and got the toner shipped on an urgent basis. When I called my contact back to tell him what was going to happen, I took one additional step: "I'm going to send out a couple of days' supply of toner from our stock here in the office just in case the branch runs dry."

This good deed cost me time and effort. Was there a direct payoff? No. I can't say, P.S., the bank was so grateful that we got a huge order as a reward. But the customer is still doing business with us. That's good enough for me.

Try it, but don't wait to be asked directly for a favor. Customers tend to be indirect. Listen closely and you'll hear. "Our Dallas district wants a system like ours, but Xerox is telling them it will be thirty days at least. You guys must be pretty busy."

Again, no request for action. It's time to take the initiative. Find out if there's a way to speed up the order. A few phone calls will probably suffice. Your interest might jog something loose. If not, the customer would probably be pleased just to know that you tried.

Even if it's your account, merely writing the order isn't enough. Were you there when the product arrived to make sure there were no problems? Did you stand by while it was being unpacked and set up to answer any questions? Did you offer some on-the-spot training to the first users to get them started? These are all functions that are supposed to be performed by people other than a sales rep. But what I hear about my best reps is, "Jill is great. She's always there when we need her."

6. KNOW YOUR COMPETITOR'S PRODUCT BETTER THAN YOUR COMPETITOR DOES.

When I was a rep, I'd go to a print shop and spend an hour or two standing there, watching the competition's equipment perform. I wanted to see how it worked, who was using it, what procedures they used, and how it differed from a Xerox product.

I wasn't snooping around. This isn't industrial espionage. I had permission to be there. Most of the people who were using the machine were more than happy to tell me about its strengths and weaknesses.

I don't care what you're selling, this kind of research is invaluable. Ask questions: "What do you like about it? What don't you like? Does it do what the manufacturer said it would? How often does it go down?" If you're lucky, the user will be familiar with your product as well. Keep asking questions: "How does mine compare? What's the best thing about their product and the worst thing about mine? Which one could you live without? Why?"

Xerox tracks the competition closely, especially at the top end of the market. It issues reams of analytical data. If your company does the same thing, it's helpful to cross-check to see if your conclusions are supported by the user's experience. Ask: "The specs indicate that the document handler will jam in some circumstances. Does it? Is the print quality erratic?" There's nothing worse than thinking that your research has discovered the competition's Achilles' heel, and then have the user or customer say, "We've never had any problems with that. What are you talking about?"

By knowing what the competition's product will do and won't do the rep is able to customize his presentations and proposals. For instance, if a potential customer is leaning toward the competition because of its lower price, a smart rep could say, "You rely on high-speed document handling, particularly card stock. Their machine has a history of jamming up with card stock. You might want to ask their rep about it."

I never badmouth the competition, but it's perfectly fair to make head-to-head comparisons on the basis of performance. I want to be able to zero in on the competition's weak spots when I'm in front of the customer: "Our machine holds more paper than theirs. And we're eight pages a minute faster. That's going to really make a big difference in this operation if your people have to stop twice as often to reload the paper, not to mention the overall speed disadvantage."

Bear in the mind that research has three prongs: one, the competition; two, your own products; and three, the customer's applications. You can control the sale if you work *all* the elements. But what often is left out is the customer's end of things. If you don't know how the customer uses the products, you can't take full advantage of the value of making comparisons. Not to load you down with copier-industry scenarios, but if the competition's machines choke on 110-weight paper and the rep doesn't know the customer uses that kind of paper, he or she can't mount an effective attack.

It makes no sense to be shy about challenging the competition. Some salespeople think it's demeaning even to acknowledge that there is such a thing as competition. Ridiculous! The customer knows all about the competition and knows why you're there—to sell a product.

7. BE EARLY FOR MEETINGS.

This one isn't as obvious as you might think at first glance. Naturally, a rep wants to be punctual. Keeping the customer waiting is not a good idea.

How's that again? Not a good idea? Make it a rotten idea; rotten through and through. Customers hate it, even though they may never complain (but they might keep you waiting the next time). They read a rep's tardiness as an indication that the account just isn't all that important.

What I'm striving for when I arrive early—five to ten minutes ahead of time—is that intercom call from the receptionist back to the person I'll be meeting announcing that I've arrived. I have a mental picture of the customer checking the clock on his or her desk and noting that I'm there early. I've scored points, and I haven't even set foot yet in that individual's office. What I'm saying to the customer is, "You're important to me. I'm prepared and ready to go."

Getting an edge is one thing, but there's another good reason: If you build in a five- or ten-minute cushion in front of each appointment—no more than that—the extra time gives you a chance to get focused on the upcoming call. Sit down in the reception area and review the account. You should have gone over the material the night before, but there's nothing like the prospect of meeting face-to-face with the customer in the next few minutes to get the juices flowing. What might have seemed routine twenty-four hours before will stand out vividly when you're on the customer's doorstep.

The rep who barrels from appointment to appointment without pause is running the risk of having one account blend into the next. It's the equivalent of the breathless tourist thinking, "If it's Tuesday, this must be Belgium." The blur is likely to lead to rote, by-the-book sales presentations. By the time the harried rep has Belgium sorted out from Luxembourg, the customer may have tuned out. Attention spans vary. I've seen estimates that range from as little as eight seconds to three minutes for the amount of time we have to persuade someone that we're worth listening to. Whatever it is, the window of opportunity is narrow. If you're struggling to focus on the who, what, when, where, and why of the customer during that first precious three minutes, there's a good chance the customer is going to switch channels.

What if you're running late and can't avoid it? Give yourself a good, swift kick in the pants—it's your fault—and call the customer to explain what's happening. Be straightforward about it, and apologize. Don't just show up a half-hour behind schedule without calling, and don't cancel the appointment at the last minute. When there is an unavoidable conflict, never cancel with less than twenty-four hours' notice; preferably give the customer forty-eight hours and try to set the date and time for another meeting. Sabotaging the customer's schedule is unforgivable; it's one of the recurring complaints I heard from disgruntled customers in Cleveland and in other problem districts. But this isn't just a unique Xerox weakness; it's a universal business problem and I bet it affects your operation the same way.

Punctuality starts with a professional attitude. What I do around the office is insist on using "Lombardi time." When Vince Lombardi scheduled a team meeting for 8:00 A.M., it meant he wanted everybody there at 7:45. If you're going to walk into one of my meetings late, don't bother. Better never than late. Punctuality is common courtesy. It demonstrates respect and professionalism. By insisting on it in my office, I am cultivating a habit. It's a discipline tool. I'm hoping that it will carry over to the way my people treat customers and become second nature.

8. DRESS AND GROOM YOURSELF SHARPLY SO YOU "LOOK LIKE A SUPERIOR PRODUCT."

The customer may not know it consciously, and he or she will never tell you directly, but clothes and grooming are important.

Why? Doesn't the product speak for itself?

The answer is no. You speak for the product, and the language is older than Sanskrit. After several thousand years, humankind still relies heavily on a nonverbal vocabulary. It's our mother tongue, actually. What's the significance of a firm handshake or whether or not your companion looks you straight in the eye? They are clues, and we use them to make a judgment. Clothes and grooming serve the same function. It's always been that way. Anthropologists will probably write to tell me I'm crazy, but it seems to me that a primitive hunter wearing a bearskin is not only keeping warm, he's telling his neighbors, "I'm rough enough, tough enough, skilled enough to have killed this bear." Or, "I'm smart enough to have gotten it away from the guy who was rough enough, tough enough, skilled enough to have killed this bear." Either way, the tribe is being told, "Mess with me and there's trouble."

Clothes don't make the man or woman. They make the message about the man or woman. The message may be accurate or absolutely misleading—but it's a message nonetheless. We're not so civilized and sophisticated that we don't notice the limp handshake, the shifty eyes, and the unpolished shoes.

I don't want my people to dress to prove that they're hotshots or overachievers. I want this message: "I'm a professional." Nothing more, nothing less. That doesn't require a $1,500 suit or $600 shoes. It comes down to a neat, crisp appearance.

I have no hesitancy about reminding reps that they need to pay attention to what they are saying to the customer with their nonverbal vocabularies. First of all, I set an example. It's easy for me because I love clothes. I get a kick out of having a closet full of many of the latest fashions in suits and ties and shirts. Looking good makes me feel good. Early in my career, when I was floundering around, one of my managers called me in to give me a pep talk. He finished by telling me to go out that weekend and buy a new suit and a new tie. Chris said I would come out feeling like a million bucks, and he was right. I knew that I looked good and looked professional, and that the customer would see me the same way. What you're getting off that clothes rack is more than just a sharp suit or a dress—it's energy and pride and confidence.

I first heard this line from my father and I use it all the time when I go into a dry cleaner and the clerk asks if I want starch in my collars: "Starch? I want to be able to roller-skate on those collars."

Some managers insist their people wear only white shirts and never loosen their ties. In Columbus, Steve Urban, whom I've mentioned for his super sales ability, used to come into the reps' training room with a starched white shirt on a hanger and say, "This is what we wear around here." He was blatant about it. But I don't have any trouble with a rep who takes off his jacket and loosens his tie once he and the customer are comfortable with each other.

Maybe I'll offend the scruffy-loafer set when I reveal this, but what the heck: I give shoe brushes and cans of polish to reps who have trouble keeping their shoes shined. I'll gently tease them about it and get the others to join in. It works, and there are no hard feelings. Once the reps start paying attention to their appearance, they realize it makes them feel good.

You don't have to be a tyrant. I don't like beards, but I've never ordered anybody to shave one off. I prefer humor. Jeff Collier, one of our printing system's managers, had a beard when I got to Cleveland. He's clean-shaven today, and we laugh about the subtle and not-so-subtle ways that I used to convince him to get rid of the beard. He fought me. It got to the point that I'd compliment him for something and then add, "I think your beard looks great, but every day you wear it, I get agitated a little more." Eventually, I inveigled Jeff into making a bet with me over something that I knew I couldn't possibly lose. Keeping his beard or shaving it off was the stake. He lost and got rid of the beard, but claimed that he was going to shave it anyway because his wife hated it.

What do I have against beards? Nothing really. I had one in college, and I'll let my beard grow on weekends or vacations.

But beards just send the wrong message when it comes to business. It's pure nonverbal vocabulary: "Here comes the guy with the beard," not "Here comes the guy from Xerox." Does that mean I wouldn't hire someone with a beard? No, but I'd tell him my views up front.

The same goes for a person who's indifferent about his or her wardrobe. Xerox spends millions of dollars projecting a professional, contemporary, high-quality, cutting-edge image. If a rep walks in the customer's door looking like an unmade bed, instantly Xerox's carefully cultivated image is undercut. We don't even wear sports jackets. There's no dress code, but a manager will take a flamboyant or sloppy dresser aside and explain. Sometimes it will be a young man or woman just starting a career, and all we have to do is say, "Let me tell you some ways to get comfortable around here and really fit in."

How does a male executive tell a female employee about the fine points of fashion and grooming? He doesn't. In Cleveland, I gave that job to Pat Elizondo, my senior female manager. Call me a coward, but call me effective. Pat handled the assignment with great tact and finesse.

9. WHEN IT'S TIME TO GO HOME, MAKE ONE MORE TELEPHONE CALL.

Excellence is not easy to achieve. It takes dedication and discipline. There's plenty of room for creativity, daring, and flair. But in the end you simply have to grind it out.

Steve Urban of the starched-white-shirt-on-the-hanger routine used to say, "Full day, full pay." We called Steve the "Bean." Bean would remind his reps that at 4:30 P.M. the competition goes home; on Friday afternoons they're on the golf course; and on Monday mornings at 7:30, they haven't even started their day. He'd pound it in that it was a golden opportunity: "You'll never know what's behind door number three unless you knock." Bean wanted us out there at the end of the day with the attitude that the one extra call we were making might be the call of the day. Instead of ending the day by coming into the office and chatting or going home fifteen minutes early, discipline yourself.

This rule is a simple way to make sure that you put in a little extra effort each day. It's too easy to just sit back and say, "Okay, I worked hard and I'm going home." Yup, you did work hard, but what would happen if you worked just a little harder? You can make five or six quick phone calls in a half-hour. Ask customers how they're doing, try to move a prospect along, see what's out there. Something will click and pay off. "Full day, full pay."

When it becomes easy to stop and go home, it will become easier and easier; 4:30 becomes 4:15, and then it's 4:00. Suddenly it's a habit, and you've lost focus and discipline.

If you want to be great, you have to pay the price—and the price is effort. There are a lot of people out there with talent who never invest the time and effort in that talent. The first 98 percent of our effort is just the price of admission. It's the next 2 percent, and the 2 percent thereafter that determines success. Too many people stop short. They've almost made it, but not quite. They go home thinking they've worked hard—and they have—but not hard enough. If you've had a good day, ask yourself, "How am I going to make it even better?" I'm the first to admit that never being satisfied is a curse. I look with a little envy at people who are lying back and basking in the glow of their achievements. It would be nice. But I know how energizing and exciting and how much fun it is to keep pushing harder.

I'm convinced that we all work well below our full capacity. It makes for a lot of squandered talent and possibilities. The true champions are the first ones out on the field for batting practice and the last to head for the locker room. They are the grinders.

10. IF YOU STAY IN THE SHOWER A LONG TIME IN THE MORNING BECAUSE YOU DON'T LOOK FORWARD TO WORK, FIND ANOTHER JOB.

Inertia is the enemy of excellence. I believe we all have the talent to succeed at something. Finding that "something" is the challenge.

Dave Leedy—I wrote about him earlier; he's an inspirational speaker—asks his audiences, "Are you the kind who wakes up at four A.M. ready to go to work? You rush out to the driveway and the car won't start, but never mind—I'll run to the office!" Everybody chuckles at the exaggeration. Yet, there's a pang of regret that mixes with the laughter. We all want to feel that much enthusiasm for the job. Wouldn't it be great to get that kind of charge from going to work?

You can. And that's really the message of this book. Don't settle for anything less.

The long sessions in the shower are a sure sign that inertia has set in. A body at rest tends to remain at rest: "Oh boy, I'm not ready for the meeting." Or, "I can't believe I have to spend the day riding with Frank." But there will be a million excuses to explain why you should stay with a job that has become a burden. None of them are valid. And it's not necessary to do a guilt trip on yourself. There's a manager and a leader who isn't doing his or her job to make work fun and fulfilling, exhilarating, and electric. Get going.

We simply spend too much time on the job not to enjoy it. Eight-hour days add up to 60,000 hours over a thirty-year career. If I told you I was going to throw you in jail for nearly seven years, you wouldn't be thrilled at the prospect. Yet we construct our own jail cells and do hard time without ever thinking that it's up to us to break out.

Ten More

I promised to give you ten more tips. No problem. I've probably got a couple of thousand to draw from. I'll make it thirteen, a baker's dozen. What I've come up with is a list that amounts to a summary of many of the concepts we've discussed so far. Use it as a refresher and a way to backstop yourself. This book is a waste of money if you don't steal my ideas and give them a try. Maybe they won't work for you. Maybe they will.

1. Make a statement early.
2. Constantly search for new ideas.
3. Trust people and empower them.
4. Get away from the desk.
5. Strive for constant improvement.
7. Assume nothing.
8. Create constant challenges.
9. Tell them the good and bad news.
10. Never, ever, back off goals.
11. Take risks.
12. Listen, listen, listen.
13. Lead, lead, lead.

8

▼

POWER SURGE:

CREATING ENERGY AND

ELECTRICITY

I have a confession to make: I swiped one of my son's toys. Yes, I know . . . what a heartless beast! When we were packing to move from Minnesota to Cleveland, I was going through Frankie's stuff and found an ugly troll doll that he obviously didn't play with very much. I knew immediately what I was going to do with it.

Since negotiating with a three-year-old is a ticklish and time-consuming business, I presented Frankie with a fait accompli. The troll disappeared, and I don't think he ever missed it.

Frankie's pal (we called him the "Wishnik") was worth a battalion of business consultants. He single-handedly—well, I had a little to do with it—persuaded my sales managers that I was serious when I said that there would be consequences for failure. At the end of each month, after we had tallied up each sales team's installed revenue, I asked each of my managers to vote on who among them deserved to get the booby prize—the Wishnik. Usually, the manager who missed plan and brought in the least revenue ended up with the troll, which had to be prominently displayed on his or her desk for the next thirty days. No hiding the Wishnik behind a Boston fern or putting him in a desk drawer.

The other way to win the honor was to be too successful. Accurate outlooking, or forecasting, is an important skill. A good manager should be able to estimate fairly closely the amount of business that will be generated by his team. The Wishnik would go, almost without fail, to managers who deliberately bagged the outlook with a lowball forecast and then far exceeded the modest expectation for the month. In that way, the doll was a way to keep everybody honest. The message was: don't mess around with the figures; keep everything on the up-and-up or you'll end up with the Wishnik.

That doll was mighty unpopular!

I decreed that the manager who won the Wishnik three months in a row would retire the prize, which turned into an ominous joke among the troops that the unfortunate manager would retire *with* the prize. The possibility was a real motivator; most of the teams dumped the Wishnik after thirty days, and those who held it for a second month jumped through hoops to get rid of their nemesis before they wound up being three-time losers.

The transfer of the Wishnik became a cause for celebration or soul-searching, depending on who was on the receiving end. There were jokes, but nobody ever shrugged it off when the Wishnik came for a visit. The best managers used the doll to galvanize their people into action. It led to healthy internal competition among the teams. Once, when the entire district failed to make plan for the month, I kept the Wishnik. It gave me an opportunity to make a statement that everyone understood: "That's the last time I'm going to have the damned thing on my desk." And it was.

In good months, when all the teams exceeded their plans and no one lowballed the outlook, the Wishnik was an orphan. When he reappeared after an absence of a month or two, there'd be a loud groan at the staff meeting and usually the recipient was really upset about getting the award. The doll could really ruin an otherwise good day. Nevertheless, he became something of a mascot and periodically would get his hair braided and face daubed with lipstick and mascara (particularly when he was about to go visit another team). One time the Wishnik appeared with a hangman's noose around his neck.

HIDE AND SEEK

Look around your own organization. Are things fairly static? The same people on top from month to month, and the same people on the bottom?

Shake it up. Many underachievers can be turned around by techniques like the Wishnik. For some people, failure isn't hard to swallow as long as it's happening in obscurity. I'll bet you know the number one performer in your business. But how about the man or woman who consistently comes in last or near the bottom? Is it Bill or Sue or Carl? The manager knows. But he or she doesn't want to embarrass anyone. Nor do I. My goal is to motivate those people by tearing away all the camouflage they've been hiding in. If you work for me, and let yourself fail, I won't let you hide from the consequences of that failure.

And isn't it better to hand out the Wishnik than pink slips? It's really just a variation on my father's trick with my lousy report cards. I got C's and, as a consequence, the report card went up on the refrigerator door. I knew that if I didn't want my aunts and uncles and cousins to see what a lazy slug I had been, I had better start hitting the books.

DO OR DIE, AND OTHER OPTIONS

Consequences. I know I've used the word before, but I've got to keep repeating it. You'll never have a high-energy, high-voltage workplace without consequences.

Don't get the idea, however, that successful management comes down to issuing bloodcurdling ultimatums. Between "do" and "die" there are several options. My use of the Wishnik is one. Another is the simple practice of ranking each person in the operation according to various indices. I do it by the total number of orders, revenue that's been generated, year-to-date and month-to-date performance, percentage over plan, customer satisfaction—there are many different ways. I want the reps and managers to know how they stack up against their peers. And I make it public knowledge. The rankings are posted and announced at each business meeting.

Be careful, though, if you use this technique. Watch out for *unhealthy* competition. When you throw everybody into the shark tank, it can bring out the best and worst instincts. If you sense that the competitive pressure is leading to an overly aggressive go-it-alone attitude, step in and tell the offenders to knock it off. Be direct about it: "Go easy—you're ticking off too many people"; or "You don't realize it, but a lot of people around here resent your behavior." I often head off trouble by suggesting that the strongest performers help those who are struggling. If I have reps who have difficulty closing a sale, I'll approach my best closers and ask them to work with those people and give them some pointers. I could do it myself, but it's better to foster interaction between colleagues. I'm dissolving and merging the isolated pockets of excellence and mediocrity. Also, the attitude that success comes at the expense of one's colleagues (talk about poison!) can be held in check.

This is a very good way to foster team spirit. It tears down the walls between individuals. Frequently a rep who's having trouble will go underground, almost like a sick or wounded animal. You've got to look for the signs and encourage his or her colleagues to offer that person assistance. In time, it will become a perfectly natural thing to do and even the biggest egos will be able to swallow their pride and say, "I'm having a little trouble here. How do you handle it?"

But it won't happen by itself; you'll have to jump-start the cooperation. People are reluctant to "meddle," so do the meddling for them.

HELP YOURSELF

Have you ever hired or promoted someone only to find out a few months later that the individual couldn't do the job? Welcome to the club. If you have a strong mutual-aid tradition going within your organization it can really help get you off the hook.

I made a serious hiring mistake in Cleveland that ended up working out all right because my team managers rode to the rescue. Instead of sniping at the person involved, the managers came to me early with warnings about the problem. I suggested they each work with the individual—a new sales manager—so that she could keep her head above water. I knew she would be reluctant to seek help from me out of fear that I would conclude she was the wrong person for the job. But having a management colleague drop into her office to chat and offer advice didn't seem strange or threatening. Eventually, she got comfortable enough to start asking for help. Her team, despite the difficulties, actually made plan. And several months later she found a more suitable slot elsewhere and left without losing dignity or respect.

It wouldn't have happened without a strong sense of teamwork. Nobody asked, "Why should I carry her?" They all knew the answer: the team would be hurt . . . that's why. There's a postscript to this story, though: Don't expect the team to do your dirty work. I made a mistake. The woman shouldn't have been hired in the first place. The team pulled together to get us over the bad patch, but I couldn't just sit back forever and expect my managers to do their jobs and hers. Once the situation stabilized, she and I had candid discussions about her best options and it worked out well for all of us.

WHAT GOES AROUND

Here's a technique that I've had good results with that you might try. Once a process has been established and functioning for about three months, throw your team managers together for an old-fashioned bull session. What I do is tell each of the managers to prepare a presentation that will update us on where the team stands to date. Is it exceeding the plan or falling short? What are the problem areas? What are the strengths? I tell them to bring a "best practice" to the meeting—i.e., something they've done that has worked well. I also want them to tell the group what didn't work.

This kind of sharing dampens unhealthy competition. I want the teams to compete, but I don't want feuding and factionalism. When they compare notes in a freewheeling atmosphere, it reinforces the notion the district is the ultimate team. Nobody wins unless we all win.

The exchange of best practices is particularly useful. I don't want anyone to hoard an effective idea just to get an edge on his or her colleagues. My goal is to make sure a best practice gets the widest possible circulation, while at the same time ensuring that the person or team that originated the idea receives recognition.

I'll give you an example. One of my young reps took the initiative after reading a newspaper article about a family-owned shoe company in her territory. She reproduced the clipping using our most sophisticated color system and sent it to the company chairman with a note congratulating him for getting such positive press coverage. She also pointed out that the copy was done on a Xerox machine and provided some information about the equipment. Bull's-eye! Lisa had taken the initiative to try something creative with the account and actually got a response from the top guy. Two days later the company chairman was on the phone requesting additional copies to send to his division managers. Before long we were doing a survey of his application needs. Lisa's success got everyone's attention.

Sending the clipping was a great idea: just the kind of thing that an intensely competitive rep might decide was too good to share with the others. Fortunately, she didn't think that way, and I immediately told everybody about it using Voicemail, praising her to the skies.

I wanted her to feel good; she deserved to. And I also intended to prime the pump of creativity by letting the group know there was recognition to be gained by those who had brainstorms and shared them.

FREE PARKING

Recognition is a consequence. I use the word in its most positive sense, although I suppose receiving the Wishnik is a form of recognition.

My preference, when it comes to a choice between the carrot and the stick, is go with the option that helps you see in the dark and wiggle your nose. In fact, I grow a gardenful of carrots and only keep a few sticks for times when all else fails.

On the days the Wishnik was handed out, the number one manager in Cleveland received a free parking place inside the building's garage. That doesn't sound like much, but for seven months a year, when Cleveland is under a blanket of ice and snow, a warm, dry parking place is a genuine treat. If there's no garage handy or if you're based in a warm climate, try presenting a $100 gift certificate to your top manager each month. It's a small investment at $1,200 a year, and you'll get it back tenfold.

Another cheap and effective form of recognition is what we called "Pictures with Paul." The Cleveland district was scheduled for a visit by Paul Allaire, Xerox's chief executive in 1991. The other Paul—Paul MacKinnon, my right-hand guy and the district's marketing manager—came up with the idea of offering a group photograph with the corporation's CEO for the reps who achieved a specific sales target. The number one rep would have his picture taken one-on-one with Paul Allaire.

Thus, we got a double bang out of his visit. It was an honor to have the CEO in the district to begin with. The incentive idea generated even more enthusiasm.

Don't underestimate the power of seemingly innocuous incentives. Having one's picture taken with the CEO is important to a person who hopes to climb the corporate ladder. What does it cost to hire a professional photographer for an hour—$150? We did several thousand dollars' worth of extra business from "Pictures with Paul." And the photos are still hanging on the walls in Cleveland as a continuing form of recognition.

HIGH VALUE, LOW COST

It's funny. If you ask reps which they'd prefer—a picture with the CEO or extra money—most will say money. But cash bonuses rarely generate the level of enthusiasm that I get from incentives with little or no financial value. In 1992, I ran one program and gave away gym bags with the logo for the Barcelona Olympics. You would have thought $10,000 cash bonuses were riding on the outcome. Everybody wanted a bag.

The money machine has always been a real crowd pleaser,

as well. I rent one of those carnival attractions that consists of a compressed-air generator and an inflatable, clear plastic chamber large enough to hold one adult. The reps who achieve the special sales target that I set for a week or a ten-day period get to go into the money machine. The air is switched on, and a cloud of dollar bills starts madly swirling around them. The winner has two minutes to grab as much cash as he or she can manage—and it isn't easy. The contortions are hilarious. We do it late on a Friday afternoon when there's a good crowd around the office to watch. We clap and chant and cheer. The chuckling lasts all weekend. It's an especially good incentive if morale is dragging.

Our turkey shoots are also popular. As Thanksgiving approaches, I set a sales goal that each rep must achieve to win a twelve-pound turkey. The prize is probably worth fifteen dollars at most. But here again, we get deadly serious competition for the birds. We issue news releases announcing the current winners, and there's no mercy for the reps who don't qualify. No sales target, no turkey. All the leftover birds are donated to charity.

FUN, FOOLISHNESS, AND MONEY

Don't try to conquer the world with every incentive program. It's nice to increase your sales dramatically, but just achieving a sense of excitement and fun can yield long-term benefits. Here's one to try that doesn't require a lot of extra effort and coordination: I bill it as the "March Madness Shootout," since I've used it several times just as the first quarter is coming to a close to spike our activity levels a little. Rent or borrow one of the scaled-down hoops and basketball gizmos that have become popular attractions in sports bars in recent years. You've probably seen them in action—the player gets two or three minutes to keep shooting at the basket and running up a score. To qualify, require the reps to bring in a couple of extra sales in a ten-day period beyond what they were already outlooking. A few days before the end of the quarter, assemble those who make it and have them shoot it out for a fifty-dollar cash prize. The high scorer wins. The qualifiers also can have the option to challenge a manager to a duel (hoops and balls at ten paces) for another fifty.

One year I had tiny megaphones made up with the Xerox logo that we gave to the crowd to add some flavor and encourage foolishness. I wonder what our neighbors in the building made of "Go, go, go . . . shoot, shoot, shoot," occasional groans of disappointment, and whoops of triumph.

THREE FOR THE ROAD

Look for big and small ways to throw your people together. Incentive and recognition events are ready-made for building camaraderie. One of my most successful is the "Cleveland Classic." It's six weeks of fun and excitement just before the second quarter comes to an end.

I start by breaking up the reps into odd three-person teams. I say "odd" because it involves scrambling the traditional business specialties and putting people together who normally wouldn't have much daily or week-to-week contact. Then, our next step is to go across the street to the VFW hall to drink some beer (alcohol isn't allowed in the office), eat pizza, and have an auction. I always bring in a professional auctioneer for the evening, and we sell shares in the teams to the highest bidders, an event known in bridge and golf terminology as a "calcutta."

The handicapping gets pretty fierce. Imagine a roomful of sales professionals sizing up the strengths and weaknesses of twenty-four untested teams: "He can't close a deal in less than two months"; "She's a great cold caller"; "He can sell Docu-Techs in his sleep." That kind of talk is going back and forth. Syndicates form to pool the money to buy entire teams outright. The proceeds of the auction are collected and divided among the teams with the best overall performances, a portion going to the investors who originally backed the winners. The pots are nothing to sneeze at; upward of $3,700 to $4,000 in some cases.

We track the teams on a weekly basis, using a weighted point formula for each sale. It gives me a chance to ballyhoo the results with news releases breathlessly updating the "neck-and-neck," "come from behind," and "upset of the century" competition. Whenever the rankings change, E-mail and Voicemail are excellent mediums for quick bulletins.

The calcutta amounts to a blitz within a blitz. The Cleveland Classic continues in the meantime, broken into two-week segments punctuated by interludes like the "Pacetta Open," an afternoon of golf for all those who qualified for the first rung of the contest, followed by a barbecue and an awards ceremony featuring minor prizes—desk calendars, fountain pens, and things like that. After another two weeks, we have a karaoke night, held outdoors behind our building, which gives all the would-be nightclub singers a chance to indulge their fantasies with a rented karaoke machine.* There are lots of hot dogs and sausages and, again, prizes for those who are bringing in the most extra business. Karaoke night is my personal favorite. It's an excuse for me to sing. I usually start the festivities with Jefferson Airplane's "White Rabbit" and close with "The Weight" by The Band.

Here's a point to remember: Don't just pay the rent with incentives. If you have to use special incentives to achieve minimal sales levels, something's wrong. Either your process is faulty or you've got the wrong people in the wrong places. A third possibility is that you or your bosses are overestimating the sales potential of your territories. Incentives won't get you out of those kinds of holes. But they will boost sales beyond the baseline after the process, the people, and realistic expectations are in place. Therefore, I advise you not to try incentives before you've been on the scene for about three months. At that point, if you've done half the things I've recommended so far in this book, a Cleveland Classic–style incentive should get you into overdrive.

Another tip: If you're going to run your own version of the Cleveland Classic, I recommend highly specific sales goals rather than going with an overall number. You may have people who are good at selling big-ticket items, and they'll always crush everyone else in terms of the total dollars involved. Give prizes out based on a mix of products or on some other formula

---

* In case you don't make the bar scene all that often, a karaoke machine lets a singer choose a song from a selection on laser disks, play the tune through a set of speakers, and sing along by reading the lyrics displayed on a video monitor —instant Frank Sinatra.

that takes into account the characteristics of your industry and district.

Finally, don't pay your reps twice. Know the sales cycles well enough to use incentives to liven up dull periods; otherwise, the deals that you're pulling down would probably have happened anyway. In my industry, June is busy, but the Classic was actually forcing the sales cycle to conclude in the middle of the month by encouraging my reps not to wait until they were up against the end of the second quarter. Otherwise, without the Classic—and this is peculiar to our situation at Xerox—if equipment sold at the end of the month isn't actually installed and invoiced by the thirtieth, it won't be counted as revenue for that quarter. The Classic gave me an extra two weeks to get the equipment in place, and it served to actually rearrange the business cycle to my advantage.

GIVING AND RECEIVING

In 1991, I invited guests from other Xerox districts and from Rochester and Stamford, Connecticut, to come in and observe the Classic, and it worked so well that I've done it each year since. The reps never know who they'll be traveling with during the six-week period. It could be a regional V-P, a big shot from the home office, or another manager they haven't worked with in the past. I really mix it up. The presence of the guests changes the chemistry and gets everybody out of their day-to-day mindset. The reps go home on the weekend and say, "God, for the next six weeks I don't know who's going to be with me in that car on Monday morning. It could be Paul Allaire, for all I know." It forces people to get cranked up and really plan their calls. The guests love it because they get a chance to break out of their routines, come to Cleveland—Cleveland?—smell the gunpowder from the front lines, and have some fun. One year, we had more than thirty guests, which meant that virtually everyone in the district was paired off and had to be at their best.

The grand finale of the Cleveland Classic is a party at which we give out the big prizes to those who have won the overall competition and to the teams that have the highest combined scores. The prizes are fairly substantial, like ten-speed bikes and

VCRs; the winning team members and investors might walk off with $600 or $800 each.

The Cleveland Classic became a district tradition and the key event in our sales year. I probably spent around $15,000 on each one, counting the golf, the entertainment, and the prizes. And if you think that's excessive, wait until I tell you how sales are affected. Normally, we do an average of 210 orders a month. During the most recent Classic, the rate jumped to 550 orders.

Is it worth $15,000? Indeed it is. During an average year, I spend more than $50,000 on various forms of incentives and recognition. Some years it's been over $100,000. I'm often asked how Xerox lets me get away with that kind of spending. Easy. The corporation's philosophy is, "If you make it, you can spend it." Xerox managers have a lot of discretion with their checkbooks as long as the expenditure ends up enhancing the bottom line.

THE CELTS, THE YANKS, THE FIGHTING IRISH, AND PASTA AL DENTE

If you go back up two paragraphs, you'll see that I described the Cleveland Classic as a "tradition." That's an important word. Most closely knit families are steeped in traditions. I was reminded of my family's rich Italian heritage on a trip to Rome in the spring of 1993, after Julie and I took part in President's Club, which was held that year in London. Our hotel overlooked the Spanish Steps, and I stood in the window mesmerized by the scene below. It brought back all the memories: my grandmother and grandfather speaking Italian, pasta al dente (always on Sundays), breaking bread with my uncles and aunts, talk, laughter, and good times.

Tradition is a history book. There's life and meaning on every page. It's powerful stuff, and business needs that power to create a common bond that brings people together and makes them want to stay together.

Sports traditions prove my point. The tradition of Notre Dame football helps the university attract the best athletes, and I would also bet that many other students who never go near a playing field are also drawn to the South Bend, Indiana, campus for the same reason. The great sports dynasties like the Boston Celtics and the New York Yankees are saturated in traditions from Red Auerbach's victory cigars to the Yankee pinstripes. An athlete who runs out on the court in Boston Garden and looks up into the rafters at Bob Cousy's and Bill Russell's uniforms hanging there like battle flags, or walks to home plate in Yankee Stadium and sees the monuments to Ruth, Gehrig, and DiMaggio guarding the outfield can't help feeling pride and the desire to do his best.

Your own family traditions are just as magical. Think of them: the Christmas holidays, Thanksgiving turkey, touch football, the Fourth of July parade and fireworks. Doesn't it feel good? Don't you look forward to them?

A workplace devoid of tradition has no heart or soul. The traditions we created in Cleveland anchored the year: the Academy Awards, March Madness, the Cleveland Classic, the Turkey Day Blitz, the President's Club campaign, Peak 'n Peak. Our people looked forward to those events year after year and plunged into them with great enthusiasm.

My favorite tradition of all is one I borrowed directly from my family. Monthly, often weekly, we break bread together. I get my managers out of the office so that we can talk and eat. Sometimes it's strictly business, often it's a little business and a lot of simple, rewarding human contact. People relax, stop playacting, and let their guards down. There's a bond created. The next day, the organization is a little closer, a little stronger.

I wouldn't think of operating a business organization without periodically breaking bread with my people. It's the one tradition I couldn't do without.

FAST START IN A SLOW SEASON

By the summer of 1988, the Cleveland jokes had stopped within Xerox. My people were coming back from training sessions in Leesburg with reports that the instructors were asking, "What do they feed you guys in Cleveland anyway?" I went to a district managers' meeting in Chicago and heard similar things. It was a generally slow year for Xerox—make that a generally rotten year for Xerox. As a result, Cleveland's performance really stood out. My boss's boss, Bud Angeles, had taken a chance when he okayed my promotion and transfer from Minnesota. During the Chicago meeting, which was rather downbeat given the poor sales results, Bud interrupted a presentation to call me up to the front of the group and, with a mixture of exasperation with his other managers and pride in what had been accomplished in a district that had been written off a few months earlier, said, "And, yeah—they can even sell copiers in Cleveland."

I took the kind words back to the district to share with the people who deserved to hear and savor them. The atmosphere in the amphitheater couldn't have been in greater contrast to our first gathering in January. The faces were mostly the same, but the fear, uncertainty, and resignation were gone. I stood there in front of them for several minutes trying to control my emotions, looking out at a group that had learned a lesson, a lesson that is the very heart and soul of this book: it's all about winning. They were winning and they loved it.

YES AND NO

After I ran through the final figures for the first half and passed along the compliments from Chicago, I set out the vision for the rest of the year: number one in the region, number one in the nation. And nobody blinked. I was confident we could stay on top in the region after our strong showing in the first half. Grabbing the top slot nationally was another thing entirely. Could it be done? Yes. Was it likely? No.

All right, let me stop here and explain something about what George Bush called "the vision thing." Small visions are a waste of time. The big ones generate excitement and enthusiasm. Without those two ingredients very little—big or small— can be achieved. In January of 1988, when I set being number one in the region as the goal, I was careful to say we'd do it over time or burn ourselves out in the attempt. Even though I left myself an out, it was as impossible a dream as coming out on top nationally was in July of 1988. If I hadn't shot for the stars my first time out, I wouldn't have even cleared the tree-tops.

It may sound cynical, but what I call "Hollywood vision" is extremely important. I'm not talking about smoke and mirrors; there has to be a rainbow and a pot of gold—in Technicolor.

Everyone in the amphitheater knew it wasn't a level playing field, for various business and economic reasons. One district's plan might be relatively low compared to another's if the last year was a bad one. Smaller districts often end up number one because they have better leverage over their territories, and Rochester isn't trying for unrealistic grand slams when it hands out the budget. Going for number one, however, was the only alternative for us in Cleveland. I couldn't very well say, "The goal is to finish second or third." What a downer!

I figured that with our momentum, and if I could keep the pressure on, I could at least catapult Cleveland into the top five and seriously challenge all the biggest districts. It would be the equivalent of the old cellar-dwelling New York Mets of the mid-sixties ending up in a World Series playoff.

Am I saying that a leader should set unrealistic and unattainable goals? No, not at all. What I'm pointing up is the need for a little bit of show business. I called on all the dramatic flair and psychological finesse I could from the likes of Vince Lombardi, Pat Riley, and Bill Parcells. All had led teams to championships; all great leaders. I doubt that they asked their players to "come in second for the Gipper."

GOALS VS. VOWS

Do you know the difference between goals and vows? Becoming the number one sales district is a goal. That's what we're shooting for. If we succeed, there's a celebration. If not, we analyze the reasons why and move ahead. It's something like a diet. Let's say I make a New Year's resolution to tighten my belt and lose ten pounds, but only manage to get rid of eight of them. I probably feel reasonably satisfied anyway. I worked hard and came close. Finishing second or third or in the top five is a pretty good showing, and therefore the goal served its purpose even though it wasn't a bull's-eye.

A vow is different. Very different. We don't hear much about vows in the business world. When I make a vow it means I'm going to do this, come hell or high water! Reestablishing the work ethic in Cleveland was a vow. I wasn't going to back off, compromise, or settle for coming close! Let's make more vows. Some things are worth going to the wall for, and can be accomplished with extra effort, unyielding determination, and the will to succeed.

There's a school of thought based on the premise that *everything* is negotiable. I don't believe that. If everything is negotiable, nothing is worth fighting for. To me, the work ethic is worthy of a knockdown, drag-out brawl; it's a defining concept without which we're nothing more than slaves to a paycheck. To pursue it as a goal leaves too much wiggle room. A vow—no surrender, no retreat—is the only way to go.

Don't be afraid of vows. When you make them with careful deliberation, incredible inner power is summoned up and released. In fact, I'm more afraid of not caring enough, risking enough, trying enough than I am of the possibly gut-wrenching struggle to achieve my vows. At the end of the day it will be worth all the effort.

Get in the habit of differentiating goals and vows. Take a piece of paper and list your goals on the left and your vows on the right. Here's what I have in mind:

Goals	Vows
• Have the number one district in the region	• Change the work ethic
• Improve customer satisfaction by 2–3 percent	• Improve my leadership skills
• All reps achieve their targets	• Make the operation a fun place to work

Vows are serious business. Make them when you're ready to move mountains. But there are no A's for effort. IT HAS TO HAPPEN.

HANDS OFF

We spent the last half of the year patting our stomachs and rubbing our heads, and then switching to rubbing our stomachs and patting our heads. Try it yourself. Not easy, is it?

This old test of coordination is an apt metaphor for the feat we accomplished by keeping our sales momentum going and at the same time drastically reconfiguring the various territories in the district.

My MSL reviews were telling me that Cleveland was trying to do too much with too little. The individual sales territories had become bloated to the point that many of the reps couldn't handle all the business without shortchanging the customers.

Part of the problem was that corporate planners have a tendency to stonewall requests for additional resources when a district is unsuccessful. Meanwhile, thanks to evolving economic conditions, the district's potential is actually growing. In time, an already beleaguered rep is totally swamped. When that happens, it's time to reduce the size of the territories and bring in reinforcements.

In 1988 and 1989, I added thirteen reps to the district to handle reconfigured territories and new business. And I made a big mistake in the process. I underestimated the impact that "the face in front of the customer"—an expression that sales managers should stop using—has on business relationships. It seemed to me at the time that the customers would shrug off the changes and adapt quickly to the new reps handling their accounts. I was wrong. I spent a lot of time in the field explaining and soothing hard feelings. Many customers had developed a real bond with their old reps and didn't like losing them.

You might keep that in mind when you reconfigure territories. What I learned from the experience is to keep my hands off territories until changes are absolutely necessary, and once those changes are made, to avoid any others for at least two or three years. Some corporations can't resist the temptation to fiddle with their sales territories. The customers are the big losers, when they are asked to take a leap of faith whenever there's a major change, and it's disorienting.

Instead of promoting good people out of a sales territory,

I'd rather see the promotions come in the form of increased compensation in return for a longer stay in the field. I think if reps have the choice of more money and less personal disruption or a fancy title, they'll take the money. It's also good for the customer, good for the rep, and good for the corporation.

A FOUR-LETTER WORD THAT MEANS SUCCESS

In the fall, I started pushing President's Club real hard. It was in Hawaii that year. I set 100 percent participation as the goal and came close to achieving it with close to thirty reps qualifying. I had an artist do a huge drawing of the interior of an airliner, and as the reps qualified, we put a picture of each in one of the seats. What I was doing—and what you need to do as a manager—is generate peer pressure as a motivational force. "If he can do it . . . if she can do it, I can do it too" is the rumbling you're trying to generate. Imagine that you're a sales rep in Cleveland and the only one who didn't qualify for President's Club. You're the lone stay-at-home, the wallflower. Not a great feeling, is it? I for one, in that situation, would start looking for another career. This is what I'm talking about when I say that if you generate a blistering pace you won't have to fire those who can't keep up. Most of them will drop out on their own.

As the list of President's Club attendees grew longer, the tension also grew within the district. When new names were added I could almost hear a sigh of relief from their managers and fellow team members. The best part was that many of those who qualified early circled back to help those who were having trouble.

And that's exactly—exactly—what all this stuff is about! Use incentives and recognition to build a team. Sure, it's great to nail down extra business. But there's more to it than that. If you're just out to boost sales quickly and temporarily by throwing red meat to the lions, the big cats will tear each other apart. You'll get the business. There will be a short-term payoff, but every incentive program thereafter will produce smaller and smaller dividends. It's fine to "eat what you kill"; however, when stomachs get full, what's the motivating factor? There isn't any without a team.

Write it down (again): T-E-A-M. Or try Notre Dame coach Lou Holtz's formula, which I put on T-shirts for my people in Minneapolis:

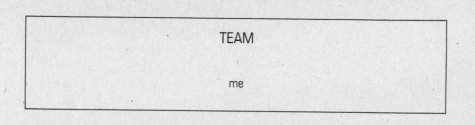

TEAM

me

HONORS AND HORS D'OEUVRES

We finished the year first in the region in terms of percentage of profit, and fourth nationally. To celebrate, I held the first of our Academy Awards nights in January of 1989. They've become a tradition in Cleveland: black tie, long dresses, klieg lights, hired camera crews, music and glamour. Everybody in the district was invited.

The "Oscars" go to the top-performing reps and managers in several different categories. I hire limousines to pick up the winners at their homes. There's a bar in back with champagne on ice and fancy hors d'oeuvres. They roll up to the club we've rented for the night, a camera crew is waiting for a sidewalk interview, the crowd cheers the couples as they arrive. Inside there are lavish decorations and food. And just like real Academy Awards, the winners are called up front to be honored, they come forward basking in the applause, say a few words to their colleagues and spouses, and some of them choke up with emotion.

I wanted to end this chapter on incentives and recognition with the Academy Awards. Every year we did them in Cleveland they got better and better. The husbands and wives of our reps and managers would tell me afterward how proud they were that their spouses worked for Xerox. The second year, for me, was the biggest kick, though. One young rep who was being honored recalled that at the previous year's Awards he had watched in awe from the back of the room as his peers were receiving their accolades. He told us he had said to himself, "I'm going to be up there someday . . . that's what I want." And he spent a year working his butt off to make the dream come true.

Tell me that this recognition and incentive stuff is hokey and a waste of money. Tell me. Tell that sales rep.

9

▼

THE CUSTOMER:

"NO" IS A FOUR-LETTER WORD

In the last eight chapters I've written a lot about customers. Now I'm going to get obsessive about them.

Since 1989, when Xerox won the Malcolm Baldrige National Quality Award, the corporation has been closely identified with the quality movement. Hardly a week goes by without someone asking me to explain what it's all about. As far as I'm concerned the best definition is the simplest definition: quality is satisfying the customer.

As you know by now, to make sure I hit the target, I always raise my sights. Hence, my personal definition is slightly different: quality is *delighting* the customer. You don't need much more than that.

In the seventies and early eighties, Xerox found itself in deep trouble because too many of our customers weren't delighted, let alone completely satisfied, with our products and service. But until we lost our market dominance, when the Federal Trade Commission came after us in 1972 alleging restraint of trade, the customer didn't have much choice. If you didn't like Xerox, you either put up with us or hired monks with quill pens to do your copying.

Without serious competition, we persuaded ourselves that the customer understood that when the copier jammed or caught fire or sent intelligent adults into screaming fits of hysterics, that was just the way things were. We knew how incredibly complex xerographic technology was and assumed the customer did too. A copier was a miraculous and expensive little box with an unpleasant personality that had to be patiently endured.

In July of 1975, Xerox and the FTC settled the government's antitrust action. Xerox agreed to forgo much of its existing patent protection on plain-paper copier technology, figuring that we had an insurmountable advantage in the marketplace and that our patents would be infringed anyway if the corporation went on refusing to issue licenses to the fledgling competition.

What's a bit of competition if you're a nine-hundred-pound gorilla?

In the next five years, 147 different copiers were introduced in the United States. By 1982, Xerox's 80 percent share of the market (based on copier installations as of 1976) was down to 13 percent. These grim figures and the story of this precipitous decline are related in *Prophets in the Dark,* the memoir former Xerox CEO David Kearns co-authored with David Nadler in 1992. The book reads like a business executive's worst nightmare come true. And it was.

One of the things that kept us afloat was the superb sales operation Xerox had built during the glory days. Almost overnight, we were under siege from at least ten different Japanese companies, many of them selling copiers for prices that were actually lower than Xerox's manufacturing costs. To make matters worse, IBM and Kodak parachuted into the upper end of the market with high-quality products that challenged our supremacy on that front. If we hadn't been on the ground with a feisty, well-trained sales force that fought hard for every sale, we would have been totally creamed.

It also helped that at first the Japanese were selling pretty shoddy products—although they were fast learning how to improve them—and IBM and Kodak were slow to get the hang of operating outside of their traditional markets. Fortunately for us, the competition's learning curve and our death spiral intersected the day that David Kearns went to Tokyo in 1982 and became interested in Total Quality Control,* a term that was then being used to describe and explain the phenomenal success of "Japan Inc."

What evolved over the next eight years—and is still evolving—was a uniquely American, uniquely Xerox-style version of Total Quality Control. The heart of it is benchmarking and its soul is the customer.

Traditionally, a high-quality product was one that was manufactured exactly to specification, passed inspection with flying colors, and could be tossed out of a window and run over with a truck and "keep on ticking." The early proponents of the quality movement recognized the customer might not want to throw the product out of a window and run over it with a truck. Armed with that insight, they concluded that quality was whatever the customer said (or thought) it was.

Kearns took this spin on quality and combined it with his belief that Xerox needed to study the competition as well as industry leaders from outside the copier business to learn how to improve our products and procedures. We started shopping for good ideas and didn't care where they came from—L.L. Bean, John Deere, Burroughs—as long as they worked.

Revolutionary notions! Kearns used them to rejuvenate Xerox.

TOP DOWN

I'm giving you a shorthand version of quality, and you've probably read enough about it by now in other books and magazine articles to understand the basics. But what you may not realize is that Xerox got lucky. If quality had been discovered by anyone other than our CEO, it never would have taken root.

Like most Xerox executives, I have spoken to hundreds—probably thousands—of people who were eager to learn about quality so they could introduce the concepts to their own business organization. Our customers ask about it all the time. I tell them they should forget about quality if the man or woman at the top isn't on board. You must have 1000 percent support from

---

* Total Quality Control was being employed successfully by Fuji Xerox in the mid-1970s. It inspired Xerox's Total Quality Management (TQM) concepts.

the CEO and senior management. The frustration level is enormous for middle-level executives who try to sell quality to their skeptical or lukewarm superiors. If the eyes glaze over and he or she rushes for the elevator whenever the subject of quality comes up—don't even try!

The other mistake about quality is impatience. It won't happen overnight. When I'm making a presentation on quality, I see the disappointed faces around the room as I explain that quality cannot be up and running in two or three years. How long? Years. And I'm not ducking the answer . . . the real answer is forever. You'll *never* be finished with the job. David Kearns aptly describes quality as a race with no finish line.

We're still running the race every day at Xerox, and sometimes we fall flat on our faces.

In 1988, the year we decided to compete for the Malcolm Baldrige National Quality Award, Xerox introduced the 5046, a mid-range copier that initially, to put it charitably, had a few problems.

On top of everything else we were dealing with in Cleveland that year, the 5046 seemed like the product from hell. There's a major law firm in the city that invested heavily in the 5046 on our recommendation. They couldn't go wrong, we said. It was a copier that combined a reasonable price, $8,000–$10,000, with substantial volume and state-of-the-art features. Just what the Juris Doctor ordered—or so we thought.

The 5046 was embarrassing. It couldn't do what we said it would. We had to pull the copiers out of the law firm and, worst of all, we didn't have a suitable replacement product. In other accounts, we survived by throwing our service people into a full-court press, but the law firm was a total loss. And to double the pain, they were nice about it; the attitude was disappointment rather than table-thumping anger. Our loss was the competition's gain.

This happened six years into the quality process. What went wrong? Remnants of the old Xerox culture still survived. An internal investigation revealed that although key people within the organization had known the 5046 had serious flaws, they hadn't spoken up and had allowed the product to be launched and shipped. Nobody wanted to be the bearer of bad tidings.

Perversely, the fiasco proved that quality worked. Our field operations' commitment to the customer was put to the test and really came through. Wherever possible, we brought in replacement machines and worked hard to minimize the inconvenience. In the old days before quality, we would have gone on selling the faulty machines and doing retrofit after retrofit in the customer's office. Quality taught us to stop the production line and not to start it again until the problem was fixed. It was the only way to restore confidence in the product. And that's exactly what we did. Eventually, the debugged 5046 turned out to be an excellent machine and is still a strong performer with high customer satisfaction.

The 5046 story is also an example of how a potential disaster can be turned around. Most sales districts, including mine, were relying heavily on the 5046 for 1988 revenue, since it played to the middle of the market. When we discovered the problems, our projections went right out the window. It was like a farmer who wakes up one morning to find that while the asparagus and lettuce are doing fine, the corn crop has failed. I decided to harvest and sell the asparagus.

I told my people that we would just have to take our hits on the 5046, but in the process we could turn the situation to our advantage. There was really no other choice. Rochester wasn't going to lower our sales plan. We were stuck with it. The answer was to go upmarket and sell the 5065, a high-volume, higher-priced machine. At first glance, it seemed we'd have to toss out our entire prospect base and start all over again because of the major price difference; the 5065 was two to three times more expensive. Fortunately, we didn't have to do that. We found that while the reps would have easily sold a 5046 with its bells and whistles because of the attractive price, for a little more time and effort, the same customer would opt for the 5065, once we pointed out its many advantages.

As a result, our revenue for the year in Cleveland got a real boost because the reps were out there pushing hard. They couldn't take their accounts for granted. In some ways, the 5046 would have sold itself, thanks to the price. That would have meant the reps were simply taking orders. Instead, they had to evaluate the customer's needs and *sell* the 5065. Even so, the extra effort was more than worth it. They would have had to move roughly three 5046's to generate the same revenue as one 5065. It forced us to go below the surface and take a hard look at our customers' applications and requirements: Were they really only mid-volume users? What was the growth potential? Did we need to talk to someone else in the organization who had the budget and the need for a 5065?

In many cases, despite its price, the 5065 was a much sounder choice for the customer. Packed with advanced features and solid as a brick wall, the machine could take a beating for six or seven years and handle a heavy work load. The copier's life expectancy was a real asset, but it's one that tends to be underappreciated by those who are looking only at a price tag. Another thing that can come as surprise to a customer is the quick escalation of copier volume once the machine is out of the carton and plugged in. There'd have to be one hell of an escalation to overload the 5065.

ESCAPE ARTISTRY

The experience proved three things: One, be flexible and move fast. Two, make sure you have the widest possible mix of products. Three, don't make decisions for the customer.

I'll take them one at a time. We didn't sit around grousing about the 5046. I knew as a manager and leader that the quickest way to demoralize the team is to waste time brooding after a setback. You can't fight what you can't fight. Our outlooks and strategies had to be revised on the fly. You can't fall in love with your game plan, no matter how good you think it is. We were geared up to sell the 5046, and saw it filling a vacuum that was developing in the middle of the market, but it was history the moment the customers started to complain that the machine was choking at key volume-bands.

Here's an important tip: Always have a fallback. In fact, I have fallbacks for my fallbacks. Call me a pessimist—it's not true, by the way—but I always assume that something will go wrong. I expect the worst. You've heard of Murphy's Law, but how about its corollary? Murphy's Law states: "What can go wrong will go wrong." The corollary says: "What can't go wrong will go wrong." Spend time building some fire escapes. You may not need them, but they sure come in handy when you start smelling smoke.

As for religiously mixing products, we never would have known about the upmarket potential if the 5046 had been allowed to dominate our strategy. I don't believe in "bread-and-butter" products, a few favorites you can sell in your sleep. Every product in the line is bread-and-butter. You're making a bad blunder as a manager if you let your people spend most of their training and selling time with a couple of products. It would have taken us weeks to get turned around if I had allowed the reps and managers to get lazy about training themselves with high-volume equipment. At Xerox, in any given year, we may be dealing with thirty unique products—many of them brand-new to the market—and it is tempting to slack off on training.

Here's a good case in point. Our DocuTech is a $250,000 machine. It's a marvelous product, but physically imposing and technically complex. To the uninitiated, just being in the same room with it is daunting. At demos, we tell the customers, "Go ahead and touch it. It won't bite." But some of our reps are intimidated and they try to avoid the DocuTech. I had a young, hotshot rep in my office one day and I asked him, "Are you up to speed on the DocuTech?"

"No, I'm going to wait for a couple of months until I go to Leesburg. I'll learn it there." Leesburg is Xerox's training facility.

"How do you demo it, then?"

"I'll get one of the analysts to help me," he said. Analysts are technical support people who are familiar with the complexities of computer software and the applications that are being used in our printing systems, which are based on laser technology. They are the ones who help the customer integrate our products with an existing computer system.

I nodded and made a mental note that the answer probably meant he did not do DocuTech demos very often. "Stop and think for a moment," I said. "What would a DocuTech sale do for you in terms of revenue?"

He sat there adding up the figures. "Three DocuTechs would make my plan for the entire year."

"Uh-huh. And you're going to wait two months until you get to Leesburg?"

He immediately saw what I was driving at. Get the training now.

I also recommend against a practice that used to be more common at Xerox than it is today. When the DocuTech was first introduced, we would designate reps to be DocuTech specialists. It seems like a good idea in view of the machine's complexity. But there are weaknesses. The specialists develop tunnel vision if they're not careful and don't see the opportunity to sell other products to the customer. It's only natural for a person who is hungry for a $250,000 deal to overlook the possibility of selling a $1,500 fax machine. After all, what's the financial incentive? And the reverse is also true. The generalist rep, who is frozen out of the big deals by the specialists, isn't inclined to make an extra call at 6:00 P.M. on the off chance that a DocuTech will drop into his lap. He may be a good corporate citizen and refer the deal to his colleagues, but he won't care quite as much. He will care a lot if there's money involved.

FAST BREAKS

We were able to get on top of the 5046 problem quickly because the launch of the 5065 earlier that year had already given us a lot of momentum. The reps knew the machine because they had been *required* to know it. No one would describe our product launches in Cleveland as lackadaisical affairs. As a rule, I always assign a team to go out and benchmark other districts that have worked with the product. I want them to find out what was done right and what was done wrong. The team then prepares an overall strategy and battle plan for the product. They learn it backward and forward, including how the competition's equivalent model stacks up against ours.

When the team is ready, we call all the reps together in the amphitheater for a presentation that will bring the whole group up to full speed on the product. With the 5065, I tried something new. After we looked at the slides and the demonstrations, I said, "Okay, we're going to get off to a fast start. Take a fifteen-minute break. Get some coffee, hit the bathrooms, and then head for your desks upstairs. I want you working the phones. Call as many customers as you can. When you come back here in fifteen minutes, I want you to have scheduled at least one 5065 demo."

In a quarter of an hour, we had lined up twenty-six demonstrations. And I mean "we." I was up there too, punching those phone buttons. Months could go by before the district does twenty-six demonstrations. We got them booked before the competition even knew the product had arrived in town! And the reps had a lot of fun with it. Instead of just sitting there nodding off, or forgetting everything they learned by the time they actually got around to selling the 5065, it was boots-and-saddle time. Get out of our way!

I'm always looking for ways to do something a little different. Nobody expected that kind of fast start, and it gave the district a real blast of excitement. Try it yourself. Be a boredom buster. When was the last time you surprised your people? Or is it the same old thing day after day? A football coach who ran the same practice drills all the time would soon have a teamful of space cadets.

Something Xerox does very well in the boredom-busting department is the "Demorama," a morning we spend having the reps demo our products to the managers. They've got to show us they know the ins and outs of the equipment. Everyone is rated, and the best get substantial prizes. It's a real challenge. If a rep can demonstrate a machine to me—and I think I've heard every objection, reservation, and excuse—he or she can demonstrate to anyone.

One requirement is that each rep must pretend to be demonstrating against a leading competitive product. Thus, they've got to know what the other "box" can and can't do. If you figure thirty Xerox products paired against another thirty from the competition, our reps don't have time to be bored.

GUESSWORK DOESN'T WORK

The third lesson I drew from the 5046 affair—don't decide for the customer—should be chiseled into a slab of granite. We assumed the 5046 was what the customer wanted, which, after all, is what quality is all about. Then why were we so successful at selling the 5065 instead? We didn't scam the customers into spending three times more for a machine they didn't need. The answer is, we didn't know customer requirements as well as we thought we did.

This is where quality either works or flops. If you want to establish a quality movement in your company, you've got to set up a mechanism for identifying customer requirements.

Raise your right hand and repeat after me: "I will set up a mechanism to identify customer requirements." Get one of your colleagues to take the pledge with you so that you'll have somebody to call in an emergency to sit with you when there's an overpowering urge to make a guess about customer requirements. Believe me, I get the urge from time to time. After seventeen years in the business, I think I know what the customer wants, and I have to remind myself to use surveys, statistical analysis, my reps' professional judgments and observations, and my own eyes and ears.

Every time you catch yourself making an assumption about the customer, pull back and ask yourself if it isn't time to call the person who also took the pledge and say, "Stop me before I guess again!"

In the case of the 5046, we decided for the customer. We decided they were price sensitive and would be more comfortable in the middle of the market. Fortunately, the machine's problems forced us to go back to the accounts and find out where they were really coming from. How? The answer to the question brings us full circle back to my penchant for asking questions.

Do you want to know the customers' requirements? Ask them. Any company that does not use its sales force as a detective agency ought to find some good bankruptcy lawyers. If you're a manager, the sales reps are your eyes and ears. They are in daily, hourly contact with the customer, and if they aren't actively seeking to determine customer requirements, then you and your company—to be politically correct—are audiovisually disadvantaged. Deaf and blind, to be politically incorrect.

The reason I ask my people so many questions is that I want them to adopt the same habit. They aren't going to be able to answer my questions until they start asking the customer questions:

- "How would you like this account to be handled?"
- "What's your biggest headache?"
- "Do you plan to expand in the next five years?"
- "Are there new products and services in the pipeline?"
- "Is your competition increasing?"
- "Is your productivity rising, falling, or flat?"

At Xerox, we require our reps to prepare formal sales proposals for each account. I take the requirement very seriously and come down hard on anyone who is slapdash about his or her proposals. It usually means that the rep is only skimming the surface of the account. If so, he or she is not functioning as my eyes and ears, and I refuse to be audiovisually disadvantaged.

As far as I'm concerned, the proposal is the most important document you have with a customer. It can make or break a deal, and make or break a business relationship.

Do you use sales proposals in your organization? I'm not talking about an order form. Dig one out of the file and see how it rates against this list of what a proposal shouldn't be:

- A one-page price quote
- Over five pages long
- Sent in the mail
- A form letter
- A fill-in-the-blanks form
- Inaccurate
- Sloppy
- Untyped
- Incomprehensible without supporting material

How did you do? I would bet most readers found proposals that were hardly more than one-page price quotes. What's wrong with that? Plenty. It reduces everything to price. Remember what I wrote a few pages back about not making decisions for the customer. That one-page price quote assumes that price is the be-all and end-all. Here's my final sermon on price competition: Repent! If you are making or selling a product or service based primarily on price, you've worked yourself into a very tight corner. The competition will figure out a way to beat your price—I guarantee it. At Xerox, we still are not over the shock of discovering the Japanese could sell a copier for less than what it cost us to make one—and turn a profit to boot. We learned through the quality movement—and it saved our necks—to put the emphasis on "total value." Some customers are price sensitive, but many aren't, and that is particularly the case when you point out to them that low price does not necessarily translate into real value. What about reliability, service, productivity? While I was writing this book, one of my competitors in Ohio decided to run TV ads stating that if the viewer had purchased a Xerox or Kodak copier, they probably paid too much. My reaction to the ad was to tell my people I hoped the guy ran it ten times a day. Make my day, month, year—compete with me on the basis of price!

WHAT MAN PROPOSES, THE CUSTOMER DISPOSES

The other common mistake is to prepare a proposal that either cannot be understood by anyone other than the one person the rep talked to on his or her sales call or needs a verbal presentation and backup material to supply the context. A proposal may make the rounds of dozens of people, and the rep won't be there to explain. Their contact probably isn't going to want to personally walk the proposal through the decision-making maze so that he can fill in the blanks. A good test is to go back five years and pull a proposal. If you can't make head or tail of it, check and see if the deal ever went through. If it didn't—now you know why.

Here's another list. This time it's what a proposal should have:

- An executive summary
- Customer input
- Benefits and key applications
- Review of customer requirements
- Comparisons
- References
- Details on service and support
- Recommendations and cost

To help you visualize the proposal, I'll give you a mock-up to work with:

The cover letter should be short and to the point. Tell the customer what he or she is about to read. Thank them for the time they've spent with you.

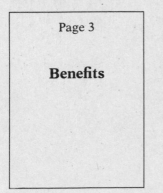

The executive summary is a must. On a single page, it lays out all the key points using bulleted sentences and phrases. Include your primary recommendation, the cost, and the customer requirements that are being fulfilled. Expect that this document will be circulated within the organization and must stand alone. Also, the summary should offer your contact a quick review of the proposal in the event that several weeks elapse between the time it is first received and crucial stages in the decision-making process. Long days, short memories.

Page 3

Benefits

This page gets into the nitty-gritty. It shows that the rep knows what the customer does for a living and what his products will do for the customer. First, do your homework.

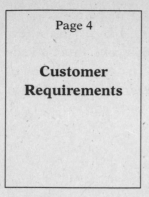

This is the customer's proposal, not yours. On your early calls you should come to agreement with the customer on the key buying criteria—speed, productivity, volume, and so on. Remind the customer that he or she sets the agenda.

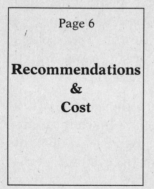

If you're replacing one of your own products, give the customer a comparison between the old and the new. If you're out to knock off a competitive product—compare, compare, compare!

This is the bottom line. Don't get carried away. Recommend no more than two options. Make sure the cost is more than just a number; include the total cost of ownership. Be explicit in showing the value of your product in the short and long terms.

<table>
<tr><td>

Page 7

Our Service

</td><td>

If you're a sell-and-run operation, you won't need this page. I hope that's not the case. This is a service economy. Tell the customer what to expect. Service will keep the customer coming back for more.

</td></tr>
</table>

<table>
<tr><td>

Page 8

References

</td><td>

A great sales tool. References really work. Let other customers speak on behalf of your product.

</td></tr>
</table>

<table>
<tr><td>

Page 9

Implementation

</td><td>

Tell them what happens next. The customer should receive a chronological rundown of order delivery, setup, and training. This is an excellent closing tool.

</td></tr>
</table>

GO LOOKING FOR TROUBLE

One of the great things about quality is that it teaches a corporation to make a fetish of solving problems. Instead of hiding from them, denying them, we go looking for problems. Constant improvement is the objective. Despite the 5046, we won the Baldrige award in 1989. In retrospect, it hardly seemed possible, given the number of warts we were discovering in our own processes. A Xerox management committee that had been set up to oversee the Baldrige competition turned up more than five hundred flaws. We are still working today to fix many of them. I would say the hardest one to resolve fully is convincing top management to loosen up on the reins and allow the field operation more freedom and flexibility.

Xerox is better in that regard than many companies, big and small. An old friend of mine left Xerox several years ago to go to work for an entrepreneur who had set up his own copier dealership. Entrepreneurs are supposed to be creative and free-wheeling, but what my pal discovered was just the opposite. His new boss owned the operation and wanted everyone to do it his way or else! The restrictions and controls were far worse than anything he experienced at Xerox.

Being small doesn't mean a company is immune to the diseases that have been sapping the strength of our major business institutions. Quality concepts and tools work effectively no matter what the size of the company. But you can't just talk about quality—you've got to go do it.

If you're not identifying and satisfying customer requirements, you're not "doing" quality.

If you're not involving and empowering your employees, you're not "doing" quality.

If there's no benchmarking or fact-based management, you're not "doing" quality.

If problem solving and constant improvement are not top priorities, you're not "doing" quality.

QUIBBLES WITH QUALITY

What don't I like about quality? Nothing's perfect, and I have two major complaints. The quality gurus, particularly Deming, condemn the practice of doing personnel evaluations. I believe the objection is based on the assumption that the reviews create stress and hard feelings that interfere with the efficiency of the business operation.

I couldn't agree more, and that's why I've worked hard to implement a personnel evaluation format that is more tune-up than terrorism. I want my people to be able to see how well they are doing against objective standards—standards they have helped devise and agreed to in advance. Their strengths and weaknesses should stand out vividly: Bill is good at writing proposals, not so good at outlooking; Nancy excels in customer satisfaction, but needs to make more customer calls. Without evaluations, how else will Bill and Nancy know what needs to be improved?

Xerox couldn't operate without personnel evaluations, and I couldn't function as a manager. But our evaluations are a basis for coaching, counseling, and constant improvement. We're not trying to tear people down; the object is to build them up. The manager who doesn't do that is held accountable for his or her failure.

My second gripe about quality is that it calls for wider spans of control. What I mean is that the ratio of managers to workers, according to the theory, should be structured so that there are more workers and fewer managers. This makes sense if power is going to be decentralized and taken out of the hands of a top-heavy bureaucracy, but I don't believe a manager can coach and counsel effectively if his team is too large. I prefer a ratio of no more than one to ten; one manager to ten reps. One to seven or eight is even better. A leader must know his people and be in constant contact with them. Wide spans of control defeat the purpose. Why bother to have a manager at all if he or she rarely sees or talks to the troops? That manager is useless as a counselor, coach, and leader.

I'd be happy if Xerox shortened its spans of control so that my boss *was* breathing down my neck. I don't want her there to second-guess me; I want a role model, an adviser, a sounding board. I want somebody to say, "Frank, you're slipping. Let me help you improve."

For many years, Xerox sales districts were subjected to annual or semiannual inspections by regional management that amounted to little more than trips to the woodshed. The regional executive would sit down and go over the sales results and ream you out for your shortcomings. They could be ugly sessions, with lots of bad blood. Also, who needed to be told that things had gone poorly? We all read the same figures. Everybody knew it had been a crummy year or quarter. Now, thanks to quality, the process is far more productive. The review is a coaching and counseling session that aims at identifying the problem areas and eliminating them. An executive will say, "Show me the process you used and let's see what went wrong." Or, "What quality tools are you employing to correct the situation? Are you benchmarking the Miami district? They did a great job with this."

If you think you'd like to initiate a quality movement in your company, don't do it unless you and the other managers are willing to throw away the book on what constitutes good management and begin to coach and counsel. Nine-one managers, a term—don't ask me where it comes from—that we use at Xerox to describe the dogmatic, take-no-prisoner types, are incompatible with quality. Why? Because if they're not willing to listen to subordinates, they'll never listen to the customer.

NUMBERS, PLEASE

Although I want to end my appraisal of quality on a positive note, there are two more negatives. One, the quality jargon can be pretty silly. At first, I thought it was another one of those flavor-of-the-month programs that come and go. Don't let it distract you. The principles are solid. Two, I was initially put off by the heavy reliance on statistical measurement. I'm no math wizard. However, the harder I tried, the more sense it made. Now I use statistical tools constantly and find they are absolutely essential. You need to be a fanatic when it comes to gathering statistics and other forms of data (but don't just collect them—use them). It's the only way to reliably identify customer requirements. To all aspiring MBAs I would say: statistics—the more the better. And for MBA candidates who pride themselves on having good instincts, this piece of advice: good instincts and good statistics are even better.

TOGETHERNESS

In the next chapter I'm going to show you one of our customer surveys, and I think it may prove the value of what the statisticians call "quantitative measurement." But I want to finish this chapter by making sure you haven't missed a key linkage that makes quality work.

Picture an old-fashioned freight train. I'm too young to remember steam locomotives powered by coal, but I've seen pictures. First, there was the engine followed by a coal car, then a string of freight cars, then the caboose at the end. In some ways, the placement of the caboose symbolizes American business BQ (Before Quality). The employees are back at the end of the train, almost an afterthought. Quality, however, links the caboose directly to the locomotive. It replaces the coal car. The employees power the corporate engine.

What I'm getting at is this: customer satisfaction and employee satisfaction are on the same line. For a long time at Xerox, customer satisfaction always appeared at the top of any priority list, with employee satisfaction several bullets down. Finally, somebody realized you can't have one without the other.

I started this chapter by saying that my personal definition of quality was delighting the customer, and that its absence was the reason Xerox got into trouble in the seventies and eighties. You don't delight the customer without delighting your employees. Can't happen.

A lot of managers are going to find that hard to swallow. There's a tradition in this country of treating the help like . . . the help. We probably learned it from the British. The old cynical question, "If you're so smart, why are you working for me?" sums up the attitude.

I like quality because it works. And because it works, I can say Xerox delights me. Until you can say the same about your job, quality is an idea whose time hasn't come.

10

The Bonus

and the Bell Curve:

Surveying Customer

and Employee Satisfaction

Did you take the pledge in the last chapter? I'll give you one last chance. Raise your right hand and repeat after me: "I will set up a mechanism to identify customer requirements." Keep that hand up. "And I will also establish a mechanism to measure and monitor employee satisfaction." End of pledge.

I used a railroad metaphor on the previous page which reminded me that every train track has two rails. We all run our businesses along such a track. One rail is customer satisfaction and the other is employee satisfaction. If either of those rails is missing or seriously out of alignment, you're headed for a wreck.

To stay with the same imagery, a manager's job is to walk the tracks and function as a gandy dancer, the guy who used to move down the roadbed resetting loose spikes into the wooden ties and tapping the rails with his sledgehammer to keep them straight and true. Somebody's got to do the job—the manager as gandy dancer—and do it every day. Otherwise, these essential parallel lines will start to buckle and bow, wiggle and weave.

I've just about exhausted my knowledge of railroad lore, so I'll just take a guess that the gandy dancer used some sort of all-purpose gauge to make sure the tracks ran parallel. I hope. If not, it gives new meaning to the phrase "Here's looking at you."

In business, anyway, you can't just eyeball the two tracks. You do need a gauge. At Xerox we use surveys to measure customer and employee satisfaction. In fact, we bombard the customer with surveys to the point where some of them complain about it. Most, however, don't mind and see the surveys as confirmation that the company is totally committed to achieving 100 percent customer satisfaction. And that is the goal—100 percent. Settling for less—say 95 percent, which seems like a respectable goal—means that with a one-million-unit customer base, you've got 50,000 dissatisfied customers out there. Think what it would be like to have 1,000 people in every state bad-mouthing your products!

No thanks. Complete satisfaction—100 percent—is the only intelligent goal. A Xerox manager's compensation hinges on customer satisfaction. The statistical people run the numbers from the surveys to come up with a bell curve, like the one you probably experienced at exam time in college, and if my district's customer satisfaction results fall significantly below the curve, I can kiss my annual bonus good-bye. By the same token, if the district exceeds the curve, the bonus rises.

This reinforces my contention that without accountability and consequences, there's no chance of success. Conducting customer satisfaction surveys solely for the sake of collecting information is a waste of time and money. If customers think they're being given the runaround when they call in for service, if there's no accountability or consequences, I might just shrug and say, "That's too bad, but it's not my problem. It's the service department's problem." But if my bank account is going to be affected, it's definitely my problem.

At Xerox we have a district "partnership." There are three top managers—one for sales, one for service, and one for administration. Their fates are tied together. If one of them screws up, all of them suffer. As a result, the partners—if they're smart—work closely together. A customer who replies that he or she is "very dissatisfied" with administrative support or technical service drags down the overall satisfaction percentile even though the same person may have been "very satisfied" with my sales reps' product knowledge.

"Not my problem" is a phrase you'll never hear from Xerox partners.

SUIT THE CUSTOMER

One of the key principles of the quality movement is that customers are not just buying a *product*, they are buying an experience. I know, it sounds a little goofy: "Give me that size forty pinstripe experience with the side vents, please. No cuffs on the trousers." But I had an experience recently when I bought a suit that needed alterations. The salesman took careful measurements and told me to come back in three days. Standard drill. I picked up the suit and made the mistake of not trying it on. When I got home, it didn't fit. I called the shop to say I would bring it back. The salesman was so perturbed that he arranged instead to come to my home immediately to refit the suit. He took it away and delivered it back in a few hours.

Would I buy a suit from him again? You bet! He wanted my business. He sold me an experience. I got a suit, I got service, I was treated with respect. I could have driven back to the shop and waited a few more days. But the salesman provided "value." That's why I talked about total value in the last chapter. Sometimes the components that add up to total value are very intangible but have a substantial impact. If the instruction manual that accompanies a new copier is difficult to understand, that subtracts from total value. If the carton it comes in is shabby and torn, that subtracts from total value. If the offices and demo rooms that the customer visits to try out the new copier are unkempt and tacky, that subtracts from total value.

As an author, I'd like nothing better than to turn my readers into total-value zealots. To be a genuine Total Value Zealot, you've got to demand of yourself—for starters—and everyone around you, that whatever is done is done first class.

AN ATTENTION GRABBER

The customer satisfaction surveys measure total value. I make the results mandatory reading. They are posted, flashed up on the screen at presentations, and talked about at almost every meeting. Why? My paycheck depends on it. Let's not kid ourselves into thinking that customer satisfaction is some sort of Zen mantra. It sells more copiers, increases profits, and puts food on the table. That's why we emphasize it.

It's so important that I would like to see every employee's compensation directly tied to customer satisfaction, not just managers'. I rarely raise my voice in meetings, but this issue is one of my hot buttons, and a few years ago I tore into my team managers during one of our outlooking sessions. My administrative partner, Tom Bill, was making a carefully prepared presentation on a new formula we wanted to introduce to the district that would cascade responsibility for customer satisfaction downward to the managers. I wanted the team leaders to agree to base at least a small part of their bonuses on customer satisfaction. I sat there listening to the feedback Tom was getting and I heard a million reasons why the proposal was a bad idea.

Normally, I encourage dissent. Actually, I not only encourage it, I fan the flames of controversy to make sure important issues are totally explored. I want to hear everyone's opinion— good and bad. But what I picked up on this occasion was that it was just fine for the three Cleveland partners—Pacetta, Tom Bill, and Tom Haywood—to have their personal finances dependent on customer satisfaction, but a different story for the managers on the next rung down the ladder.

Finally, I stood up and walked to the front of the conference room. Tom is taller and outweighs me by more than a few pounds. I swept his slides off the overhead projector and onto the floor. "That's it," I said. "We're not going to talk about this anymore. We're doing it." Poor Tom was trying to get his slides back in order and go on with his reasonable, rational exposition. "I'm sick of hearing you guys whine," I declared. "It's done and we're not talking about it anymore."

I wasn't putting on a show. I was legitimately angry, but my outburst served a purpose. Every person in the room knew exactly how much importance I placed on customer satisfaction. It wasn't just a passing fad with me.

TAKING THE CURE

If a manager is merely paying lip service to customer satisfaction, he or she will live to regret it. I know, because I, in fact, lived to regret it. I've written a lot in this book about the need to establish a process, but in 1990 I belatedly woke up to the fact that I didn't have a process to deliver customer satisfaction in my own district. Not that it wasn't a priority. I spent major chunks of my time mending fences with customers and responding to complaints. But that was after the fact. I lacked a before-the-fact process.

The wake-up call came in the form of an 83 percent customer satisfaction rating for 1990. And 1991 was starting off even worse; the monthly figures were in the seventies.

What was wrong? Good question. Unfortunately, when it was asked, we didn't know the answer. What I'm about to tell you may seem obvious, but when you don't know what the problem is, you've got to find out. There's no other choice.

Actually, there is a choice and it's the one most people go with. Instead of curing the problem, they treat the symptoms of the problem. Customer dissatisfaction is not the problem, it's a symptom. For two or three years I attacked symptoms until I started listening to Tom Haywood, who was a zealot on the customer satisfaction issue. He took Tom Bill and me by the throats and kept shaking until we agreed that we had to drop everything else until we figured out what was going wrong.

That's customer satisfaction lesson number one: invest the time in identifying the problem. I've warned you about assumptions, and I'll warn you again: don't assume the problem can be explained away by blaming the shortcomings on a particular product or group of people. Beware of easy answers. The quick fix can be a killer. I know the last thing a busy manager needs is hours or days of research into the roots of an intractable problem. It's worth it, though, believe me.

The three of us jointly called on our top twenty-five accounts in a nonselling mode and asked them how we could do a better job for them. You know what happened? In all twenty-five accounts, our customer satisfaction index immediately jumped by several percentage points. Without setting out to do it, we had devised the semblance of a controlled experiment. While the partners were off listening to twenty-five accounts, it was business as usual for all the rest. Big improvements for the top twenty-five, zip for the rest.

Now I'm going to contradict myself—or seem to. You didn't have to be a rocket scientist to realize what was happening. There was a disconnect between the customer and our district operation. Easy answer, right? Schmooze the customer and everything will be okay.

Not so fast. Schmoozing wasn't going to do the job. We realized that a mechanism was needed for continued two-way communication. Selling wasn't our problem; we were selling just fine. But we were not plugging into our customers until they had something to complain about. We weren't hearing the minor rumbling until it developed into full-blown criticism. Better listening and customer contact was all well and good, but the district needed to react to the little glitches, the minor annoyances, the petty irritants before they escalated into major grievances.

Xerox collects every customer complaint, totals them up at the end of the month, and does a breakdown by district, team, service and sales rep, and machine. Nobody can hide from the numbers. The trouble was that when a complaint was logged it was too late. Sure, a rep might be able to fix things, but the goose egg still stood. The Cleveland partners' experience with the twenty-five top accounts persuaded us that the answer was to be more proactive about dealing with embryonic complaints to head them off at that stage.

We set up interdisciplinary teams to identify customer "dissatisfiers" and develop a strategy for dealing with them. I immediately told my sales team leaders to get out into the field and start talking to their accounts—all of them.

One manager, Cindy Fowler, developed her own customer satisfaction questionnaire and response form that her reps started using at the end of every call. No matter what they were there for, at the end of the call they religiously pulled out the form and worked through it. Cindy's team saw its customer satisfaction rating quickly move upward from the low seventies to the mid-nineties. The other teams immediately picked up on the idea.

Just as I did with sales figures, I opened each month's business meeting, attended by the whole staff, with the customer satisfaction standings. Whoever was number one that month got public recognition and a thank-you.

To lock in the priorities, I junked a sales contest that had been set up in the first quarter of 1991 after the district failed to meet its customer satisfaction target one month. In terms of sales, the reps were cooking. They had sold and installed enough equipment to meet the contest requirements. But instead of prizes they got nothing, and that grabbed everybody's attention.

And there's customer satisfaction lesson number two: consequences. If the hottest sales rep in the district doesn't make his customer satisfaction number, I'm not going to say, "Well, that's okay, you made up for it with the extra sales." Selling is only part of the job.

STAT. SAT.

Tom Bill increased his administrative manpower to collect and crunch the numbers. The extra statistical ammunition gave the special customer satisfaction teams the data they needed to analyze and strategize. Service discovered to its amazement that the one machine everyone thought was our strongest product was in reality the weakest.

New lesson: The more data, the better the fine tuning.

SWATING THE REPEAT OFFENDERS

The ghost of 5046 was still with us in 1991, but service was doing a good job of doctoring the machine with a special software program. The cancellation rate practically disappeared after Tom Haywood's field service managers started using a customer satisfaction process that had been built around a deceptively simple concept—find the customers' technical problems before they do, and fix them.

Service also instituted an "escalating call system" that eliminated a major customer gripe. Instead of just sending out a technician to fix a repeat problem two, three, four times—driving the customer nuts—the second call is automatically escalated so that a specialist goes out. If that doesn't work, the third call brings out a service SWAT team. At each level there's a heavier commitment of manpower, expertise, and resources. At any point, the people on the scene have the power to make a decision about the best way to resolve the problem, including pulling the machine and replacing it.

In all three arms of the partnership, people were empowered to take action on the spot to satisfy a customer. There was no time wasted while decisions were bucked from level to level.

And that's the next lesson: customer satisfaction starts with you. It isn't a game of hot potato. Several years ago, when David Kearns was still CEO, he decided that top management would take turns answering the customer hotline in Rochester. Nobody was exempt, not even Kearns. He and the other executives got a gigantic dose of reality, and, what was even better, each person was required to do something to personally solve the customer's problem. The buck—trivial or tremendous—stopped there. Kearns said it was bad enough to field all the incoming complaints but even worse to experience how frustrating it could be to get his own corporation to resolve a legitimate grievance.

That brings us to the final customer satisfaction lesson: You live and die by follow-up and follow-through. Many companies are pretty good at figuring out what they should be doing—they just don't do it. Inertia is a tremendous obstacle. Important matters fall through the cracks. What we do to combat inertia is to use our computer system to track decisions that have not been made. Anything that is supposed to happen, but doesn't, is identified and pushed through the management chain. As it "ripens," this orphaned piece of business gets higher and higher priority. It could be something basic like a call to a customer to see if he or she is pleased with a new machine. If the rep doesn't make the call, it goes to the next level. If the team manager doesn't respond, it keeps moving upward until it reaches me or one of the other partners. Do I call the rep and chew him out? No, I pick up the phone and call the customer to check on the new machine. Then I talk to the rep's manager about improving his or her follow-up and follow-through process.

PEST CONTROL

Our system uses the partners as the ultimate backstop. If no action has been taken on a lower level, then we handle it. Ideally, nothing "ripens" to that extent, but if it does we go back to see if our empowerment mandates need to be tweaked so that decisions are made at earlier stages.

It's a good system, and I recommend that you work with your computer people to come up with something similar. Want to make a bundle of money on software? Here's a free idea. Design a must-do list that automatically blinks each item that hasn't been acted on after an hour. The rate of blinking increases every hour thereafter. If the workday passes without action, the item moves to the must-do list of the next person in the management chain, where, tagged according to its source of origin, it appears in a different color and starts to blink after an hour of inaction. And so on, all the way to the CEO's computer screen. To stay honest, must-do's would have to be conscientiously put in and inspected. The list could appear in a small box in the corner of the screen once every hour as a reminder, or whenever applications begin or end.

I'd buy the software. High-tech, low-tech, anything to enhance follow-up. As it is, I'm the master of low-tech follow-up. I use my trips to the men's room for that purpose. If you listened in as I move through my office, passing the reps' cubicles, you'd hear "What about . . . ?" "Have you . . . ?" "Any word on . . . ?" George Urban, whom I credited in Chapter 4 for persuading me to take the district on an early "road trip," was once asked what really bugged him about my management style. George said I drove him crazy by asking again and again about pending business. He'd go into the men's room, the door would open, and there'd I'd be beside him at the urinal asking, "What's the status of . . . ?" George admitted that in sheer self-defense he'd wrap up whatever issue was still outstanding to shut me up.

I concede I'm a pest when it comes to follow-up. I think a good leader and manager has to be. Procrastination is part of human nature. People put things off until tomorrow and tomorrow and tomorrow. Some executives manage by procrastination: put it off long enough and the issue will die a natural death.

I'm just the opposite. I want the issue resolved today; or, if not resolved, then given a major push toward resolution. When I leave the office at night, my desk is literally and figuratively clean. That's how I enjoy my family in the evenings and sleep soundly at night. There's nothing hanging over me waiting to explode. Try it for the next thirty days. If the decision cycle normally takes three days or a week, cut it in half. Go back at the end of the month and review the results. Were the decisions too hasty or did you increase your productivity? I think you'll find it far more productive.

THE GOLD STANDARD

A leader has to provide role models for the behavior he or she wants to see in action. The reason our customer satisfaction figures were poor was that the three partners were poor role models on the issue. When we got our acts together, the district did too.

One of the more gratifying aspects of the improvement program was to see how the employees reacted. It's easy to relate to customer satisfaction. We are all customers. We've all been frustrated by poor products, service, and support. All a good leader has to do is some basic show-and-tell. Tell the employees a customer with a problem blows out all other priorities. Everything else takes a back seat. Then *show* them, by treating that disgruntled customer—I'm talking about you, Mr. Manager—as the most important person in the district at that time. Once that happens, the customer satisfaction obsession will spread like wildfire. It really is the golden rule: do unto others as you would have them do unto you.

CUSTOMER SATISFACTION DIVIDENDS

The devotees of the quality movement preach that in a highly competitive environment, businesses do not have time to make mistakes. You have to do it right the first time. When you have to stop to fix something, that adds a hidden cost that comes right off the bottom line. I suggest that you turn your computer whizzes and accountants loose to figure out exactly how much. The figure will be hefty, and it may motivate you to get busy.

I've said it before—what you don't know will hurt you.

I don't believe it was a coincidence that 1991 was the best of five years financially in Cleveland (I'll give you those figures later). By driving hard on customer satisfaction, we got extra momentum that went directly into the sales effort. For starters, we weren't wasting time and effort fixing problems. Then, the relationship that we had with our customers was totally transformed. It wasn't adversarial anymore. Have you tried to sell lately to an adversary? Not much fun.

By the end of 1991, our half-year customer satisfaction index stood at 101 percent. It was the largest increase of any district in the country. Xerox sent a crew in to do a training film based on our example. It was titled *North by Northeast,* playing off the Alfred Hitchcock classic and our designation as the Northeast Ohio district. The format was a spoof on the hard-boiled detective genre. The narrator was a young female gum-shoe, Bess Practice. She interviewed many of us, trying to ferret out our "secrets" for a mysterious client. In the end, Bess concluded there were no secrets—just constant hard work and a dedication to continuous improvement. The mysterious client turned out to be a Xerox district manager who was having trouble with customer satisfaction, and thanks to Bess Practice he was clued in to Cleveland's best practice.

A FIRE STARTER

What about the other rail—employee satisfaction? Starting in 1993, the manager–gandy dancer at Xerox was given a good reason for picking up the old sledgehammer and going to work. Our bonuses now rise and fall according to how well we satisfy our own employees.

Until '93, there wasn't any money riding on it directly, but a manager's poor showing in the extensive surveys that were conducted each quarter with his people would have an impact on job performance ratings and promotion possibilities.

Think about it. What manager in his or her right mind gives subordinates that kind of power? A smart manager, that's who.

A leader without followers isn't a leader; he or she is a tyrant, a crank, and a menace. I don't buy the idea that good managers are, in fact, good managers even if they are held in disregard, contempt, or ridicule by their people. In that case, top management has decided to turn a blind eye toward the executive's serious deficiencies as a leader. Whether they choose to recognize it or not, those shortcomings are undermining morale, productivity, performance, and profitability. If you don't believe that after having gotten this far into the book, I recommend you use its pages to light the charcoal for next weekend's barbecue.

I'm not saying that managers have to be loved or win popularity contests. Employee satisfaction must rest squarely on professional respect.

I'm going to show you how we measure it at Xerox. Here are the figures from a survey that was conducted with the eight team leaders who reported to me in May of 1991, just short of three and a half years into my tenure in Cleveland. These are the people who bear the brunt of my pestering on the way to the men's room.

Effective Management Survey

	Percentage Favorable
• My manager keeps me well informed about what's going on in the business.	100
• I have confidence in my manager's decisions.	100
• I can depend on my manager to honor the commitments he/she makes.	100
• My manager shows his/her personal appreciation for my contribution.	100
• My manager explains the reasons for business decisions that affect my work.	100
• My manager gives me honest feedback on my performance.	100
• My manager treats Leadership Through Quality as the basic Xerox business principle.	100

- My manager treats people with dignity and
  respect.   100
- My manager is straightforward and honest
  with me.   100
- When I ask, my manager helps me with ca-
  reer planning.   100
- My manager is committed to resolving the
  concerns identified in this survey.   100
- My manager delegates the right amount of
  responsibility to me.   100
- My manager does not show favoritism.   100

The above is an example of just one of several specifically targeted surveys. While I'm proud of the 100 percent ratings, I'm not showing them to you to brag. I got dinged in some categories. My lowest overall score in that cycle was on a survey measuring satisfaction with pay and benefits. It averaged a total of 90 percent. On the question "I understand the company's pay philosophy," I pulled a 63 percent, which told me that I needed to do a much better job of understanding it myself and communicating the knowledge to the managers.

I have selected some more questions at random from other surveys to give you a better feel for them. Here goes:

Organizational Process
- The communication process in my organization is effective.
- In my work group there is an atmosphere of openness and trust.
- I feel free to speak up when I disagree with a decision.

Customer Satisfaction
- My manager will not compromise his/her commitment to customer satisfaction in order to achieve short-term business results.
- I do not sacrifice customer satisfaction in order to achieve other targets.
- My manager rewards people who satisfy customer requirements.

Use of Quality Tools
- My manager acts as a positive role model for Leadership Through Quality.

Sales Compensation
- Incentive promotions motivate me to act in my best interest.

In reviewing the figures, I just noticed that my lowest mark in the job satisfaction survey was on the statement "Based on my performance, I am paid fairly for what I do." I drew 50 percent. Considering how hard my managers were working that year, I was not surprised. I probably gave my own boss a similar rating when I filled out his survey. Pay is a sensitive subject, and it's one reason I told the reps and managers in Cleveland when I arrived that I was determined they would make more money than they had in the past.

And you thought it was all about winning? It is. In terms of employee satisfaction, it's all about money, too. One of the reasons I spend so much time fine-tuning the sales territories, developing fair sales plans, and training my management staff is that the effort directly impacts the reps' paychecks in the form of the bonuses they receive each year. If they don't make money, Xerox doesn't make money.

I guess that mediocre 50 percent rating motivated me a little. By the end of 1991, many of my people were looking at bonuses that put them among the highest-paid Xerox reps and managers in the country.

11

The Night Before

Christmas:

Even Santa Has to Ask

for the Sale

Now I've done it. We've taken a gigantic three-year leap from 1988 to the end of 1991. So much for chronological story-telling. But I'd need to write five books—one for each year—to take you through the high points and the low points in the precise order they occurred.

I'll backtrack a bit, though. Cleveland ended 1988 number one in the region and fourth nationally. We exceeded our profit plan by 18.9 percent. Cleveland was back for real! Needless to say, I got out the black ski cap and we headed off to "Peak 'n Peak" to celebrate. The outing was memorable for my rendition —so I'm told—of "American Pie" late one evening (early one morning?) to a roomful of mellow managers, reps, their spouses and significant others. The party was all the sweeter because we had had a bad scare at the end of the third quarter. Our September had suddenly gone down the drain. Several major deals fell through and we missed the plan; I was convinced the whole year was finished.

I tend to be emotional. Okay, time out while you laugh and say, "No, Frank. You're emotional? Could have fooled me."

Well, I am. Most everyone had left the office when the September figures came in and I was—and I'm not exaggerating—devastated. I went back to my private office, sat on the couch without bothering to turn the lights on, and told myself that I was nothing but a flash in the pan, and everybody was going to know it. As it happened, Fred Thomas was still around. He looked down the length of the murky corridor and saw me sitting there in the twilight. For a moment, he later told me, Fred considered trying to cheer me up but decided against it.

"You looked just terrible," Fred said. "Like somebody had died."

I get so wrapped up in the game that I just can't step back from it and shrug off the disappointments. I went home that night and told Julie I wasn't as good a leader as I thought I was. I said that everything was falling apart. That night I couldn't sleep fast enough. I wanted the morning to come quickly so that I could get back to the office and fix things.

As emotional as I am, I rebound fast. I don't agonize for long. It's a trait I learned from my mother. She took care of my brother Joey and our elderly grandmother year in and year out and never wavered. My sister and I never saw a flicker of doubt or despair or anguish. She got up each morning and gave it 100 percent.

That's what still gets me out of bed. I recognize how lucky I am to be healthy, to have had the education I did, and received the breaks that came my way in the early days at Xerox, when I was young and green and stupid. I have an obligation to get out of bed early and enthusiastically; a debt. I pay it off every day with, I hope, interest. Maybe I can help somebody else get lucky.

And so I scared the hell out of my managers at our next meeting. I told them that they—we—had blown the whole year by screwing up September. Everything they had worked for since January was going up in smoke.

October, November, and December were very good months.

AFFLICTING THE COMFORTABLE

Then what? For me, that question is the worm in the apple. Success does spoil winning teams. In many ways, it's easier to get to the top than to stay there. When you're losing and desperate, working hard is about the only alternative. A moderately talented leader can build a team under those circumstances simply by standing up and saying, "Follow me." Once the immediate danger is past and the good times roll, however, the same person will stand up again and say, "Follow me," and the answer will be: "Why should I? Things are comfortable right here."

It's one explanation for the rapid ups and downs of many companies, and the reason why executives who specialize in quick corporate turnarounds make sure they move on to a new assignment before the effects of their miracle cures wear off.

If you stop and consider the principal tactics used to rescue ailing companies—fear and money—boom-and-bust cycles are almost unavoidable. If you tell me I'll have to bust a gut to save my job—pass the Maalox. But once I perceive my job is safe, if that's the only motivator, I'll start coasting again. The result is C-C-C: crisis, comeback, crisis.

Money works the same way. I can throw money at a problem and use it to squeeze out extra effort. Eventually, though, the money loses its appeal. Overtime pay is the best example. Initially workers are eager for the extra cash, but after a while they start to grumble that the money isn't worth the time they spend away from their families and TV sets.

I can hear you say, "Frank, you told us in the last chapter it was all about money."

I did, and it is.

"And you said it was all about winning."

Right again. The successful leader can't forget that we go to work to earn a living. George Bernard Shaw said, "Lack of money is the root of all evil." Shaw had it right. But the Bible tells us that "without vision the people perish." The same leader must constantly change the definition of what constitutes winning. You've got to keep moving the goalposts. Yesterday's vision—Cleveland as number one in the region—was old news as of January 1, 1989. The challenge was, and is, to keep the vision fresh and alive in order to create a permanent culture of success.

FLAG WAVING

By turning Cleveland around in 1988, I was under pressure to demonstrate it was not a fluke. The life that fate determined for one brother in Far Rockaway, and not for the other—that's a fluke. My business process isn't. It's simple, tight, and repeatable.

I was determined to do it again in 1989, only better. And that is what happened. Our numbers continued to grow: sold revenue was up by 20 percent over 1988 to just under $30 million; * total revenue gained 24.9 percent; in 1990, we brought home another 23.5 percent upward bounce in sold revenue and 14.3 percent in total revenue.

The turbocharger switched on in 1991. We opened the year with a kickoff at Kent State University. We rented one of the main halls in the university's conference center. Paul MacKinnon got hold of dramatic World II battle footage from old newsreels and other films of that vintage. The conference room featured a huge video display screen and a terrific sound system. The two of us spent hours picking out the right dramatic music to go with the clips of fierce naval engagements in the Pacific.

Paul found a huge shot of an American flag that we projected onto the screen as in the opening scene of *Patton*. We enlisted Tom Bill, our business partner, to dress the part of General Patton with khakis and an old helmet. But I gave the speech. I'm going to go easy with this, since, as I put it down on paper, I can see that you had to be there. Some people will read these paragraphs and say, "Give me a break."

The reaction on the scene, however, was all that we had hoped, and more. We cranked up the big speakers and blasted "Born in the U.S.A." as I entered down the main aisle wearing a leather aviator's jacket and holding a riding crop (Hey, play the part, loosen up, have some fun!).

I'm tempted to pull back here and give you a sociological explanation of the reasons stuff like this works: e.g., a steady diet of TV has awakened an appetite for larger-than-life experiences

---

* Sold revenue measures the dollars taken in by way of actual sales in the fiscal year rather than total revenue from sales, existing leases, supplies, and other services, that is, new sales vs. continuing income.

. . . etc. Forget it. Don't take yourself so seriously that you can't give them something to laugh about and to cheer about.

I gave the district a vision for 1991 as I stood in front of that screen with the flag and the big guns flashing, pilots revving their engines for takeoff, and flaming fighter planes spiraling into the sea.

Fighter planes? I'll stop being diplomatic: Japanese Zeros. I think you can guess what my message was. We were not just going to win against other Xerox districts, we were going to beat the Japanese competition.

A roar went up when I issued the challenge. I turned to look over my shoulder, at the screen, where, with perfect timing (and dumb luck on my part), a kamikaze was torn apart by cannon fire and fell out of the sky.

Now that I've offended the Japanese and wrecked any chance of selling the publishing rights to this book in Japan, turn down the soundtrack for a minute and consider the reality of those images. There was one clip that Paul and I took from the film *Tora, Tora, Tora,* showing masses of modern-day samurai warriors ready to strike. For a roomful of Xerox people that was red meat. In the 1970s and 1980s, we had been deliberately targeted by the Japanese for extinction. And they almost pulled it off.

Television and VCRs were invented in the United States. We don't make them here anymore.

Copiers were invented in the United States, and we *do* make them here. But if Xerox hadn't started fighting back in 1982, the copier would be just another huge debit in the balance-of-trade deficit.

Pure John Wayne. The combat footage that showed the cross hairs of an American Hellcat fighter lining up on an emblem of the Rising Sun was our vision in 1989. "Born in the U.S.A." was our theme song.

EVERY DAY IS SUNDAY

While I was writing this book, Dave Myerscough, the president of Xerox U.S. Customer Operations—the BOSS, visited my district. At the end of the day he spoke to the troops. (Here's a tip:

Never let the brass come and go without exposing them to a question-and-answer session with your people. It's good for the boss, good for them.) Dave is a fine communicator. He picked up on my theme of being number one, but cautioned the group not to become fixated on internal competition and forget about going after the external competition.

It was an excellent point. In many ways it's easier to evaluate yourself against your brothers and sisters than it is against the guy from the next neighborhood who is the real threat to the family's well-being. You may be the biggest kid in the house but a midget outside in the real world. At our next staff meeting, however, I told the managers that while I respected Dave's views and understood where he was coming from, I didn't want any confusion—we were still going to shoot for being the number one district.

I think you must do both. External *and* internal competition are essential. Internal competition gets you sharp and keeps you sharp. It's the equivalent of daily practice drills on the football field; run the plays, block and tackle. The object is to prepare the team for Sunday afternoon.

The great thing is that in business our Sundays happen Monday through Friday. We can compete against each other internally and beat the brains out of the competition at the same time. I share Dave Myerscough's concern—and he was reflecting the position of Xerox's top management—that an overemphasis on internal competition can lull a company into thinking that its people and policies are the best in the business, when, in fact, they're not being realistically tested. However, the fallacy of going too far in the other direction is that the external competition ends up setting the rules of engagement; you become reactive rather than proactive.

I also believe in being so much better than the competition that there is never a danger of sinking to their level of mediocrity. We've all seen sports teams that play in a league or division against such weak competition that they never really achieve greatness; they don't have to. There's no challenge, and they just go through the motions season after season. Those are the teams that rot from within and suddenly collapse.

My sales teams should be able to beat Kodak and Toshiba in their sleep. But I want them wide awake. It's the only way to achieve double-digit revenue growth. Don't just beat the competition; crush it. Over the course of five years in Cleveland, we all but drove Kodak out of the market. Today, they hardly show up on the radarscope. I couldn't have done that if I hadn't pumped up the district by concentrating on intense internal competition. Where else was the stimulus going to come from? Kodak certainly didn't provide it.

NEW BUSINESS

After I had spent three years team building, my 1991 Kent State kickoff was designed to unleash the sales power that had been created and send it lunging at the Japanese competition. I wanted what we call in the copier industry "net turnovers." All too often, when we sell a new product, we are replacing a previous generation of our own equipment. The goal is to supplant the other guy's machine while at the same time upgrading your existing customers. That, in a nutshell, is how to increase market share.

The problem is that there is no "organic" incentive to knock out a Canon, Ricoh, or any other competitive product. A sale is a sale. For a lazy sales organization, it's easier to churn your own equipment than to achieve turnovers because of the existing relationship with the customer. A rep doesn't have to start from scratch. If he or she is conscientiously working the account, the rep knows what hardware can be profitably and legitimately upgraded based on the age of the equipment or the customer's changing requirements. The sale is booked—a one-for-one swap —without the need to go out and beat the bushes for new business.

I used to do that all the time as a young rep. New business, old business—what difference did it make to me? It makes a lot of difference to the health of the company. Grow or die.

As far as I'm concerned, new business is synonymous with growth. When my people turn in their thirty-, sixty-, and ninety-day plans, I want to see new names. Conceivably, a rep could close the loop and work the existing accounts to generate enough business to keep him or her comfortable. But I won't let that happen.

"Where's the new business?" I ask.

"I'm just swamped. There's so much going down this month I haven't been able to do any prospecting."

"Oh, what are you going to do next month?"

"Things are looking pretty good sixty days out."

"And then you're done. The cupboard will be bare. Don't you think it would be smart to take an hour today—I know you're busy—make some calls, and get one new name, that's all. Do it again tomorrow and you've got two new names."

Common sense dictates that an unending stream of new names, and hopefully new business, should be pumped through a sales organization. But the live-for-today mentality often prevails. Today is marvelous; business is booming. Like clockwork, in two or three months there's a dry spell. How did that happen? You let it happen.

Here's some advice: When things are going great today, it's time to panic about tomorrow. I told you not to assume anything, but it's never wrong to assume that the grasshoppers outnumber the ants. What I mean is that Aesop's fable about the industrious ant and the happy-go-lucky grasshopper is an accurate representation of what goes on in most sales operations. After the harvest and when winter comes, the grasshoppers perish because they didn't stock up like the ants.

If things are booming, I always get nervous and start increasing the effort to insure that new business will be there in the future. Don't slough off on this chore. Get the ants stirred up. If the average number of new names for each rep every month is five, ask for seven or eight. That's not a horrible burden. And inspect to make sure they're not just pulling names out of the phone book—it happens! Ask a few questions to see if there's depth of knowledge. Another way to defeat the grasshopper mentality is to run sales contests with rewards for those who bring in the most new business.

PUSH AND PULL

They used to make fun of me in Cleveland because every time I saw a rep I would ask the same three questions:

1. "Any orders today?"
2. If there was an order, "Was it forecast?"
3. And, of course, "Any new names?"

The second question is the one I like most of all. My people know I always congratulate them for an order, but if they want me to really light up, they need to tell me it wasn't on the outlook. Then it's special. Accurate forecasting is extremely important, but beating your own outlook—unless the projections are overly cautious—indicates that the process is operating at peak efficiency.

As for the "new names" question, I want to come back to the subject for one last pass. I'm out to make converts on this one. I believe in keeping the bucket full of prospects at all times. The only way to do it is to systematically gather new names that can be culled and filtered until viable prospects emerge. Out of a dozen new names, there may only be one real prospect. And this touches on a point I really want to emphasize: a new name is not automatically a prospect. There must be—at minimum—contact to determine the customer's requirements and how you can meet them with your product. Furthermore, there are prospects and closable prospects. There's a big difference. Once customer requirements are ascertained, the product must be demonstrated, the key decision maker brought into the transaction, and a final proposal and implementation plan submitted; then, and only then, is the prospect closable.

As the rep goes through the requisite steps, the transaction will start moving through the sales cycle. The faster the steps are performed, the faster you get to a close. By using a thirty-, sixty-, ninety-day plan, which I've mentioned before and strongly recommend, you can track the evolution of each deal and get a good feel for where the operation will stand three months or more down the road. But the whole thing starts with new names. It's like planting a seed. If there's no seed, there's no corn.

By inspecting a rep's thirty-, sixty-, ninety-day files—and we do it every month—we can see exactly what's happening and what isn't. In addition, we inspect the rep's activities each week to see if there's adequate follow-through. We're deadly serious about this process, and for good reason. If he or she isn't making enough calls or delivering proposals or holding demos, the sales projected for any given slice of the cycle just aren't going to happen.

I see the process as a mathematical equation. I preach it, teach it, and screech it to make sure my people never lose focus:

New Names + Activities = Closable Prospects + Activities = **SALES**

The thirty-, sixty-, ninety-day plan is also a good fail-safe mechanism. If I lose a deal unexpectedly this month, I can try to recover by turning to something that's still in the sixty-day mode and bringing it to a rapid boil. Maybe the rep needs to meet the key decision maker or hold another demonstration. Put the pedal to the metal, and do it now, rather than miss the thirty-day target.

Even if everything is on track, don't be afraid to mess with the plan. You might want to write this down: Always seek to pull business forward. If it's next year's business, see if you can pull it forward to this year. If it's ninety days out, how do we pull it forward into the sixty-day zone? If it's on tap for next month, let's get it this month. Make your organization run faster and faster. There's no such thing as a speed limit.

I can hear the question coming: Won't that have an adverse impact on old business?

Yes, it will—if you allow it to. Organizations that push for new business without closely monitoring customer satisfaction —among old and new customers—run the risk of having their customer base crumble without warning. All customers are created equal. If a healthy flow of new business is threatening to swamp your ability to service and support existing customers, don't, don't, don't ever get suckered into making a choice between the new and the old. Instead, make the case to your senior management that the new business argues for additional personnel and resources to better handle both the old and the new.

What if they won't listen?

Speak louder and more effectively.

If that doesn't work?
Show them the customer complaints.
And if it still doesn't work?
Get a new job.

SAY WHAT, SAY WHO, SAY HOW

My theatrical kickoff in 1991 could have been stripped of its editorial content and presented solely in terms of obtaining new business. Every rep and manager in the hall knew that was the bottom line. Perforce, going after the Japanese competition meant bringing in new business; bringing in new business meant going after the Japanese competition.

I could have soft-pedaled the Japanese angle and stayed generic. But I don't believe we must be so "businesslike" that we can't give our competition a real name and a nationality. Don't be cowed into treating the Japanese with kid gloves. That doesn't mean we should bash them. Beat them fair and square. We can't do that, though, if we buy into the notion that it's xenophobic or racist to remind our people that Japanese companies are deadly serious business adversaries. They give no quarter and take no prisoners. Every time they win, we lose. That's not xenophobia, that's capitalism. If we're too timid to tell our people who's who and what's what, that it's time to compete and to fight for profits, jobs, and the welfare of our families, then we deserve to lose, and we will.

THE ART OF THE AMBUSH

Did the Kent State kickoff work? Something worked. While our 1991 figures weren't as flashy, we managed a 10.7 percent sold revenue gain and pushed ahead with an 8.6 percent increase in total revenue despite a recession that was hammering the U.S. economy throughout the year. We were on a roll and perfectly positioned to withstand the body blows the recession was dealing out to American business.

I'm convinced that we kept our edge by staying on the offensive rather than retrenching. Ron Onorato's "sneak attack" against Toshiba vividly demonstrated the advantage of going for new business and net turnovers at the expense of the Japanese. I put quotation marks around sneak attack because that's how it was described by *The Wall Street Journal*. Here's what happened:

Our printing systems people were wooing Packard Electric, a unit of General Motors based in Youngstown, Ohio.* The Packard executives who had to sign off on the deal were invited to our offices to see a demonstration of the equipment. And . . .

I'm going to interrupt my own story, even though it's only just begun, to do an advertisement for teamwork and communication. If the individual teams had been allowed to just do their own things, a demonstration arranged by the printing systems team would never have come to the attention of anyone else. But our monthly outlook meetings alert everyone—including the team managers—to our business activities across the board. Communication breaks down when pockets of information are allowed to exist in isolation. You've got to wire up your entire team to avoid the If-I-had-only-known syndrome. That doesn't mean burying people in paper. It's all done verbally during my outlook meetings and only takes a few minutes a month. End of advertisement.

Back to our story. The outlook meeting alerted Rob Onorato, whose team sold copiers, to the fact that Packard executives—flesh and blood, living and breathing Packard executives, not disembodied voices on the phone—were going to be on the premises in a few weeks. Rob knew that a demonstration is an important event in any sales cycle. It shows a meaningful level of interest when a customer is willing to leave home and travel across town to get a look at your product. It can take weeks or months of work to get the customer to that point.

Net turnarounds, I should point out, are labor-intensive. They usually happen one or two at a time. Rob's reps were working with Packard, but it was slow going. We knew Toshiba had eighty-two machines in there. A little legwork had turned up reports that the operators weren't entirely satisfied with the performance and service they were getting from Toshiba. An open, all-out campaign to knock out those machines would have sent

* Printing systems use laser and computer technology integrated with the customer's own computer hardware and software as opposed to stand-alone copiers.

Toshiba into overdrive. The possibility of losing all those machines in one fell swoop, at a price of around $7,000 a unit, would not have been taken lightly. The Japanese secret weapon in a situation like that, at least for those companies we compete against, is price. If there's an all-out price war, and there surely would have been one over Packard, Xerox usually loses. Our U.S. production people have turned dazzling somersaults to cut costs, but Xerox's manufacturing costs were at the time higher than those of the Japanese. Rob didn't have to be told that he would need to forestall a price war to make inroads at Packard.

Hence the sneak attack. When the Packard executives showed up for the demonstration, Rob was waiting for them. After the printing people put on their show—and our printing systems can knock customers' socks off—Rob was introduced. He asked what it would take in terms of price and other requirements to get Packard's copier business that day. He wasn't going merely for a foot in the door—can we start talking about this?— he was out to rip down the door and the wall by stipulating that we wanted to do business *that day*.

As a sales tactic, it was brilliant: the close was built in. If the customer came back at us, all we had to do was meet Packard's terms and it was a done deal.

They could have said, "We'll have to think about it," but they didn't. The executives laid it all out for us, although they did not reveal the exact terms of Toshiba's bid (which would have been unethical on their part). We had roughly six hours to make it work. Rob, my two partners, and I frantically crunched the numbers and worked the phones to Rochester. We had done our homework by finding out the financial parameters of other recent Toshiba deals around town. That gave us a ballpark figure to work with. Initially we ran into the classic corporate stonewall: "The margin is too small . . . no way." But I had a good friend running interference for us and I told him not even to bother responding if headquarters couldn't make their figures roughly correspond to ours.

Many times, selling the customer is only part of the job. You've got to sell your own bosses. More deals go south because salespeople are afraid to sell internally. It's never easy, and it surely wasn't in this case. What turned the tide was my contention that while we were looking at small profits today, Packard was a prime candidate for additional business in the near future.

We finally got the okay and the deal went through. Our victory was significant in that we were able to compete against Toshiba and still make money. Based on the feedback we received from the customer, our emphasis on total value rather than price was the key. It made Packard feel comfortable with Xerox. Total value, we realized, isn't just a handy slogan—it's a potent weapon.

WHITE KNUCKLE CHRISTMAS

In terms of our best years, 1989, 1990, and 1991 were the high-water marks. Total revenue went from around $57 million in 1988 to almost $90 million in 1991.

Even so, Christmas 1991 was a manic-depressive affair—or, I should say, a depressive-manic affair. As usual, we had fun celebrating the holiday. Paul MacKinnon did his Santa Claus number complete with whiskers and red suit. Paul found a videotape of a blazing fire, and we projected it onto the screen in the amphitheater where we gathered to sing Christmas carols and unwrap presents. Everyone who was at 100 percent of the special December order standard was on the gift list, and those who were ahead of the curve were stack-ranked according to percentage and allowed to pick a gift corresponding to their place in the ranking.

We also did our annual turkey shoot, but I had learned my lesson from a previous fiasco. Last time, many of the reps and managers who had won turkeys didn't pick them up on Friday evening. The office had been closed over the weekend, and when we got in on Monday the place stank like a poultry slaughterhouse. From then on, I made sure the turkeys went into the refrigerator of the restaurant on the ground floor of the building.

Despite the festivities, there was tension. The year's success was literally riding on one deal that hadn't happened yet. We were rapidly running out of time. The hang-up was that a large insurance company was on the verge of accepting our bid for a major printing system package with a price tag of well over a million dollars, but final approval kept eluding us. Two divisions within the company were involved with the decision; one was ready to go, the other wasn't. When Christmas week rolled around, we were told key executives were going on vacation; consummation would have to wait until after the first of the year.

Bah, humbug! To the customer, the delay was a trivial matter. To us, our yearly profit plan was about to go out the window. The day before Christmas, a Tuesday, Paul MacKinnon and I were sitting in my office mulling over the bleak situation. There was still a chance of salvation if we could shoehorn the deal into the few business days between Christmas and New Year's. We had been told the key decision maker would be back in the office the following Monday.

I suggested we call and set up an appointment, even though there would only be two days left to iron out all the wrinkles. Paul picked up the phone and dialed the guy's office, expecting to deal with a secretary. Instead, the executive personally answered. Paul nearly fell out of his chair. We had heard he was on vacation and were calling to arrange a meeting with him on Monday, Paul explained, to see if we could complete the deal before the end of the year. No way, the man replied. He was officially beginning his vacation on Monday—our information about his schedule was backward—and, in fact, he was going to take Thursday and Friday off as well.

I frantically scribbled a note to Paul. I held it up where he could see it. "How about right now?" Paul asked the executive.

"It'll have to be quick" was the response.

"We'll be there in twenty minutes," Paul promised.

We made it with a few minutes to spare but didn't have time to track down the rep who was handling the account before leaving the office. Fortunately, he was on the phone by the time we got to the customer's office to bring us up to date on the negotiations.

It turned out to be a friendly and productive meeting. I reviewed the terms of the deal, summarized the benefits, noted that Xerox had worked hard to meet his company's requirements, and finished by saying that I believed we had earned the right to the business. The executive said he agreed and would sign off on the deal as soon as he got back from vacation.

· Grabbing the guy by the lapels and shouting "No, now!" wouldn't have been helpful, so I explained the problem and suggested that the unusually flexible pricing concessions that had been granted did not have a long shelf life. The customer countered that he needed to run the numbers past a few more people. He graciously offered to change his plans and do that the day after Christmas.

Now, to avoid creating the impression that I was taking advantage of the customer's kindness, let me explain my next move. As I've said before, I always assume the worst. I knew that Murphy, as in Murphy's Law, would be the Grinch who stole Christmas if I wasn't careful. If one of the executive's colleagues pulled a disappearing act on Thursday and Friday, we would be finished. Therefore, I told the customer that the suspense would absolutely ruin my Christmas. "How about getting everybody on board today?" I asked. He said he would try.

" 'Twas the night before Christmas and all through the house not a creature was stirring . . ." and the phone rang at 9:15. We had a deal and a very Merry Christmas. December set a record for Cleveland with close to $9 million in sales in one month.

12

FINE-TUNING:

HIRING, FIRING, AND FINESSING

I told you about the occasional quizzes I spring on my reps. Now, I'm going to do it to my readers. Just a quickie.

Based on your understanding of this book so far, what is the most important word a manager and leader should always keep in mind that begins with the letter "P"?

Jot down your answer on a scrap of paper. If you said "process," and if you're in the office, stand up and stick your head out the door. Look to the left and look to the right. You'll see the correct answer to the quiz. It's not process. The answer is people.

There's no substitute. Sports is living proof. A coach can be the greatest motivator, organizer, strategist, and taskmaster, but he or she is ultimately dependent on the talent, courage, and dedication of the people recruited for the team. It's one thing to cultivate talent—it's a leader's job—but the ingredients have to be there in some form in the first place. Earlier I quoted Casey Stengel's famous lament about the hapless Mets of the early 1960s: "Can't anybody here play this game?" Stengel was a good coach who was stuck with the limitations of his individual team players. He could drill them, browbeat them, inspire them, but in the end the players were the ones who had to go out onto the field and win or lose.

We've spent a lot of time dealing with process. And it worries me. If just one of my readers closes this book and says, "I get it. All I need is a tight process, a little vision, execution, accountability, follow-up, and I'm all set," then I've blown it. Those things are important—very important—but you'll wallow around in mediocrity unless and until you find the best people.

I'll show you how to do it in this chapter.

SNIP THE SNAP DECISIONS

In the first half of 1988, I tried to avoid making wholesale personnel changes in the Cleveland district while I established a process. Notice I said "wholesale." There were changes. One rep was terminated for an ethical lapse, I pulled another off an unproductive assignment, a few others left the district on their own when they saw the days of late breakfasts and early golf were over. By and large, though, it was not a drastic shakeup in terms of personnel, and a superficial analysis of the results might lead someone to conclude that by going from the cellar to number one in the region within six months I proved that "good management" can do the job no matter who's on the payroll.

Wrong. Six months is nothing. From the very first day, I was planning for the long haul. Good management and an effective process got us up and running, but we couldn't have sustained that performance for an extended period without finding the best people and putting them in the right slots. In addition, there would have been no way to ride out the recession of 1990 through 1992 successfully if I had tried to rely exclusively on process. Why did I wait? For one thing, you have to start somewhere. Cleveland didn't have a viable process. For another, I needed time to see my people in action. And that's perhaps the most important lesson of this chapter: Don't rush the "people decisions."

More harm is done by managers who feel they have to start rearranging bodies, hiring and firing, before they really know what's going on in their operation. Had I done that, I probably would have lost some of my best people by underestimating their true potential based on past performance. Snap judgments alone would have tripped me up. Fred Thomas, probably my most successful manager, would surely have been a goner. Fred is so unconventional in the way he approaches his job that I would have misread him if I hadn't waited to see for myself what kind of results he could produce. It's easy to shoot from the hip. In troubled organizations, the holdovers are blamed for the mess and promptly executed. The slaughter is indiscriminate and unproductive. Before going down that road, ask yourself three questions:

- Is it a process problem?
- Is it a leadership problem?
- Is it a people problem?

Don't jump to conclusions. Find out. It could be all three combined. But you've got to find out *before* you apply a drastic solution that doesn't address the real circumstances of the situation.

NO TANKS

Even in successful organizations, new managers feel they have to make a statement no matter how disruptive it may be. When my mentor, Neil Lamey, left the district manager's position in Columbus, the members of his management team, "Neil's boys," as we were known, were quickly moved elsewhere. The district, and Xerox, paid a high price for the upheaval because the Columbus sales operation lost its edge and eventually went into a slump.

That experience, combined with the trauma of losing three managers in one three-hour period during my first week in Minnesota, taught me to take my time when it comes to personnel decisions. How much time? Unfortunately, there's no hard-and-fast rule. Too much, and inertia sets in; too little, and there are half-cocked decisions. At the end of the first quarter, I had a fairly good feel for the strengths and weaknesses of the people I'd inherited, but my inclination was to give it a full six months, especially since the district was making progress. I deliberately built in some time to allow people to get used to the new regime and to grow.

Look at it this way: If a rep or a manager—any employee—has never been asked to perform, shouldn't you first ask and then see what happens? He or she may turn out to be a superachiever. If you flip back and review the early chapters of the book, you'll see how much emphasis I put on setting a high level of expectation. If you do that at the outset, the decisions that must be made about your people will be a lot easier. There won't be any gray areas.

Isn't that the bottom line of every personnel decision: Can he or she do the job? However, you can't be unfocused and ambiguous about expectations. By announcing that each manager and rep would be expected to pay the rent each month by achieving the sales plans, I wasn't leaving any doubt about what was going to be required. No exceptions, no loopholes. If you leave one, they'll drive an Abrams M-1 tank through it: "Business is slow for everybody"; "It's a recession"; "I exceeded the plan last month"; "I'll get well next month." If you tolerate the excuses, it's as if you've taken your only yardstick and snapped it across your knee. From then on, there is no effective measuring device. You've gone from a people problem to a leadership problem.

OTHER PATHS

The best thing about setting a blistering pace is that it's easy to spot the stragglers. Most of them, in fact, see what's happening on their own and make other arrangements. And that isn't always a traumatic parting of the ways. One of the advantages of working for a major corporation is that there are many alternative career paths. Just because a person is having difficulty in sales doesn't mean there isn't another suitable slot within the district or elsewhere. Not everyone can "play this game," and a person should not be stigmatized if he or she can't keep up. Coach them, work with them, help them in every way, but don't cheat them by propping them up and hiding the truth.

THE LOST AND FOUND

Even though I don't like one-size-fits-all approaches, I'm going to say that if you have been in a new management job for six months and haven't begun to address the question of how best to deploy your people, don't delay another day. Get on it. You're probably rationalizing the delay: "I need far more information before I act." No you don't. You're ducking the hard and unpleasant task of telling people things they may not want to hear.

If you can't do it, you're in the wrong job. And if you don't do it, your failure will become painfully obvious to everybody in your organization. It doesn't take X-ray vision to spot the dead wood. If you flinch from moving the dysfunctional people, the message is demoralizing: "Hard work is for suckers." It's basic human nature. Why should I knock myself out when the guy next door is allowed to coast?

The old saying "He who hesitates is lost" really applies in this area. Once a manager knows what needs to be done, he or she has to go do it. The longer you wait, the harder it gets and the more damage is done to the organization. Before much time goes by, the honeymoon is over. It's your meter that's clocking up the failures. People start asking, "Is he blind?"

Start making the people decisions today. Is there one person who isn't doing the job? Assemble the facts, call him or her in, and, in a dispassionate, courteous manner, provide an honest evaluation point-by-point. What I do is tell the person that the record speaks for itself, and that it just doesn't look like he or she is going anyplace in the company.

"What do you think?" I might ask.

"I think you should give me a couple more months."

"You've had six months and there's been no improvement. Your accounts aren't producing. I can move you to some others that aren't as critical, but the question is will you be professionally satisfied with that?"

"I'd hate to give up my territory."

"You're going to have to, but if you can get cranked up on these other accounts, I could eventually justify letting you take on more important business. You'll have to prove that you can do it."

And so on. I give the rep honest feedback. And in real life, I wouldn't have let it go for six months. He or she would have been hearing the message in various forms as soon as I spotted the deficiencies.

That's why I say, "He who hesitates is lost." Hesitate and you've lost business momentum, credibility, and the possibility of turning the rep around. The more often you bite the bullet, the easier it's going to be the next time.

If you're having trouble, try giving feedback to one of your best people. Tell him or her what you like. That should be enjoyable for both of you. Now, tell that same person what could be done to show improvement. The rep might bristle at the implied criticism, but you've paid the price of admission: you're there to help.

Isn't that exactly what you're doing with employees who have more serious problems? Get in there early and help them save their jobs. When and if the time finally comes to cut them loose, you'll know—and so will they—that there is no other choice.

SALVAGE OPERATION

Xerox has a corrective-action process that I swear by. It's simple and fair. There are four basic steps. First, a manager informally counsels an employee: "Your order rate is falling way behind the others on the team, Ken. It probably wouldn't hurt to expand your prospect base. I'll check back with you next week to see where you stand." It's usually as easy as that. I prefer, however, to make informal counseling a little more formal to avoid misunderstandings. I put it in writing after I've talked to the employee. It's still informal; just a brief note or memo in the file so the rep doesn't misconstrue the meaning of our conversation. I want him or her to know that the corrective-action process has begun. The piece of paper says it all.

The second step is full and formal written notice that the employee is on corrective action. Again, there's a face-to-face conversation at which time the manager lays out the areas that need correction and what the employee should do about them. Then there's an additional and very important action. The manager makes a commitment to assist the employee in remedying the deficiencies.

Gotcha! It's now the manager's responsibility to work with the employee, not to just lean back and watch rigor mortis set in. This keeps everybody honest. The manager can't just say, "I warned him," and then wash his hands of the responsibility. His job is to do everything in his power to save the employee. If the manager can't or won't coach and counsel his people, why does he have that job? If I have a manager under me who isn't the greatest communicator or teacher, I'll step in and work with the rep myself and coach the manager to improve his or her skills.

A word about empowerment and delegating responsibility: inspect. I'm not going to sit idly by and lose a potentially valuable employee just because I've empowered a manager to work with that person. If you think the situation is being mishandled, move in and correct it. You'd better. If there's a screw-up—empowerment or no empowerment—it's your fault. There's much to be said for learning from our mistakes, but mistakes involving people's lives must be headed off even if it means stepping on toes. Use the near miss as a learning situation for the manager: "Here's what would have happened if I hadn't intervened." And move on from there.

PULLING THE TRIGGER

The next step in the corrective-action sequence is formal notification that the employee is on probation and has thirty days to correct his or her poor performance. We get to that point when the facts show there has not been adequate improvement. By and large, most people never arrive at that stage. They get to work and fix the problems before it's too late.

Finally, if all else fails, the employee is notified that he or she is to be terminated. Firing at Xerox is very serious business. If an employee has been with the corporation five years or more, Paul Allaire, our CEO, must sign off on the paperwork. If he doesn't like the look of it, he can stop the termination.

I've never been overruled, and one reason for that is I'm scrupulous about basing a termination squarely on the facts. I work with personnel every step of the way. Here's an important tip: Don't try to slip a termination through quietly. You've got to be open and aboveboard. Personnel should never be blind-sided. Even if I think I will ultimately be able to save a problem employee, I immediately tell personnel what's happening. I get on the phone and say, "We're probably going to be able to pull this one out, but just in case, I want you to know about it."

Another tip: Don't ever fire anyone in a fit of anger. In fact, don't do anything in a fit of anger. I've had to teach myself that, and it hasn't been easy. But I've found that if I'm enraged by something and wait twenty-four hours, although I'll probably feel just as angry, the execution of the decision will be smoother and more effective. I use the breathing spell to examine thoroughly the probable consequences of the action I'm about to take. I run a what-if exercise. What if he or she hasn't been coached properly? What if I don't have all the facts? What if I can't find a replacement right away? I want my managers to go through the same exercise. If I have a trigger-happy team leader under me, and all he or she wants to do is fire the rep and get it over with, I force that manager to think it through: "Have you documented the deficiencies? Personnel is going to complain if you haven't. Do you want that hassle while you're struggling to make plan? Are you sure of the facts? Maybe you don't know the full story, and you'll end up looking unreasonable and unfair." Usually, I don't have to countermand a decision; the cooling-off period results in the exercise of sober judgment. If not, I get involved. Is that a black mark against the manager? Not necessarily. I'd rather pull a manager off a rep than have to push him on. It's hard to teach aggressiveness, but I can temper and channel it.

HOTHEADS AND HOT DOGS

Even the most flagrant provocations need to be thought through. In Minnesota, I didn't realize an impulsive decision to fire one of my reps could have gotten me into deep trouble. It didn't, but I was lucky.

There was a young guy in the office who was having a hard time. Although he was on corrective action, there hadn't been much improvement in his performance. Tim came to me—I've given him a fictional name—and asked for time off. He wanted to go skiing in Utah. "Do you think that's a smart idea?" I inquired. "You're going to have to make plan this month." He assured me he would and that he really needed the time off. I told him to go ahead, figuring he probably wasn't going to make it anyway and he might as well use his vacation time. The next week, I was downtown eating a hot dog for lunch on a street corner with another rep. Who did I see walk by in a suit and tie, as though he were going to work? You got it, my boy Tim. I tossed the hot dog into the trash and said, "Come on, Mary Ann, let's see where he's headed." We followed him to the headquarters of a large insurance company. I had a hunch. I wrote down the name, and when I got back to the office, called to see if he worked there. The receptionist assured me that he did and rang his extension. I hung up, and was I ever angry!

I called Tim's answering machine, described what I had seen and confirmed, and fired him.

I shouldn't have. If I had waited twenty-four hours to examine the consequences, I would have seen the potential danger. First, I really didn't have the authority to fire Tim; my boss had to sign off on that. Secondly, what if he hadn't actually been on the insurance company's payroll yet? People can do what they want with their vacation time. I already had him on corrective action, but the hasty decision could have undermined the process and possibly reversed it.

The lesson here is that even if it's cut and dried—cut it and dry it one more time.

A KILLING KINDNESS

Some Xerox managers are reluctant to use the corrective-action process. I'm not. When I got to Cleveland, almost two-thirds of the district's reps were not making plan, but only one of them was on corrective action. When I asked the team managers why they weren't using corrective action, I got a variety of excuses, ranging from "He's a hard worker," to "I don't have time for all the paperwork." Basically, they didn't want to hurt anybody's feelings.

Feelings? How would those people feel if they got fired out

of the clear blue? How would you feel, as a manager, if you were fired because the team didn't perform month after month? I do not look at the corrective-action process as inevitably leading to termination. It's a way to *avoid* a worst-case outcome. At the first sign of trouble, therefore, I implement corrective action. I don't want the employee to miss a single day that he or she could be using to improve.

At first, the employee might flare up: "You're just trying to get rid of me, Frank."

"No. I'm not. I can't afford to get rid of you. We've spent thousands of dollars on training. I just want you to be the person you said you'd be when we hired you. But if that's not possible —and I think it is—I owe it to your team to get someone in there who can do the job."

I use corrective action to hold people accountable. Go back and take a look at Chapter 6. The contracts that I discussed are the perfect benchmark. If the rep isn't fulfilling the terms of his or her contract, it's time to act. Why wait? Waiting means the district slides deeper into the hole. Waiting means the person isn't being helped. Waiting means the customer is hurt. Corrective action has nothing to do with being "a nice guy." It's not nice to fail. It's not nice to allow others to fail. One year, I had more people on corrective action than any other district in the region. I also sent more reps to President's Club than any other district.

WHEN BONDING TIES YOUR HANDS

By postponing people decisions too long you start running into another problem: friendship. Bonding happens, whether you want it to or not. And you do want it. The friends I made in Cleveland will last a lifetime. In fact, I knew my team-building process was working well when I started to see solid friendships on and off the job developing among the managers. Some of them went from cold and distant business relationships to actually being best friends.

That sort of camaraderie is great, but it can be paralyzing when it comes time to break the bad news. If I had waited eight months or a year to tell George Urban that I thought he'd be better off giving up his team, I probably couldn't have done it. I've mentioned George before. He and I had become close friends. But I felt he was better in front of the customer—and he is, particularly working at the highest levels in an account—than he was as a leader. George was so good that he actually carried his team and did too much for them. I wanted to make a change. The idea was to move him laterally to handle several big national accounts. George tried to talk me out of it. One day we spent hours hashing it over. Finally, we got out of the office and took a long walk. I told him there was no choice.

Today, if we were putting together a Xerox all-star team, George would be one of my first selections. He'd be doing fine, but he wouldn't be nearly as successful if he had stayed where he was in Cleveland. I come back to the adage "He who hesitates is lost." If I had hesitated beyond the time I needed to size up George's situation, our friendship would have become a barrier. In the end, there would have been three losers: Xerox, out one star player (and never even knowing it); George, deprived of the opportunity to excel; and me. What would I have lost? A friend. I never would have been satisfied with his performance, and the bond couldn't have survived the pressure I'd have brought to bear.

POOL MAINTENANCE

Here's a quick way to determine if your organization has a people problem: Look in the recruitment file. When was the last time a job candidate was interviewed? If it was more than a month ago, you've got people problems.

When I arrived in Cleveland, the recruitment cupboard was bare. I told my managers that we were going to start interviewing and never stop. Recruitment isn't a chore; it isn't drudgery. It's an absolute necessity.

If you don't have the best candidates at all times, you're going to end up rushing to fill a vacancy from a shallow, lackluster talent pool. And you've probably seen it happen as many times as I have: "I'm desperate, just give me a warm body." In time, all those warm bodies proliferate and failure is inevitable.

Many executives resist getting involved in the hiring process because they think it is not a productive use of their time. On the contrary, a few hours a month can pay huge dividends. One month, two of my young trainees sold a couple of modestly priced, low-volume machines—the first sales they had ever made. We wouldn't have achieved our plan that month without those two machines. Was I glad we took the time to hire them? Better believe it.

Was I glad I spent more than six months trying to convince Pat Elizondo to move from Xerox's Chicago office to Cleveland? * Not only did I get an exemplary team leader, Pat served as a role model for other women. She was a magnet that drew the best female talent to Cleveland. And that's what happens—excellence attracts excellence. When managers tell me, "We just can't find qualified women and minorities," I have no sympathy whatsoever. They're not trying hard enough. There's no magnet. They expect the minority superstars to wander in off the street and say, "Hey, there are no minorities here . . . must be a great place to work."

Having said that, let me add something. Don't, repeat, don't hire minorities or women just to fill a spot or a numerical quota or so that you'll feel you've done your civic duty; it's a disservice to those you hire and to the organization. "I had to fill the corporate quota" is nothing but a cheap and lazy excuse. If an effective and conscientious process is in place for recruiting minorities and women, finding the right people for the right jobs will happen as a matter of course. If it isn't happening, the fault is not with the lack of qualified women and minorities—I wouldn't buy that lame cop-out in a million years—the fault is the recruiting process or, what's worse, far worse, that yours is an organization where women and minorities don't feel welcome and probably aren't welcome. Take your pick. There are only two explanations, and both are unacceptable.

I've said repeatedly that I want you to steal my ideas. Steal Xerox's idea on this one. It's a truly color-blind, gender-neutral, ethnically impartial operation. And how did that happen? Not by accident. Not by a halfhearted process. We made it happen. We worked at it until it was second nature. One of the reasons that Xerox is again a healthy corporation is the diversity of our

---

* I wasn't poaching; Xerox prohibits it. Chicago couldn't match the opportunity and I had her boss's permission.

work force. If I ever had any doubts about that, all I'd need to do is walk around Wright-Patterson Air Force Base with our account rep, Bev Smith, an African-American woman, and marvel as we're greeted by nearly every person who passes by. She's an impressive sales professional. Bev could serve as a role model and benchmark for the type of person we look to hire.

REAP WHAT YOU SOW

Make recruiting a top priority, and don't delegate it to others or expect the personnel department to handle the dirty work. If you owned a major-league sports team, you wouldn't think twice about spending huge amounts of time and money on recruiting athletic talent. Some coaches say a third or half of their job is recruiting. It's not just a matter of burnout or injury or aging. They've got to find the best people and put them out on the field for every game. If they don't, the competition will.

There is no difference between sports and business when it comes to the hiring process. Slipshod recruiting will give you a slipshod organization. Take a sheet of paper and write down your five biggest business headaches. Which of them would never have occurred if the right people had been hired in the first place? I'll bet three of the five would come off the list. I wouldn't be surprised if it was five of five. We put the wrong people in the wrong places and expect to get by using a process, hard-nosed management practices, or the latest flavor-of-the-month business concept. It doesn't work.

Do some benchmarking. Identify colleagues who have been notably successful at hiring good people and get them to tell you how they do it. Put out the word that you want to hear about best practices in the recruiting area (also the worst practices). When you walk through the front door of a business establishment that's humming with enthusiasm and competence, whether it's a dry cleaner or day-care center, take the time to find out how they rounded up the talent. Talk to your vendors. The dynamite salesperson who stops by each month to sell you brand X didn't fall out of the sky. How was he or she recruited? It isn't surprising that many companies are happy to share their procedures. For one thing, it's a great advertisement.

Collect recruiting techniques the way some people collect stamps. What a great hobby! It will make you allies, friends— and money.

THOU SHALT COVET
THY NEIGHBOR'S . . . BEST PEOPLE

Early on in Cleveland, I got caught in the shallow end of the talent pool and I vowed never to let that happen again. Now, if two weeks go by and I'm not being asked by my managers to interview a job prospect they're considering, I'll start checking to make sure that we haven't forgotten about recruiting. Although we may not be actually hiring that month or quarter, I'm constantly on the lookout for good people. I have an informal scouting organization. I talk to personnel, check with fellow managers, and ask customers to steer people my way. A lot of screening—both in and out—can be done this way.

There's a point that needs to be emphasized: Your customers know all about the competition. Find out who they're most impressed by and hire them. If a rep tells me his competition is good, my first reaction is to say, "Let's see if we can steal her away."

The reverse is also true. If your reps are negative about a job candidate, listen to them. I didn't do that in Minneapolis once and learned a painful lesson. I wanted to hire a guy who worked for the competition. Several reps told me to forget it. I went ahead anyway, convinced that I had made the right decision. The guy just waltzed through the screening process. A month or so later, my brand-new hire just up and disappeared. He didn't show up for work one day, and that's the last we ever heard of him.

Listen to the reps.

SELL ME, SELL MY DESK

I believe in consensus hiring. A candidate is interviewed by each of my managers. I ask the managers for a thumbs-up or -down. If one of them says not to hire, the candidate is rejected. It's got to be unanimous. I want to be able to have the flexibility to put the new employee on any team. The last thing I need to hear is "I don't have faith in the guy," or "I told you I didn't like her, give her to somebody else."

You'll never build a team if you either ram people down the throats of your managers or allow them to pick and choose haphazardly without any reference to the overall organization.

I interview the candidate once he or she has been okayed by the managers. It's usually pro forma at that point; I rarely overrule. What I figure is, unless they throw up on my desk, a person who has gotten that far is probably a safe bet. Even so, I want to see how they will perform in front of the customer. If they collapse on me, they'll probably collapse on the customer.

One of my patented questions is to ask the candidate to sell me my desk. Or I'll point at the TV and say, "Let's role-play. Get me to buy that television." Some people stutter and stammer, others show poise and creativity. What I'm looking for is their ability to think on their feet, to stay calm and cool.

Today, many job interviewees are preprogrammed and carefully prepared. I want to strip off the facade and see what's underneath. I ask for their role models, get them to talk about their parents, and encourage them to elaborate on the toughest moment in their lives.

One young woman, leaning forward and growing extremely intense, responded that her toughest moment was when her sister died. I sat there feeling like a jerk for raising the subject, but she went on to explain that the tragedy had forced her to suddenly mature and rally her stricken family.

I like to find out how the candidate financed his or her college education. If mom and dad paid all the bills, I wonder if the person is ready to confront the real world. I know I wasn't. My father was too generous. Many of the problems I experienced as a young rep grew out of having a safety net there when I was irresponsible.

My role-model question is also important. If the candidate doesn't have one—and it happens—I suspect he hasn't thought about what he wants out of life. He may lack standards and direction.

I asked Lisa Huston the role-model question and her response led me to break my rule about rubber-stamping the managers' unanimous recommendations. She came into the interview with me having passed all the others with flying colors. But she was nervous and got even more so as the session proceeded. I asked about role models, and it was all over. She grew red in the face and started gasping for breath; tears welled up. I thought she was going to faint or actually throw up on my desk. I ended the questioning right there. It was over. When Lisa got control she explained that her role model was her father and that he had been very ill recently. The pressure of the interview and that particular question had been too much of a strain.

I went back to the managers and told them what happened. I vetoed their hiring recommendation. I didn't want to take a chance that Lisa's emotions would crack in front of a customer.

Instant uproar! Every manager in the room told me I was nuts. Pat Elizondo demanded to know what I had said or done to set Lisa off like that. I thought I was going to be tarred and feathered. "All right, all right," I said. "Start all over again. Go back to the beginning and assure yourself that this incident was just a fluke." Pat volunteered to take charge of the process.

A few weeks later we hired Lisa. I never regretted it. She's a brilliant salesperson. But now I'm a little gun-shy every time I ask the role-model question.

13

Cold Comfort and a

Hot Product:

No Surrender, No Retreat

Okay, you hired the best talent. Now what? Send them out on cold calls.

Sink or swim. Actually, I'm not that heartless. At Xerox, new employees go through weeks of training before they're exposed to the customer. There are very few corporate training facilities that even approach the one we run in Leesburg, Virginia. It's a business university. Many of the young people who join us straight out of college are shocked by the intensity of the experience. A kid walks in the front door and six weeks or so later an adult walks out.

All of us end up in Leesburg from time to time for refresher courses, and our best reps and managers are rotated through the facility for stints as faculty members. There's a lot to learn and to teach. It never ends.

All I can say about training is that if you're not providing it to your people—shame on you! If your people aren't gulping down every morsel of training you provide—shame on them!

The return on the investment in training is astronomical. I've seen figures that show every dollar spent on training yields something like a thirty-dollar dividend. Companies are shortsighted—no, make that just plain stupid—to begrudge their employees adequate training.

On the other hand, workers who resist training aren't showing a lot of smarts either. In Cleveland, before our people left for Leesburg, they were told it was their responsibility, their job, to learn. That admonition was absolutely serious. We weren't going to tolerate anyone who went through training with a closed mind. Corporate America is crawling with know-it-alls. They sit back at seminars and roundtables, saying, "What else is new?" You've seen them. The outright hostility to educational enrichment and training is astonishing.

As a manager, I make it quite clear that when the trainee returns to the district, I expect to see what he or she learned put into action. I'll surprise a rep or manager by asking them to stand up at the monthly business meeting and summarize the high points of their Leesburg sessions. I know right away what was absorbed and what wasn't. I'll also assign a newly trained rep to teach a refresher course on aspects of Leesburg's curriculum.

The training process continues back in the district. It has to. One-shot educational binges are very inefficient. Training must be an ongoing process, otherwise skill levels become spotty. A rep will handle a few products or services well and bumble through the rest. I want consistency across the full range of products and throughout the organization.

Track your average training time. If it comes out to about a half-hour a week, you're just about hitting the national average of 1½ percent of total employee hours, which I think is lousy to begin with. Double that to a full hour and get serious.

Does that mean there's an hour of formal instruction each week? No, not at all. I include a training module in almost every presentation I make to my district. It doesn't have to be anything more than flashing a slide on an overhead projector showing a page from the Xerox Account Management Process form and explaining why we want certain bases covered. I tell my managers to conduct training in the car while they're traveling from appointment to appointment with their reps: "Here's what I thought you did well at the last call. Now, what you need to concentrate on is this . . ." In fact, whenever a manager travels with his reps the whole day should be one long training opportunity. If not, what's the point—a guided sight-seeing tour for the manager?

There are other ways to train on the fly. I do what I call "chalk talks" in the morning. Just before my managers are about to leave the office for the day, I'll pull them in for a quick session that's part training, part tactical briefing, part critique. If I think they're starting to sleep-walk, I'll jolt them awake. Once, when we suddenly lost a $100,000 deal and I first heard about it from my secretary—whose husband was the purchasing agent for the customer—I just told them I was thoroughly disappointed with their performance and sent them on their way. For the next nine hours I had a group of managers doing wheelies all over town. The rubber met the road that day!

Strictly speaking, that's not training. But I'm introducing the managers to leadership techniques that they should know about and use for the rest of their business careers.

KNOCKS—HARD, HARDER, AND HARDEST

If Leesburg is a business university, cold calling is boot camp. All of our new reps (the beginners in the trade) spend the first year on the job cold calling. It's the hardest thing in the world to do. Experienced salespeople can spend an entire day making twenty-five or thirty calls and not even getting in front of a single decision maker. We like to see how a young person survives the experience.

I tell them to put on a leather skin because they're going to be subjected to one rejection after another. They can't let the battering get them down. While it's an important lesson, there's more to cold calling than just learning how to roll with the punches. Developing the ability to get past a good screen takes practice; there's no way to learn from a book.

One method is to do a little homework and come up with a name. Walk in and tell the receptionist you're there to see John Doe.

"And your name, sir?"

"Frank Pacetta."

That's all. Don't say what company you're from or fumble around with the name and title of the person you want to see. If you're lucky—and you probably won't be—the receptionist will assume that you and Doe are old friends.

"He's very busy" is the standard put-off line. Cold callers hear it in their sleep. "I understand that, but Xerox has some exciting new products that he's really going to want to hear about. I can wait fifteen or twenty minutes until he's available."

This is sales at its most basic level. In the end, often the best you can do is to leave your card and some promotional material. An effective salesperson always leaves *something*. I'll ask if there's a good time to catch John Doe when he isn't so busy. If the receptionist goes for that, she is semicommitted to letting you through the next time. Try to get Mr. Doe's telephone extension. The idea is to come out of that cold call with something you didn't have when you walked in.

Talk to the receptionist. She may be able to steer you to another decision maker, or, as is often the case, she may be a good person to be in contact with anyway. The nature of the copier business is such that actual operators of the equipment have a lot to say about purchasing decisions, and many times they're not being protected by the screen (or they are the screen). "Let me ask you a few questions," I'll say to open. "How much copying gets done around here on an average day?"

He or she may balk, but it's worth a try. Sale or no sale, it's never a waste of time to gather information. But shoot for a close —any close: "Can I send you more information?" "May I telephone next Tuesday?" "What would be a good time . . . ?" If they agree to take a call, get your calendar out and write down the date and time so they see you actually intend to follow through. If I were writing a sales manual, I would have several chapters on the art of closing. Probably each one that's ever been published includes the old huckster's line "Will that be cash or charge?" That's a close. Get the person to commit in some *way* to some*thing*, large or small.

I think of the sales sequence as a long stairway. To get to the top, I've got to proceed step-by-step, close-by-close. A good salesperson, when the situation is right, will run up the stairs. Other times the climb can be painfully slow, but he or she is always going for the next step, the next close.

Some reps never learn how to do it. They're well organized, conscientious, have rapport with the customer, know the products, but shy away from closing. The reluctance is almost a phobia. I think it's a fear of rejection or dread that the customer's objection is really a reflection on the rep's ability and value as a human being. To overcome the anxiety, I push new reps hard to make small closes. I want them to get in the habit of closing so that when it comes time to take the final step, arrive at the top of the staircase, and obtain the deal, it will be instinctive: "I've brought the paperwork with me today. Why don't you look it over and sign off? We'll deliver the equipment next Tuesday"; or, even more directly, "I worked closely with you. I've met every one of your requirements. There's nothing left to do or say. Let's put this one to bed today." There may be an objection. If there is, the stairway just got a little higher, that's all.

I'm spending so much time on cold calling and closing because I'm doing missionary work on behalf of the Ancient and Honorable Society of Drummers, Travelers, and Professional Mendicant Classes of All Nations. You may not be in sales directly, but I want you to get a feel for what the salespeople in your organization have to do for a living. It cracks me up when I talk to engineers and production people who are so proud of their product that they assume the customer is waiting for the salespeople with a red carpet and a brass band. I wish!

Going into sales is like joining the infantry. It's grimy work, and as combat veterans will tell you, the only way to really understand what the battles are like is to be there yourself. That's why I go out of my way to invite nonsales executives from Rochester and Stamford into my districts so that they can "be there." I tell the reps to take them out into the field and not to bring them back until their tongues are dragging the ground. If you're in sales, do the same thing. Issue an open invitation to all the ivory-tower types who could use an education in the art, science, and black magic of knocking on doors until the knuckles bleed. If you're not in sales, take a few days every year to join the infantry and see the world.

THE IMPORTANCE OF BEING ~~ERNEST~~ ENTHUSIASTIC

These days, telemarketing is touted as a way to avoid the agony and inefficiency of cold calling. There's some truth to that; however, for sheer training purposes, I would hate to see cold calling eliminated. The novice salesperson learns quickly that the most effective approach is to emphasize the value of the product to the customer. The message has to be that you, the rep, are there to make life easier for the customer. After several days of cold calling, the rep is so conditioned to push that button that it is second nature. The first thing the rep says, the initial benefit statement, as it's called, is usually the key to the sale. Years later, customers will say, "I remember when Linda first walked into the office. I was really impressed." They may not be able to recall the details, but the energy, the enthusiasm, the level of knowledge are indelible.

Here's some advice for dealing with salespeople who are trying to sell you something on a cold call, or at any time. If they're zombies, forget it. You can usually judge the quality of a product by the sales rep. If the rep is not excited about the product, you should be very wary. Yes, perhaps it's a bad day. But maybe that rep and his company make a habit of having bad days. By the same token, if I sense that my own sales force is down on a product, I immediately try to find out why. Experienced salespeople know a dog when they see one; it doesn't have to bark or bite. It's a foolish executive who expects to shove an inferior product down the throats of the salespeople and make them like it.

ACCEPTING (BUT NOT EXPECTING) YES
FOR AN ANSWER

There are other benefits to cold calling. When you finally make a sale, it is absolutely thrilling. Veteran reps who routinely sell $250,000 machines will get just as worked up when they receive an order on a cold call for a $2,000 copier. The hunter comes home with dinner.

Even more exciting is what happened to me in 1991. I still go out with my reps on cold calls a couple of times a year. If you're a sales manager you should too. I insist that my managers keep their cold-calling skills sharp so that they will experience what's going on in the field. There's no better way for getting a feel for the marketplace and a sense of what the reps have to deal with on a day-to-day basis.

In this case, I went out with a young guy named Joe Dean, who was cold calling in Lorain, Ohio. We got out of the car, and since it was a cold, blustery day, I said, "Let's start here," pointing to a real estate office right across the street. We walked in, and fifteen minutes later we had a sale. I still get a buzz thinking about it.

The first call of the day! There is *nothing* like getting a sale right out of the box when you're cold calling. Doors can be slammed in your face for the next eight hours and it doesn't matter. Joe just couldn't believe it. He had scar tissue two inches thick to show for all the rejections he had experienced, and there was a sale first thing in the morning when he's traveling with his boss.

That was the high point of the day. We picked up some names for future use and were rebuffed several times. We walked out of one place where the woman in charge flatly refused to see us, and I said to Joe, to cheer him up, "Imagine that . . . we're here to help that lady and she won't even give us the time of day. What a shame." We chuckled and went on our way. Nothing could spoil the day.

When we got back to the office, word immediately spread about the sale, and I had a ball teasing the reps: "You grouse about how hard cold calling is, but my first day out and on the very first call, I sell a machine. What's the big deal about cold calling?" They couldn't believe it. Of course, I didn't tell them how lucky we had been. The reps were hoping that Joe would run me ragged, but instead we got that order right out of the box. I was pumped for the next two weeks.

DECENT EXPOSURE

You may be in a business where cold calling is inappropriate. Off the top of my head, I can't imagine what it would be—embalming? For most companies, I think it is a necessary evil that will never be completely supplanted by telemarketing or direct mail. You can cover more ground with the phone or mail, but there is a tremendous amount a rep can learn by going out and getting kicked around, meeting with people, being disappointed. It's a great toughening process. Experienced salespeople all look back and say, "Boy, I'm glad I'm not doing that anymore." But I don't know anyone who would contend that cold calling didn't help along the way. It introduces the new rep to one of the occupation's most important skills—instant objection handling. There's no better way to learn how to respond to the million-and-one reasons customers will cite for not buying a product. Poise under pressure can't be learned out of a book, nor does a salesperson grow the essential hard shell—I call it the rejection skin—that he or she needs to survive from day to day.

OUT OF SMALL BEGINNINGS

Another necessary evil is the small order. If I were selling jet airplanes or nuclear power plants, I'd be tempted to invent another product on a more modest scale to allow my sales force to write small orders. I want to get my reps into the habit of constantly writing orders. If they wait for the big deals to come along, it could be months or years before something happens. In the meantime, if you have a monthly sales plan to meet, that rep isn't contributing.

Often, your most experienced people will develop a taste for major deals. After all, they have the depth of knowledge and savvy needed to get them. You will end up ghettoizing your operation once that happens, however. And that's disastrous if you're trying to hang on to market share across the full range of your product line.

Demand a mix of small and major orders. It's smart psychology and strategy. I don't care what the price tag is, most salespeople get a kick out of selling. It's a payback for all the hard work. If I have to wait a year for the payback, no matter how high the commission, I find it's harder and harder to come to work in the morning. Strategically, a manager who becomes dependent on major deals is asking for trouble. All you need to do is miss one and it's "trouble in River City." The perfect example is the story I told in Chapter 11 about our struggle to get a huge order for printing systems from an insurance company before 1991 ended. If we had lost that deal, the whole year would have been blown. Smaller deals will give you a cushion or a margin for error.

The other advantage is that small deals, which often involve small customers, have a way of evolving. I pushed hard to win approval from Xerox for flexible financing for Office Max, back when the operation wasn't much more than a scruffy little warehouse and big, glitzy plans. At my first call on Office Max, I sat there in amazement when the company's founder, Michael Feuer, proposed to us that we grant special credit terms that only go to our largest customers. When we left the meeting, I said to the rep, "That guy sure has a lot of nerve. He says we should go for it because he's going to be the number one retail office supply operation in the country . . . fat chance!" By the time we got back to the office both of us were saying, "Maybe he can do it." I urged Rochester to take a chance and got the go-ahead. Today, Office Max has come damned close to fulfilling Michael Feuer's dream, with more than 200 stores and leases for 300 of our copiers. Some customers stay small forever and some don't.

A SPEED BUMP

Constantly writing small orders keeps a sales force revved up. By 1991 the Cleveland district had so much RPM that we were able to overcome the almost crippling handicap of a difficult sales plan (I described it in more forceful terms to my wife) and the introduction of a new product with a six-figure price tag that many people thought was guaranteed to induce massive sticker shock.

Success has its rewards and its punishments. We had turned in such solid performances in the three previous years that the inevitable happened: the Xerox powers-that-be decided to load on a sales plan that was so ambitious it provoked consternation and outrage in everyone in Cleveland when we got a look at it.

As I mentioned earlier, a salesperson's level of compensation at Xerox is dependent upon making plan. If I sell $5 million worth of products, for example (which could be twice what I did the previous year), but the plan calls for $5.1 million, my income could actually decrease. There is an understandable temptation to take the most successful districts' plans and bump them upward. Why not? You've got to grow the business. However, the bump should be justified by reasonable expectations of growth and potential in the marketplace. And that's the Catch-22. One executive's reasonable plan is another's nightmare. When the formulation of the plan takes a wrong turn, the salespeople are in the frustrating position of running harder and faster just to stay in place, and in some cases, despite the extra effort, they'll actually lose ground. A plan can be appealed, criticized, and cursed; in the end, the sound and fury usually don't do any good.

We were stuck with the 1991 plan. Even so, I decided to opt for an unusual tactic. I told my bosses that I was going to hold back part of the plan. Instead of divvying up the whole thing among the teams, I cut the total down to make the goal seem achievable. Rather than forcing them to run a marathon of twenty-six miles, three hundred and eighty-five yards, I rounded it off. Actually, the cut was around 10 percent.

This move took considerable pressure off the reps, who would have thrown up their hands in despair at the size of the original plan. In essence, I was shielding them from taking a hit in the wallet by giving them numbers they could reach. They'd still have to stretch, but it was possible. I told them what was going on and explained that I was depending on everyone to surpass the adjusted plan. My gamble was that if each rep did a few percentage points over the plan I would have enough margin to make the original figure. I was doing a psychological soft shoe in the hope that a pumped-up and eager sales force could be squeezed just enough to reach the goal, while a demoralized, angry team wouldn't even come close.

To Xerox's credit, my bosses allowed me the leeway to try what, at the time, was an unorthodox approach. My timing was fortunate in that we had been designated as one of a handful of districts to participate in the corporation's "Leap Out" program (also known as Vendor of Choice), which involved granting extraordinary levels of empowerment to test just how far Xerox could afford to go in terms of allowing its units the independence to act in areas that had once been the sole purview of top management. Cleveland and seven other districts were assigned to a special VOC region, which meant we were going up against formidable internal competition. Denver, Cincinnati, and mid-Ohio were always dangerous, and Atlanta was very tough, seeing that it was twice the size of Cleveland. The others—Pittsburgh, Phoenix, and St. Louis—could never be taken for granted. The program, by the way, was a smashing success, with the specially empowered districts scoring solid sales and revenue gains against the other districts that were operating under tighter control.

The double irony in Cleveland's case was that although my tactics paid off—we actually beat the plan—the next year I was refused permission to again hold back a portion, and the district didn't make it. In 1993, Dave Myerscough, the customer operations president, announced that henceforth he was going to withhold a piece of the sales plan on a nationwide basis. It gave my partners and me the satisfaction of knowing that while we had taken a risk a year earlier, it had been the right thing to do for our people and plowed new ground for the entire corporation.

KISS OFF

Despite the difficulty with the plan, 1991 was my favorite year in Cleveland because of the way the district slam-dunked the launch of DocuTech, a $250,000 hybrid copier product that moved Xerox head and shoulders—as well as hips and heels—above its competition.

Technically, DocuTech is a copier, but it also uses laser and computer technology. It's an awesome machine, sleek and stylish, the length of a subcompact car, with a video display monitor amidships that gives the impression a salvo of Patriot missiles is about to be launched. There's never been anything like it. An office worker can sit at his or her desktop computer, writing, editing, creating graphics, and at the push of a button send a one-hundred-page document (or more) to DocuTech for printing, duplication, folding, and binding. It provides high-speed, high-volume offset quality that most companies couldn't come anywhere near equaling with their in-house printing operations.

Rather than feeling intimidated by the six-figure price tag, we couldn't wait to get our hands on the product. In fact, we didn't wait. DocuTech wasn't due on the street until May, yet in February the Cleveland district was already demonstrating the machine. We didn't have one in our possession, which made for interesting demos, but the team was really cranking.

Our first move was to identify potential customers. Not everyone can afford a $250,000 copier. Surprisingly, though, we came up with a long list of prospects, many of them businesses that sent their work to outside offset printing shops. This gave us the possibility of expanding the customer base, since we weren't cannibalizing already existing copier utilization. DocuTech gave us extra "clicks," as we say in the copier business. Given its incredible quality and productivity, this impact on traditional offset machines convinced many industry analysts that DocuTech was our most important product introduction since the ground-breaking 914 in the 1960s.

We put out the word that everyone was going to be involved in selling DocuTech. Our official plan called for selling eight of them. Based on the initial enthusiasm from the managers, I set the district goal at twenty-plus. Each manager was required to act as a role model by selling at least one DocuTech. The DocuTech launch team sent out a memo asking every rep to furnish names for an invitation list to a DocuTech symposium that we decided to use as our kickoff. The teams came up with so many guests that we had to run morning and afternoon sessions at a ballroom in a nearby hotel. Ninety people came, representing forty-three different companies.

To make up for the lack of a demonstration unit, we ran a film, and Bill Valentine, the chief engineer for the DocuTech production project, was the featured speaker. You have to remember, nobody makes a major investment in a new copier without kicking the tires and honking the horn. Knowing that, many Xerox districts had decided to hold their fire until the first units arrived. Our idea gave us almost a three-month head start.

The symposiums (there were a total of three), *sans* machine, even produced a couple of presale agreements. The customers were so hot they didn't need to see the equipment. They authorized us to get started on the paperwork. When we actually took delivery two and a half months later and demonstrated Docu-Tech to many of the same people who had attended the symposiums, we had eight deals immediately.

In some ways, DocuTech in the flesh is almost overpowering. It weighs two tons, and to the uninitiated appears menacing, as if by pushing one wrong button you would wind up orbiting around Venus. Customers stood there gaping, afraid to get close enough to touch the machine. Bill Hookway, who handled the demo, did a good job of demystifying the product. He and the other key players at the demo had gone through two full weeks of training on the machine. Instead of allowing the complexity to blind the customers to the product's benefits, we followed a KISS strategy: Keep It Simple, Stupid. Don't get bogged down in things like networking and technical jargon; DocuTech is a production machine that works fast and saves a lot of money; no more extra charges for quick turnaround at an outside print shop; no more waiting, and no more paying through the nose for small lots. One of Bill's more impressive flourishes was to run the customers' own applications and material through DocuTech and, while the output was being admired, he'd inform them the machine was simultaneously processing two other jobs, all at ferocious speeds of 135 copies per minute.

We also won goodwill by giving the operators good-looking white shop coats with the DocuTech logo on the breast pocket. The early customers were so impressed by the ease of training provided by a special Xerox team that whenever a prospect was nervous about the machine's complexity we referred them to people who could speak objectively and from experience.

By the end of 1991, in the middle of a deep economic slump, we had achieved our ambitious DocuTech goals. In an odd way, the recession probably helped us. The emphasis on value made sense to executives who were being forced to do more with less.

With the DocuTech, Cleveland outsold districts that were far larger than we were, and our total revenue for the month of December, nearly nine million dollars, was the highest in the nation. We ended up being benchmarked within Xerox for both the DocuTech launch and our customer satisfaction improvement program.

Yes, 1991 was a year to remember.*

* The results confirmed my opinion of the 1991 plan. We had a long string of number 1 and number 2 rankings in the various sales categories, exceeding the plan in some cases by more that 200 percent. Even so, in terms of the percentage over plan, we only finished in the top ten nationally and did not take the top spot in the region. And don't forget the close call in December. If I sound like I'm complaining, it's because I am. An artificially high plan—once you've knocked yourself out achieving it—forms the baseline for all succeeding years. It never goes away, and it's a classic disincentive. My own superiors at Xerox won't like reading this, but they should know how their decisions affect people in the field.

14

Bell Ringers:

Self-Conceit and

Self-Destruction (Almost)

"**P**ersistence, Hard Work, and Confidence" was my motto in Cleveland (stolen from Neil Lamey). I used it as a tag line in memos to the district. As I reviewed the files for this book, I discovered one dated January 8, 1992, that displays the '91 year-end statistics. Regionally, out of fifteen sales categories, we finished number one in nine of them, number two in five others, and third in the last index that measured total high-volume-copier orders (the high-volume order percentage was number one, which indicated that the bigger districts had sheer size going in their favor).

We had a lot to be proud of, and I concluded the memo with this exhortation: "I would like to thank everyone for the year-long Persistence, Hard Work, and Confidence you displayed. You have made 1991 a standard setter for us to chase and shatter in 1992."

Less than five months later, in a hotel room in Palm Springs, California, I slammed down the telephone and wheeled around to tell Julie what I had just learned from my Voicemail. Paul MacKinnon left word that the district had missed its plan for April, and missed by a mile.

We were at the resort for President's Club, and about thirty-five of my managers and reps were en route from Cleveland for what amounted to a celebration of our 1991 success. I fumed about the April results for most of the morning, left a scathing critique in each person's Voicemail box, and threatened to have nothing to do with the Cleveland contingent when it arrived later that day. Julie heard me out and announced that if I was going to wreck everyone's vacation, she would take the next plane home. That shut me up.

The first event of President's Club was a pool party at another hotel. As we circulated, Jeff Collier approached and asked, "Do I dare get close to you?" We laughed about it and ended up having a good time with the group. But everybody knew that when we got back to Cleveland the fun would be over. As I put it at the time, "We are going to work harder than we have ever worked in our lives."

A LIFE SENTENCE

I blamed myself for April. I had let the district sit around feeling self-satisfied and triumphant when we should have been out hustling. It's tempting to ease up when you come off a string of successes—hell, we earned it—and I succumbed. Many of the motivational and leadership techniques that I described in previous chapters were not being used with peak effectiveness. I wasn't inspecting rigorously, since I assumed the team was functioning so smoothly I didn't need to.

Take my advice: Never stop inspecting. Take another piece of advice—please: Increase your inspections after there's been a highly successful run. A letdown, or feeling of anticlimax sets in, with devastating effects. You mustn't ease up. If success is predicated on hard work, team building, high expectation, enthusiasm, accountability, and communication, the absence of any one of those ingredients is ruinous.

What I learned from the experience was that there is no such thing as a perpetual-motion machine. You can't expect to get your organization to peak performance levels and then keep it there by lapsing into a sort of caretaker mode. Organizations do not simply run themselves, no matter how good the process or previous track record. The best of them lose momentum very quickly; perhaps even faster than mediocre teams that never take risks or set high standards in the first place.

If I've convinced you in the last thirteen chapters that it is all about winning, I now have to break the bad news: it's all about winning *all* of the time. Once you climb on the escalator, you can't get off. There are only two options—up or down. In some ways, Malcolm Lowry, the novelist, was right when he said, "Success is like some horrible disaster, worse than your house burning." The more successful you are, the more the house burns, and the fire department never comes.

I wouldn't want it any other way. My point is that it is easy to start thinking that success breeds success. It doesn't. Unremitting effort breeds success. It's a life sentence, with no time off for good behavior.

THE CAN'T-DO PHILOSOPHY

When we returned from Palm Springs, I immediately convened a business meeting of the entire district. I told the group, "The ox is in the ditch and it's going to take an extraordinary effort on everyone's part to get it out." I said I doubted whether we had enough time left in the remainder of the second quarter to do the job.

The note of pessimism caught the district off guard. The reps and managers had grown accustomed to my can-do rhetoric, and I was deliberately throwing a change-up pitch. I wanted to shake them out of their complacency. Also, I half believed it myself. The fast and furious start is one of my specialties. Since I was raised in the Northeast and have spent my adult life in the Midwest, I know that the winter doldrums can cost a business organization three or four months' worth of momentum. There's a tendency in those regions to hunker down when the weather is cold and nasty, do the necessary paperwork, training, and other chores until spring finally breaks. When the weather improves, many organizations come out of hibernation, but precious time has been lost. My mistake in 1991 was to allow a long winter's nap to take place, and there was a possibility that the alarm clock hadn't gone off in time.

THIS IS NOT A DRILL!

If we were talking face to face, I'd ask you to predict my next move. By now, you should be pretty good at anticipating what will happen next. I hope so. The reason I wrote this book was to give readers the leadership tools for use in a crisis. I have an image of *Don't Fire Them, Fire Them Up* displayed behind a pane of glass with a sign that reads "In an emergency break glass, read book."

I began the equivalent of an assault on Mount Everest, handing everyone ice axes, coils of rope, and crampons, with the instruction, "Start climbing." I told the district the goal was to install $7 million worth of copiers in May and June. Keep in mind that for all of 1991 we installed just under $2.2 million worth of machines, an average of $183,000 a month. I was proposing roughly a 2,000 percent increase.

For a moment there was dead silence in the room, and then a rustling sound like water coming to a boil.

GHOST BUSTERS

I used the $7 million number as a red flag. It was everywhere: cubicle walls, bulletin boards, the reception area, at the top of memos, and mentioned at every meeting. Our cleaning people could have told you what the number was. I wanted the reps and managers to wake up their spouses in the dead of night mumbling in their sleep, "Seven million dollars . . . seven million dollars."

Instantly, the joint was jumping. The reps needed every order on their thirty- and sixty-day outlooks and then some. My four years of harping about pulling the deals forward from ninety days out really started paying off. One of the keys was that the managers had learned to distinguish between "suspects" and "prospects" when their reps submitted thirty-, sixty-, and ninety-day plans. Here's how it works.

A rep might say, "This account has expanded fivefold in the last two years. He's going to need a new mid-volume machine within ninety days. I'll put him down as a prospect."

I want the manager to ask, "Have you talked to him about his plans?"

"No."

"That's a suspect, not a prospect. When you talk to him, he might tell you the company is ready to retrench or make a big change in its product line. In that event, the existing equipment could handle the job. The customer is a prospect only when he confirms that he is ready to consider your proposal."

No shortcuts. Long- and short-term planning documents are useless if they are allowed to be compromised with phantom prospects. A name doesn't belong on a thirty-day outlook unless it is closable—barring nothing less than an act of God—that month. The sixty-day outlook is reserved for prospects that are 90 to 95 percent of the way through the sales cycle, with a few last decision-making hurdles to clear. At ninety days out, the reps should have initiated the sales cycle by actually contacting the prospect for an assessment of his or her requirements and received encouragement to proceed to the next stage.

Using that sort of control, we purged the plans to such an extent that what we saw on the page was what we got thirty, sixty, or ninety days later.

A day didn't go by without good news—and bad. The ship captain's bell was ringing so much I began wondering whether it wasn't a hallucination or a practical joker. I'd count the number of times it rang, multiply by the remaining days, and go out into the office and say, "I don't think we're going to be able to do it."

I wouldn't have even attempted such a formidable goal without backup from my district partners. The whole enterprise would have ground to a halt if the business operation had been unable to process the deals we were throwing at them. The corporate paper chase can grind down the fastest and strongest runners. Tom Bill's people never faltered. The documents were there when we needed them with all the *t*'s crossed and *i*'s dotted. The service side of the district was also running flat out. It's not a game of horseshoes. Close doesn't count. If the equipment isn't installed, the deal can't be booked. Tom Haywood's managers ramrodded a carefully orchestrated installation program that put a technician on location when the equipment was delivered—just-in-time installation!

THE TRUCK STOPS HERE

"How are we doing?"

"The number . . . what's the number?"

"Are we getting close?"

The questions were coming at me from all sides as we advanced deeper into June. I eased up on the pessimism just enough to trigger a final rush of energy. On Saturday, June 27, the final weekend before the end of the half, I was in Paul MacKinnon's office, looking over a printout of figures from other districts in the region.

"St. Louis is going to edge past us," I said.

Paul didn't respond immediately. He shook his head, still studying the figures. Paul talks like John Wayne—low and slow. "St. Louis is on a roll, but our district is working today and theirs isn't."

The bell kept ringing. On Monday and Tuesday, I was climbing the walls. Several orders were hanging fire. The customers had given us the okay, but last-minute details were still pending. At times, all of the phone lines were jammed as reps and managers conferred with Rochester or conducted conference calls with their accounts' principals. Reps who had exhausted their own prospect base were working the phones on behalf of their colleagues. Barb Mullen, for one, wasn't going to make her bonus that quarter, but nevertheless spent five hours sitting in the office of another rep's customer waiting for the deal to drop so she could contribute to the district's goal. Orders that even Paul and I figured didn't stand a chance started tumbling our way.

Signed orders or no signed orders, I arranged for the delivery trucks to be loaded with equipment and made ready to move out before the ink was dry on the contract.

And the bell kept ringing. A cheer would go up; applause; then the hubbub of activity would resume with another few ergs of enthusiasm behind it.

By Tuesday afternoon, with less than eight hours to go, I brought in backup delivery trucks in case of breakdowns. The last thing I needed was a flat tire to botch things up. I ordered the trucks to circle the block around the prospective customers, the drivers on cellular phones waiting to be told that the deals had been signed.

That evening, as was customary at the end of the month, we had our pizza-and-potato-chip vigil, a combination of work and play that can mean the difference between nosing across the finish line or falling short. Last-minute orders are accident-prone: the documentation might be incomplete, a form filled out incorrectly, a handwritten addendum illegible. Since my earliest days in Cleveland, I had turned the last night of the month, and particularly the last night of the quarter, into parties with snacks, cold cuts, pizza, and soft drinks to encourage the reps and managers to pitch in and help fight the bureaucratic brush-fires that flare up. There's nothing worse than going home at 5:00 P.M. thinking you've just managed to make plan for the month, and then to come in the next morning and find out that the crucial order never made it into the system because you weren't around to answer a question from Rochester or fill in a blank spot for the district administrative people.

Usually a couple of dozen people showed up. This time we were packed. I was still bouncing from admin to service and back to the reps' cubicles by the time 10:00 P.M. struck, the deadline for inputting orders. We all stood around the buffet table, letting the tension dissipate, still ready to respond if Rochester called to report a glitch.

Somebody rang the bell one last time before we headed home.

FLASHBACK

It was a long night of tossing and turning for me. I was in the office early the next morning to receive the report as soon as it was transmitted from Rochester. Our monthly business meeting was scheduled for 8:00 A.M., and the entire sales force, including the analysts, were in the amphitheater waiting, while I paced around Tom Bill's office waiting for the figures. Finally, after what seemed like hours and was probably only ten minutes, the results appeared on the computer screen. The number was unbelievable. I read it three times to make sure. Our monthly totals were second in the region, just behind Atlanta, which was twice the size of Cleveland.* We had written more than 500 orders in the last month alone, and hit the $7 million mark. It was a stunning success.

I went down to the amphitheater. A hush fell as I entered. As I stood there, gathering my composure, the memory of the first meeting with the Cleveland district flashed through my mind ("Close your eyes and imagine what it's like to win, to be the best. . . ."). I read the numbers, afraid my voice would crack, stepped back, and listened to the cheers.

FILLING IN THE BLANKS

So then what? I thought you'd ask that question. Having fought and won, like the infantry, the district went right back into the battle. And I decided the troops needed another general.

In the aftermath of the midyear turnaround, I did some serious soul-searching. Drivers who just manage to avoid head-on collisions with a hair-raising display of virtuoso skills at the wheel should congratulate themselves and then have their eyesight and reflexes checked. April wouldn't have happened if I hadn't let it happen.

The hardest thing for a leader to come to terms with is deciding when it's time to walk away. Early in 1992, sensing that I was beginning to lose focus, I had started putting out feelers. I was approached about going to Italy for Xerox—my last name ends with a vowel but I'm not fluent in Italian, which turned out to be a prerequisite; the company had some other intriguing ideas. After June 30, I knew I had taken the district as far as I could. I was thrilled by the May and June performance, which confirmed that the team was in its prime. Paul Mac-Kinnon has a special golf club, an iron, that is hinged to bend during practice sessions to warn the player that his backswing is faulty. If your form is really bad, it's like trying to hit the ball with a wet shoelace. Paul once went into a tournament after working with the special club and shot a hole in one off the first

* By this time, we were in the Vendor of Choice program (see Chapter 13 for my discussion of "Leap Out," the specially empowered sales districts), and our region was no longer a geographic entity but one that was composed of all the other VOC districts from around the country.

tee. His partners whooped and hollered, but Paul stepped back, smiled, nodded, and gave the thumbs-up sign, just as he had pictured himself doing in all his practice sessions with the club. Paul was prepared for the hole in one; prepared mentally and physically. He knew exactly where the ball was going to go and what he would do in response.

Preparation. The district was prepared to pull it out in the second quarter, and they did. I knew they would the moment I told them that I thought it was probably too late to recover. It never should have reached that point, though, and the greatest disservice I could do for them was to let them think we could go on playing come-from-behind ball.

If you're a great crisis manager—congratulations! But stop long enough to ask yourself, "Am I creating the crisis in the first place?" All too often the answer is yes. It may be burnout. Leading, whether you're a football coach, president of the United States, or a top business executive, is grueling. It eventually takes a toll. And if it doesn't, you haven't been working hard enough. My top ten tips in Chapter 7 apply to everyone. If it's hard to get out of bed or out of the shower in the morning, it's time for a new job.

Burnout may not be the problem, however. For a leader, every day is a new day. What worked to motivate and to energize your team yesterday may not work today. The challenge is to constantly come up with something new. It's probably the most demanding part of the job. The danger is not so much that the leader "hits the wall," as much as that he is "drawing a blank."

When I sat down in July and August of 1992 to review the situation one more time, I was drawing a blank when I asked, "How do I raise the bar on this group?"

Familiarity may not necessarily breed contempt, but it does result in complacency. After three or four years of "March Madness," "Cleveland Classic(s)," chalk talks, straight talk, and "talk like you walk," even the best team can start to go numb.

Here's the bottom line:

> Keep It Fresh

WARNING SIGNS

Write this down. Eventually, the magic fades. Expect it to happen. Look for these signs:

- The same mistakes—yours and the team's.
- Inconsistency.
- The basics aren't being executed smoothly.
- Extraordinary efforts are needed to accomplish ordinary goals.
- Your superstars start marking time.
- Meetings go dull and flat.
- Too much reminiscing about last year or last quarter.
- You put off decisions or hesitate to offer tough but fair criticism.
- You're the last to hear about a problem or important development.

REPETITIVE COMMOTION SYNDROME

Start at the top of the list. Repeating the same mistakes over and over again is a clear indication that you are not inspecting. When we launched the ill-starred 5046 in 1988, I made a mistake. I delegated responsibility to Bill Hookway, who, taking his cue from me, delegated to a specially chosen team of reps. Then, he and I sat back while the whole launch was fumbled. It was painful to watch. I almost got up and left the room. I also considered stopping the whole thing midway. And that's what I should have done, but I didn't want to hurt anybody's feelings. The reps had worked hard on the presentation.

What I learned from the experience was that a product launch is too important to treat as a "learning experience" or as an exercise in empowerment. I should have stood up, halted the proceedings, and explained why. More than six years after the fact, I discovered when I commented aloud about the disastrous 5046 launch that there were managers and reps in Cleveland who were under the impression that it was an effective launch.

Had I spoken up at the time, that notion would have died on the spot.

Contrast the 5046 with the DocuTech launch. I watched the preparations like a hawk. I asked those involved for updates every day. We never had a product launch fiasco after the 5046. If we had, it would have told me that it was time to play pin the tail on the donkey—and that I was the donkey.

But remember, I'm talking about making the *same* mistakes. If you take chances—and you must!—there will be mistakes. When Friday rolls around and I haven't made a mistake that week, I begin to worry that I haven't been taking risks, and haven't been creative. I try to avoid holding formal meetings, but I'll convene them in a shot to review mistakes. The operative question is always, "What went wrong and how do we prevent it from happening again?"

THE OLDEST CON: INCONSISTENCY

The purpose of developing and executing a process is to maintain consistency. Ralph Waldo Emerson said, "A foolish consistency is the hobgoblin of little minds." But there's nothing foolish about a consistent process.

When things start turning erratic, look at your process. Very often it means you have one but you aren't using it. There are more processes out there than junk bonds, and many of them are orphans.

When I first got to Cleveland, the district wasn't bothering to using XAMP—Xerox Account Management Process. Why? No one could answer that question. It wouldn't have been so bad if XAMP had been ignored in favor of a better, homegrown process. There wasn't anything. Talk about inconsistency! Every major account rep and manager had a different way of doing business —some good, some bad. One month, a rep would be flying high, the next month he or she would crash in flames.

BLESSED ARE THE BASICS

Blocking and tackling are what football is all about. If the basics aren't sound, everything else crumbles. When Cleveland was digging itself into a hole in the winter and spring of 1992, its order rate was falling off. That should have told me trouble was brewing, but I ignored it. I probably could have gone back at that time to see if the reps were still making their minimum number of four calls a day. I bet they weren't. My assumption was that any team that had broken so many sales records would as a matter of habit keep making a high number of calls. Dream on!

EXTRAORDINARY-ORDINARY CAUTIONARY

This one is a dead giveaway. We had an extraordinary-ordinary incident in 1991 that did not escape my attention, and it was one of the reasons we had such a good year. The district was about to close the largest single copier deal in its history. All the terms had been worked out. There was nothing left to do but sign on the bottom line and uncork the champagne. My boss, Joe Valenti, even flew in for the occasion.

It was a big day for us and for the customer, Nancy Vetrone, president of Original Copy, Inc. She was as happy as we were. The appointed hour arrived, we gathered in her conference room for a last read-through of the contract, and what happens? Sh— happens, that's what. Remember the corollary to Murphy's Law (what can't go wrong will go wrong)? We had messed up the contract—big time. What she thought we understood, we didn't understand. What we thought she understood, she didn't understand. Ordinary communication had broken down. As I attempted to patch the problems, other errors popped to the surface. The rep got so rattled that Fred Thomas took him for a walk to settle him down. Fred later told me that once they were alone, he asked him, "What the hell did you do with that contract????"

Meanwhile, my boss was flipping out, and I could hardly blame him. Joe suggested we back off and return to the office before the deal went belly-up permanently. Again, I turned to Fred and whispered, "Get him out of here . . . I'm not leaving until we sign this thing." Seven hours later, I was still at it. Finally, we put Humpty-Dumpty back together again.

Weeks later, Joe Valenti encountered one of our reps in an

elevator. He was still brooding about the situation. "You guys sure messed that one up," Joe growled. As the door opened and the rep got out, he said, "Ah, Joe, they're all like that." I laughed when he told me about it, but if they had all been like that I would immediately have asked for a transfer.

STAR GRAZING

The superstars are the first to notice and react to a leader who has lost his or her edge. There won't be a drastic decline in performance, but the overachievers will start throttling back. I'm not sure why; one possibility is they're not getting the care and feeding they need—or the pushing and prodding—to maintain peak performance.

One way to look at it is in terms of an analogy with a formula-one race car. If that machine isn't getting tune-ups, meticulous maintenance, and the highest-octane fuel, it will probably make it around the track, but its record-breaking days are over.

Another factor is that an organization's top people are operating near the outer limits of their skills and capacity, always pushing themselves as far as they can go. The slightest change in the level of support they receive is significantly magnified.

MEETING MALAISE

A dull meeting means two things: you're having too many of them, and they aren't accomplishing anything. As far as I'm concerned, meetings are a last resort. I only call them if there is no other way of achieving the objective. My meeting phobia is a reaction to a corporate culture—Xerox's—that once treated meetings with the same reverence communion receives in the Roman Catholic Church. The all-day meeting used to be quite common, but in recent years we've taught ourselves to make better use of our time.

I use meetings to test-market ideas, brainstorm, and problem-solve. They tend to be very freewheeling. I want controversy and clashes; yet I expect the participants to listen to and respect contrary opinions. When a decision has been made and we leave the room, we leave united.

Looking back on the runup to the April '92 flop, I'd say our meetings turned into mutual-congratulation sessions without the snap, crackle, and pop of the previous three years.

PAST PERFECT

When you start strolling down memory lane, the best days are behind you. For one thing, it tells me that the present isn't as satisfying as the past. The lack of truly challenging goals will trigger a nostalgia trip. We spent a good four months reliving the glory days of 1991, and if half of that wasted time and energy had been redirected to 1992, there wouldn't have been a problem.

MR. OR MS. MAÑANA

Procrastination is one of the leader's deadliest sins. The more you delay, the worse things get. But one reason you fall into the trap is to avoid rocking the boat. After all, the boat just won the America's Cup.

Believe me, as your organization becomes more and more successful, it does not get any easier to make tough decisions that affect people's lives or to step up and deliver bad news. It gets harder, actually. Friendship, shared experiences, war stories, you-were-there-when-I-needed-you camaraderie become major impediments.

CIRCUIT BREAKERS

If the leader is the last to know, his communication system has short-circuited. Fortunately, this hasn't happened to me, at least to my knowledge (maybe I'm the last to know?). I have the opposite problem: I'm often the first to know. My office seems like a confessional some days. I hear about marital breakups, alcoholism, and other serious problems. One day, a rep starting talking about suicide. Want to be a leader? Okay, but you'll never know what's about to walk through the door.

But—but—if those sorts of things aren't walking through the door it probably means you are not making contact with your people. There's a barrier they can't get over or around. When was the last time one of your people came to you for advice about a personal matter? Months ago? Never? Ask yourself why.

THERE WE ARE

I bombarded myself with questions for the rest of the summer. "What next?" was foremost among them. My bosses were encouraging me to get my ticket punched by doing a few years in Rochester. Julie and I talked it over and talked it over again. She's a Columbus, Ohio native, and Rochester is a long way from home. She had moved without a complaint to Minnesota and then to Cleveland.

By August, we had decided. Unbeknownst to the others in the district, Pat Elizondo was officially designated as my successor. I had brought her to Cleveland in the first place and had been saying openly for more than a year that if and when I made a move, Pat would get the district manager's job. It wasn't my decision to make, but wisely, Xerox saw her tremendous abilities and there was never any doubt. Before the change was announced, Julie and I threw a party for Fred Thomas, who was also being promoted to a top job as a national account manager. We pulled out all the stops. The whole sales management staff was there. We ate and drank and danced. At three in the morning we were standing shoulder to shoulder in the kitchen singing James Taylor songs. Looking back, it seemed a little like the last episode of "The Mary Tyler Moore Show"; misty-eyed, mellow, just right.

I didn't mention my plans. I'd do that in September, in the amphitheater one last time to introduce Pat to her new district team. That could wait for a few more weeks, though. It was

Fred's night, but it was our way to say thank you to all of them
—thank you and good-bye.*

* The wind blows hard off the lake in Cleveland and it can pierce the heaviest
garments. But, Cleveland, I will always remember your warmth. Let me recognize the men and women of the Cleveland district one last time and let you
know that I owe all my success to you. You met every challenge and put up with
me for more than four years. I miss you—thanks again.

15

TOUGH LOVE:

A LETTER HOME

I'm a golf nut. It's a wonderful sport, and good things always happen when I'm out on the golf course, even if my game is off. In the spring of 1992, I was on a putting green in Hilton Head, South Carolina, with my boss, Joe Valenti. We were making small talk about business. Between practice shots I said, "If anything opens up in Columbus, keep me in mind." Six months later, I was manager of the central Ohio district and Julie was house hunting in her hometown.

Aside from being the birthplace of Jack Nicklaus, Columbus is an important city in Xerox's scheme of things. It's the hub of a booming area that's headquarters for several major national and international corporations, the campus of Ohio State University, the capital of Ohio, and the site of the sprawling Wright-Patterson Air Force Base.

In business terms, the district is slightly smaller in size but roughly equivalent to Cleveland and northeast Ohio—or should be. The reason Joe pounced on my comment was that he had a problem with Columbus. For the previous three or four years, the district's performance had been about as lackluster as Cleveland's record was prior to 1988. I became the solution to Joe's problem; and another one, as well: how to rejuvenate Columbus, and what to do with the "maverick manager" with the "rebel style," to use a couple of phrases from *The Wall Street Journal*'s September 1991 article about the Cleveland comeback.

The *Journal* story provoked praise and, unfortunately, hard feelings. Paul Allaire, our CEO, immediately called to congratulate me, but a few others thought I was slamming them personally when I was quoted as saying that Xerox's financial managers "sit up there in an ivory tower and don't know the potential of a business."

It was a controversial thing to say, particularly when a newspaper writer homes in on the zippiest quotes, which stand out vividly in a 2,000-word article, whereas the same comment would probably go unnoticed in another context. Basically, what I was getting at was my aversion to the word "no." I never think of no; instead, my preoccupation is what can be done to meet the customer's legitimate requirements and get the business.

As I noted in the introduction to this book, the *Journal* created the impression that I was a gunslinger. I'm not, and I hope you agree after having come this far with me. After the article appeared, the people from Cleveland who went off to Leesburg for training or to other Xerox functions would run into comments like "Hey, you sure must hate working for a guy like that." The arguments that followed tended to be pretty heated, and I heard that my reps and managers would get so angry that they'd almost end up in fistfights.

I'm ambitious. I'd like to run Xerox someday. However, Paul MacKinnon, to whom I owe about 99 percent of my success in Cleveland, says that the moment the *Wall Street Journal* article appeared, I no longer had a future at Xerox. I hope Padre's wrong. I believe you get ahead in this country by doing your job well. If that ever stops being the case, we're in big trouble.

By opting to go to Columbus, I passed up several other enticing offers from Xerox. Julie had misgivings about leaving Ohio, and in the end I couldn't stomach the idea of sitting in Rochester at a desk and not being out on the front lines. My allergic reaction to corporate politics and bureaucracy is my greatest weakness as a fast-track executive. Maybe I've swerved into the slow lane, and maybe that's where I belong.

In the first half of 1993, the central Ohio district went from nearly dead last in the region to second in the nation. Sound familiar? The methods I've been discussing in this book work. Want to see me do it again? I'll take any five Xerox districts—I'm talking about the ones that are in the bottom third of the sales standings—combined into a single region or other administrative entity, and double their revenue in five years. What happened in Cleveland, and again in Columbus, proves that the leadership and management techniques I've been sharing with you in this book will work anywhere. Cleveland didn't just turn around on its own. Nor did Columbus. They were *turned* around, just as we can turn around troubled and failing businesses and industries all across this country if we just . . . go do it!

It Ain't Over Till It's an Overview

Just go do what? First, reread this book. Actually, you don't have to; I'll make it even easier. In the next few pages, I'm going to break out some of the tips and techniques we've been discussing and present them outside the text and narrative in which they were originally presented. I want to give you a quick refresher and overview of what we've been considering. The bad thing about books is that important stuff gets lost in all the verbiage. I've told you how I strip away all the camouflage, so there won't be any hiding places and excuses for failure. I'm doing the same thing here: ripping out the verbal undergrowth so you can be the best manager and leader that you can be.

First Things First
(from Chapter 1)

- Make changes immediately.
- Reestablish the work ethic.
- The first order of business: start *doing business* again.
- Set a blistering pace at the outset.
- Make a statement.
- Tell 'em where they're headed.

- Keep the lines of communication short, simple, and direct. Trickle-down communications guarantee confusion and misunderstanding.
- Recognize. . . . Praise doesn't cost anything and it yields big dividends.
- Tell someone (every day) that he or she did a good job and that you appreciate the effort.
- Benchmark: if it is being done elsewhere, do it too and do it better.
- Listen hard. Then look at what other people are actually *doing*.
- Call a major account and ask questions: "What's wrong and how can you and I fix it?" You'll get an earful from your customers.
- Never assume anything (unless it's the worst).
- Gather statistics.
- Don't be afraid to ask questions . . . questions, questions, questions.
- Impose consequences. If there are no consequences for failure to achieve minimum standards, then those standards will not be met.
- Expect and inspect.
- Don't allow support functions to get in the way of business.
- Find some powerful symbols and use them.
- Relentlessly pursue excellence.
- Don't let anything stop you from reaching your goals.
- Be who you say you are.
- Show no tolerance for cynicism, backbiting, finger-pointing.
- Satisfy the customer.
- Offer a vision: a leader must give his people a vision that will motivate them to do their very best.
- Be tough, be fair.

TOUCH IT, TASTE IT, FEEL IT
(from Chapter 2)

- The more people you put on the fast track, the more fast-track talent will be attracted to your operation.
- Find a mentor. Find a dozen. Use them as role models and sounding boards.

- Get the operation up and running while the competition is still in bed.
- Take it personally when the competition scores.
- Accept the fact that there will always be some cynics, but don't be intimidated by them into silence, and keep talking to the good ones.
- If you don't mind being beaten by the competition—then you'd better get used to losing.
- Remind everyone how good it feels to win.

A VISION OF WINNING

Here's a technique for rediscovering the thrill of winning that I often use to open meetings. I've put together a videotape of final, exciting moments in football games; a collage of action shots and excitement: players racing across the goal line and flinging down the football, clenched fists and high fives, the crowd going wild. I play the tape with the sound track cranked up full blast. When it's over, I ask the people in the room to stand up and celebrate. "You've just gone over the top. You're the number one district in the United States—boogie!"

- In taking over a new, troubled business organization it is safe to assume that the will to win is either absent or badly depleted.
- Maybe you're the problem. Have you failed to simply state your minimum level of expectations?
- Having fun on the job is the most effective preventive medicine.
- The absentee rate can work as an accurate barometer if you compare it with previous years and other parts of the organization. If it's up, start wondering whether your people are looking for reasons why they shouldn't come to work. It's your responsibility to make the working environment exciting and irresistible.

- Customer contact is the lifeblood of sales.
- Ask yourself what it is that drives your business. Once you've identified it, you'll know what has to be done every day, day in and day out, to keep the doors open.
- Less is not—not, not, not—more! More is more. The more a sales force gets out in front of the customer, the more things happen: leads begin to materialize, the rep's familiarity with the territory grows, he or she learns to present the product more effectively, and success starts breeding success.
- Ask your best people, the strongest performers, to do more.
- Listen closely to the shop talk that is going on around you. What are the managers and reps talking about? If I start hearing a lot of complaints about the customers, I get worried.
- Those with a well-developed will to win aren't talking about problems; they're talking about opportunities.
- The quickest fix is to start with yourself and make sure that you're totally focused on making success happen.
- Mistakes. Don't be afraid to make them—once.
- Transform setbacks into the basis for the next success.

THE TALLEST SHIP: LEADERSHIP
(from Chapter 3)

- Are you a manager or a leader? There's a difference, a big difference.
- Slashing away at people is a favorite short-term expedient. It actually can scare an operation into action, but not for long.
- Leadership starts with people.
- What you need in a turnaround situation is respect for people. If it's not there, please do something else with your career. Forget management.
- Tell them what has to happen. Don't pull your punches. Make them straight and hard. I call it hardball with a heart.
- I want the strongest performers to help energize the not-so-strong.
- A leader has got to walk like he talks. Don't just tell them, show them.
- Words aren't enough. Action. Action that implements the words. Both have got to be absolutely clear and unmistakable.

- What a leader must establish is that the unusual is now usual.
- Get out of the office to gather firsthand information.
- Give your people backup and support . . . you are a resource.
- If you don't plan to win, you plan to lose.
- The rep should be there not just as an order taker but as a resource for the customer.
- Ask the customer, "Where do we stand?" "How long does it take the purchasing committee to grant approval?" "What can I do to speed up the process?"
- Listen to the customers. They will tell you exactly what's going on.
- Learn the art of impatience. Keep pushing for action and answers now.
- Learn the art of patience. Keep trying, pushing, probing. Never give up. Quick results always make me wonder if the objectives were too cautious and easily obtainable.
- The art of leadership is mastered by those who get their hands dirty practicing the craft of leadership.
- Two words come to mind to describe effective leaders: passion and premeditation.
- Six more leadership words: devotion, vision, communication, fairness, toughness, responsibility.

BUSINESS IS A CONTACT SPORT
(from Chapter 4)

- Get in contact with your customers and stay in contact.

COMMON CUSTOMER COMPLAINTS

- "We're not treated like a major account."
- "Your own team members don't talk to each other."
- "I didn't appreciate the way your rep went over my head."
- "I don't trust the proposal that has been delivered."
- "You're just trying to jam products in . . . we've been oversold."
- "You're inflexible."
- "You didn't understand my requirements."
- "You were sore losers when we chose another vendor."
- "I didn't know you offered that product."
- "I haven't seen anyone from senior management in ten years."
- "I don't feel that I'm important to you."

- Don't create a fool's paradise by isolating yourself from the customer.
- Drop everything when a customer calls.
- Expose your bosses to the customer.
- Keep a list of "must do" chores, and put this one on it: Tell everyone that a surefire way *not* to win points with the boss is to withhold unpleasant information.
- Hate surprises.
- Winning isn't much fun if nobody knows about it. By making each deal a public event, you ensure that the successful people get a little instant recognition and gratification.
- Listen to advice and keep an open mind—and don't be afraid to change it.
- Make it fun!
- Ask: "Do you enjoy coming to work?" An honest answer will

explain almost everything. It will explain why productivity is down and absenteeism is up, why quality is poor and customer satisfaction so abysmal, and explain the reason for high employee turnover, low stock prices, and angry shareholders. Why? It's not fun to come to work.

- A leader must step up to this responsibility even if it means erecting a wall that inhibits friendship. It's one of the hazards of the job.
- I'll fight for my people when they're right, and when they're not—I'll tell them and work with them to find an acceptable accommodation.
- Tell your people explicitly what you are going to do *for them*. Don't weasel around.
- Make a commitment. Hand it out, post it on the bulletin board, and live by it. Never back off.
- Review your accounts, top to bottom. "If it wiggles, I want to know about it."

REVIEW, POWER VIEW
(from Chapter 5)

- Carefully timed incentives boost sales performance higher and higher.
- Random, scattershot incentives are counterproductive.
- If the basic process is not in place and functioning smoothly, incentives can be a distraction.
- Major Suspect List Reviews: the objective is to force the reps to take a cold, hard look at each customer, spread out over 365 days.
- Set specific targets for each account and the next question is simple: "What are you going to do to generate that level of business?"
- I refuse to accept generalities. Generalities tell me the rep is winging it.
- The MSLR forces the rep to put his or her accounts and assumptions under the microscope. They should be doing that as a matter of course—but they probably aren't. No one has ever asked them to. What you have to do as a leader is ask.

ACCOUNT REVIEW QUESTIONS

- Tell me what's going to happen ninety days from now.
- Show me what each account has and tell me this: What are you doing for each one?
- What's the organizational structure for each account?
- Who makes the decisions?
- What's the competitive situation?
- What help do you need?
- What are you doing to knock out the competition?

- Don't bother doing the MSLR if you aren't going to follow up. It's like going to the trouble of inventing a cure for cancer and then never using it.

WHY REVIEW?

The object is to get the accounts—and the rep—up to potential. I rarely raise my voice. It's much more effective to say, "You can do better than this," pointing out the fact-based reasons why. And implicitly—or explicitly—the next line is: "And I'm here to help you do it." If you don't have the background and the skills to assess the situation accurately and to help that individual, he or she should be the manager—not you.

- Go to your strongest person—the one with depth of knowledge, high energy, and confidence—and throw him or her smack-dab into the middle of the district's toughest assignment.
- Give the best people visibility, rewards, and running room.
- Inexperienced or mediocre reps simply do not get beneath the surface of their business. The good ones do.

- There's no team without team leaders. The Major Suspect List Review process will supply you with potential leaders—providing that you are willing to put those individuals where they belong.
- Get help! You can't do it all yourself.
- First you find good people—*then* you empower them.
- The idea of empowering untrained, unmotivated, untested people is ridiculous. You're asking for a disaster.
- I want my people to act as though they were independent entrepreneurs.
- I pass along as much of my power as possible to the managers under me, and they are expected to hand it down to the reps.
- Look around and determine how you can strip yourself of power.
- The process I'm presenting to you in this book is based squarely on *continuous* inspection. Anybody who would empower without inspecting would probably enjoy a nice little game of Russian roulette.

TALK TO ME
(from Chapter 6)

- Most business organizations communicate badly.
- I force my managers to chunk (organize and absorb information) at the end of our monthly outlook meetings by going around the table and asking them to give me instant feedback on the meeting. I want them to tell me what we accomplished, whether we wasted time, to prioritize decisions that have been made.
- Open your ears and cruise the office several times a day. I'm listening all the time: snatches of phone conversations, the banter that's being exchanged between reps, shop talk.
- An office is like a baseball dugout. The chatter is very revealing. There's a healthy hum—you know the sound when you hear it—and an unhealthy silence or rumbling.
- Quick forays out into the office also give me time for mini-inspections. A few brief questions will tell me who's following through and who isn't.

GET PERSONAL

When I stop at a rep's desk, I always begin by asking about his or
her family. And I'm not just doing it for the sake of politeness.
What I hear about the family tells me a lot about how that person
is functioning on the job. If I pick up the scent of family problems,
and it comes as a surprise, I know that either my managers haven't
been keeping me informed, or they're not informed themselves.

- I want to be the first to know of a birth, an illness, a divorce,
  or a death. Why? I want to be able to provide whatever assistance I can. It's the right thing to do.
- As a manager, you cannot expect people to give 150 percent
  and to work long hours that might otherwise be spent with
  their families if you aren't going to be there when they need
  you. When your people know that, they will break down walls
  for you.
- You can have the most powerful vision and the greatest process, but without effective communication you're dead in the
  water. Cruising the office is one way to cross-check information from other sources. Managers who limit themselves to a
  few channels of communication are always in danger of being
  fed misinformation—advertently or inadvertently.
- Constantly communicate overall objectives.
- Don't be afraid to repeat yourself. Drive the message home.
- Use manager-rep contracts to communicate. The contract is a
  simple one- or two-page document that outlines what the *individual* will do to deliver the team's plan.
- The reps' contracts are the basis for the overall business plan.
  The manager merely coordinates, orchestrates, and fine-tunes.
- Buy-in is essential.
- Arbitrarily imposed standards from the top—particularly
  when it's a question of going beyond minimal levels of expectation—make it difficult to achieve voluntary and enthusiastic
  compliance. The contract promotes buy-in because the individual sets the terms to start with.

- Meet with each of your employees at length at least twice a year for personnel reviews (use the contracts), general information gathering, and feedback.
- If your personnel reviews are used as an instrument of terror and torture—don't waste your time.
- If your personnel reviews are a headache and a burden—don't waste your time.
- If your personnel reviews are subjective and unquantifiable—don't waste your time.
- You choose either communication or isolation. There's no alternative.

NAIL IT TO THE MAST
(from Chapter 7)

TOP TEN TIPS

1. Prepare customer proposals on weekends and evenings.
2. Never say no to a customer—everything is negotiable.
3. Make customers feel good about you, not just your product.
4. Meet customer requirements, even if it means fighting your own bureaucracy.
5. Do things for customers you don't get paid for.
6. Know your competitor's product better than your competitor does.
7. Be early for meetings.
8. Dress and groom yourself sharply so you "look like a superior product."
9. When it's time to go home, make one more telephone call.
10. If you stay in the shower a long time in the morning because you don't look forward to work—find another job.

WORK IN PROGRESS: TEAM BUILDING
(from Chapter 8)

- If you work for me and let yourself fail, I won't let you hide from the consequences of that failure.
- I want all reps and managers to know how they stack up against their peers. And I make it public knowledge. The rankings are posted and announced at each business meeting.
- Tear down the walls between individuals. Build a team.
- Once a process has been established and functioning for about three months, throw your team managers together for an old-fashioned bull session.
- I want the teams to compete, but I don't want feuding and factionalism. When teams compare notes in a freewheeling atmosphere, it reinforces the notion the district is the ultimate team. Nobody wins unless we all win.
- The exchange of best practices is particularly useful. I don't want anyone to hoard an effective idea just to get an edge on his or her colleagues. My goal is to make sure a best practice gets the widest possible circulation.
- Don't try to conquer the world with every incentive program. It's nice to increase your sales dramatically, but just achieving a sense of excitement and fun can yield long-term benefits.
- Look for big and small ways to throw your people together. Incentive and recognition events are ready-made for building camaraderie and team spirit.
- Don't just pay the rent. If you have to use special incentives to achieve minimal sales levels, something's wrong. Either your process is faulty or you've got the wrong people in the wrong places. A third possibility is that you or your bosses are overestimating the sales potential of your territories.
- Small visions are a waste of time. The big ones generate excitement and enthusiasm. Without those two ingredients very little—big or small—can be achieved.
- Am I saying that a leader should set unrealistic and unattainable goals? No, not at all. What I'm pointing up is the need for a little bit of show business. Every leader needs some.

QUALITY TIME
(from Chapter 9)

- Leadership Through Quality is Xerox's version of Total Quality Control. The heart and soul of it is the customer.
- Quality is whatever the customer said (or thinks) it is.
- Forget about a corporate quality program if the man or woman at the top isn't on board.
- The other mistake about quality is impatience. Quality doesn't happen overnight.
- Quality cannot be up and running in two or three years. You'll *never* be finished with the job.
- You can't fall in love with your game plan, no matter how good you think it is.
- Always have a fallback. In fact, I have fallbacks for my fallbacks.
- Assume something will go wrong.
- Always look for ways to do something a little different.
- Be a boredom buster. Surprise your people.
- Don't decide for the customer—and that should be chiseled into a slab of granite.
- To establish a quality movement in your company, you've got to set up a mechanism to identify customer requirements.
- Do you want to know customers' requirements? Ask them.
- Any company that does not use its sales force as a detective agency ought to find some good bankruptcy lawyers. The sales reps are your eyes and ears.
- The reason I ask my people so many questions is that I want them to adopt the same habit. They aren't going to be able to answer my questions until they start asking the customer questions.

The proposal is the most important document you have with a customer. It can make or break a deal, and make or break a business relationship.

What a proposal shouldn't be:
- A one-page price quote
- Over five pages long
- Sent in the mail
- A form letter
- A fill-in-the-blanks form
- Inaccurate
- Sloppy
- Untyped
- Incomprehensible without supporting material

And what a proposal should include:
- An executive summary
- Customer input
- Benefits and key applications
- Review of customer requirements
- Comparisons
- References
- Details on service and support
- Recommendations and cost

- Make my day, month, year—compete with me on the basis of price!
- If you're not identifying and satisfying customer requirements, you're not "doing" quality.
- If you're not involving and empowering your employees, you're not "doing" quality.
- If there's no benchmarking or fact-based management, you're not "doing" quality.
- If you think you'd like to initiate a quality movement in your company, forget it unless you and the other managers are willing to throw away the book on what constitutes good management and begin to coach and counsel.

- You need to be a fanatic when it comes to gathering statistics and other forms of data (but don't just collect them—use them).
- To all aspiring MBAs I would say: statistics—the more the better. And for MBA candidates who pride themselves on having good instincts, this piece of advice: good instincts and good statistics are even better.
- You don't delight the customer without delighting your employees. Can't happen.

CAN'T GET MORE SATISFACTION
(from Chapter 10)

- Complete customer satisfaction—100 percent—is the only intelligent goal.
- You've got to demand of yourself—for starters—and everyone around you, that whatever is done is done first-class.
- It's so important that I would like to see every employee's compensation directly tied to customer satisfaction.
- If a manager is just paying lip service to customer satisfaction, he or she will live to regret it.
- Customer dissatisfaction is not the problem—it's a symptom of the problem.
- Invest the time in identifying the (customer satisfaction) problem. Beware of easy answers. The quick fix can be a killer.
- Selling is only part of the job. If customer satisfaction is being neglected, you're not earning your paycheck.
- Customer satisfaction starts with you. It isn't a game of hot potato.
- You live and die by follow-up and follow-through.
- Be a pest when it comes to follow-up.
- A leader has to provide role models for the behavior he or she wants to see in action.
- Tell your employees a customer with a problem blows out all other priorities.
- In a highly competitive environment, businesses do not have time to make mistakes. You have to do it right the first time.
- I'm not saying that managers have to be loved or win popular-

ity contests. Employee satisfaction must rest squarely on professional respect.

BEFORE THE FALL
(from Chapter 11)

- Success does spoil winning teams. In many ways, it's easier to get on top than to stay on top.
- The successful leader—to remain successful—must constantly change the definition of what constitutes winning.
- The challenge was—and is—to keep the vision fresh and alive in order to create a permanent culture of success.
- Don't take yourself so seriously that you can't give your people something to laugh about and to cheer about.
- Never let the brass come and go without exposing them to a question-and-answer session with your people. It's good for the boss, good for them.
- External *and* internal competition are essential. Internal competition gets you sharp and keeps you sharp. It's the equivalent of daily practice drills on the football field; run the plays, block and tackle.
- If external competition sets the rules of engagement, you become reactive rather than proactive.
- Don't just beat the competition—crush it.
- New business is synonymous with growth.
- Grow or die.
- When my people turn in their thirty-, sixty-, and ninety-day plans, I want to see new names.
- When things are going great today, it's time to panic about tomorrow.
- If business is booming, get nervous and start increasing the effort to insure that new business will be there in the future. Don't slough off on this chore.
- Always seek to pull business forward. Why wait sixty or ninety days? Do it now!
- Organizations that push for new business without closely monitoring customer satisfaction—among old and new customers—run the risk of having their customer base crumble without warning.

- Don't be cowed into treating the Japanese with kid gloves. That doesn't mean we should bash them. Beat them fair and square.
- Communication breaks down when isolated pockets of information are allowed to exist. You've got to wire up your organization to avoid the "If I had only known" syndrome.
- Many times, selling the customer is only part of the job. You've got to sell your own bosses. More deals go south because salespeople are afraid to sell internally. It's never easy.

REAL PEOPLE
(from Chapter 12)

- You'll wallow in mediocrity unless and until you find the best people.
- Don't rush the "people decisions."
- Don't rearrange bodies, hiring and firing, until you really know what's going on in your operation.
- The best thing about setting a blistering pace is that it is easy to spot the stragglers.
- If you flinch from moving the dysfunctional people, the message is demoralizing: "Hard work is for suckers." It's basic human nature. Why should I knock myself out when the guy next door is allowed to coast?
- Get in there early and help stragglers save their jobs. When and if it finally comes time to cut them loose, you'll know— and so will they—there is no other choice.
- Poor performance? Put it in writing.
- It's the manager's responsibility to work with the employee, not to just lean back and watch rigor mortis set in.
- The manager's job is to do everything in his power to save the employee. If the manager can't or won't coach and counsel his people, why does he have the job?
- Don't try to slip a termination through quietly. You've got to be open and aboveboard. Personnel should never be blindsided.
- Don't ever fire anyone in a fit of anger. In fact, don't do anything in a fit of anger.
- I do not look at a corrective-action process as inevitably lead-

ing to termination. It's a way to avoid a worst-case outcome. At the first sign of trouble, therefore, I opt for corrective action. I don't want that employee to miss a single day that he or she could be using to improve.

- Corrective action has nothing to do with being "a nice guy." It's not nice to fail. It's not nice to allow others to fail.
- One year, I had more people on corrective action than any other district in the region. I also sent more reps to President's Club than any other district.
- Here's a quick way to determine whether your organization has a people problem: Look in the recruitment file. When was the last time a job candidate was interviewed? If it was more than a month ago, you've got people problems.
- Recruitment isn't a chore; it isn't drudgery. It is an absolute necessity.
- If that recruitment file isn't chock-full of the best candidates at all times, you're going to end up rushing around trying to fill a vacancy out of a shallow, lackluster talent pool.
- Make recruiting a top priority, and don't delegate it to others or expect the personnel department to handle the dirty work.
- There is no difference between sports and business when it comes to the hiring process. Slipshod recruiting will give you a slipshod organization.
- Do some benchmarking. Identify colleagues who have been notably successful at hiring good people and get them to tell you how they do it.
- Collect recruiting techniques the way some people collect stamps.
- Your customers know all about the competition. Find out who they're most impressed by and go hire them.
- If a rep tells me that his competition is good, my first reaction is to say, "Let's see if we can steal her away."
- I believe in consensus hiring. A candidate is interviewed by each of my managers. They're asked for a thumbs-up or -down. If one of them says not to hire, the candidate is rejected. It's got to be unanimous. I want to be able to have the flexibility to put the new employee on any team. The last thing I need to hear is "I don't have faith in the guy," or "I told you I didn't like her, give her to somebody else."

- Job interviews: What I'm looking for is candidates' ability to think on their feet, to stay calm and cool.
- Today, many job interviewees are preprogrammed and carefully prepared. I want to strip off the facade and see what's underneath. I'll ask for their role models, get them to talk about their parents, and encourage them to elaborate on the toughest moment in their lives.
- I like to find out how the candidate financed his or her college education. If mom and dad paid all the bills, I wonder if the person is ready to confront the real world.
- My role-model question is also important. If the candidate doesn't have one—and it happens—I suspect he hasn't thought about what he wants out of life. He may lack standards and direction.

SMARTS
(from Chapter 13)

- Training: If you're not providing it to your people—shame on you! If your people aren't gulping down every morsel of training you provide—shame on them!
- Companies are shortsighted—no, make that just plain stupid —to begrudge their employees adequate training.
- As a manager, I make it quite clear that when the trainee returns to the district, I expect to see what he or she learned immediately put into action.
- Training must be an ongoing process, otherwise skill levels become spotty. A rep will handle a few products or services well and bumble through the rest.
- I include a training module in almost every presentation I make to my district.
- I tell my managers to conduct training in the car while they're traveling from appointment to appointment with their reps: "Here's what I thought you did well at the last call. Now, what you need to concentrate on is this. . . ."
- Cold calling is boot camp.
- Telemarketing is touted as a way to avoid the agony and inefficiency of cold calling. There's some truth to that; however,

for sheer training purposes, I would hate to see cold calling eliminated.

- Always go for the close. Get the person to commit in some *way* to some*thing*, large or small.
- I think of the sales sequence as a long stairway. To get to the top, I've got to proceed step-by-step, close-by-close.
- Fight the bureaucracy: issue an open invitation to all the ivory-tower types who could use an education in the art, science, and black magic of knocking on doors until the knuckles bleed. Take a few days every year to temporarily join the infantry and see the world.
- Here's some advice for dealing with salespeople who are trying to sell you something on a cold call, or at any other time. If they're zombies, forget it. You can usually judge the quality of a product by the sales rep. If they're not excited about what they're selling, you should be very wary.
- The big-deal hang-up: Demand a mix of small and major orders. It's smart psychology and strategy.
- Strategically, a manager who becomes dependent on major deals is asking for trouble. All you need to do is miss one and it's "trouble in River City."
- Constantly writing small orders keeps a sales force revved up.

MAIL IN THE KEYS
(from Chapter 14)

- Take my advice: Never stop inspecting. Take another piece of advice—please: Increase your inspections after there's been a highly successful run.
- You can't expect to get your organization to peak performance levels and then keep it there by lapsing into a caretaker mode.
- Organizations simply do not run themselves no matter how good the process or previous track record. The very best of them lose momentum very quickly; perhaps even faster than mediocre teams that never take risks or set high standards in the first place.
- I now have to break the bad news—it's all about winning *all* of the time. Once you climb on the escalator, you can't get off.

- It's easy to start thinking that success breeds success. It doesn't. Unremitting effort breeds success. It's a life sentence, with no time off for good behavior.
- Know the difference between suspects and prospects. No shortcuts. Long- and short-term planning documents are useless if they are compromised with phantom prospects.
- The hardest thing for a leader to master is coming to terms with deciding when it's time to walk away.
- Leading, whether you're a football coach, president of the United States, or a top business executive, is grueling. It eventually takes a toll. And if it doesn't, you haven't been working hard enough.
- What worked to motivate and to energize your team yesterday may not work today. The challenge is to constantly come up with something new.
- Eventually, the magic fades. Expect it to happen.

TIME TO GO? HERE ARE THE SIGNS

1. The same mistakes—yours and the team's.
2. Inconsistency.
3. The basics aren't being executed smoothly.
4. Extraordinary efforts are needed to accomplish ordinary goals.
5. Your superstars start marking time.
6. Meetings go dull and flat.
7. Too much reminiscing about last year or last quarter.
8. You put off decisions or hesitate to offer tough but fair criticism.
9. You're the last to hear about a problem or important development.

THE CODE

I suppose every book must answer one question to be worth reading: Why? Why did the author bother to write the work in the first place?

For me, the question is double-barreled: Why did you write the book and why did you live it? I can't think of a better way to respond than with an open letter to my two children. "Why" is a child's favorite word. As a father, I'll never grow tired of hearing those wonderful whys. And as an author, I owe them an answer most of all.

To my children, Alexandra and Frankie Pacetta:

Alle, you're two years old now and I suspect that in fifteen or twenty years, if you have any memory of the period when I was writing this book, it will be the frustration of being locked out of my study each evening. Sorry, baby, I had to do it. The "terrible twos" and writing don't mix. You'd have colored all over my notes. And, Frankie, at nine years old, you were disappointed that Dad couldn't play with you in the evenings or that we couldn't watch sports on TV together for several months. It probably seemed like a lifetime of waiting for the book to be finished so that we could get back to normal.

Well, it's finished. I hope you'll read it someday and understand what was happening upstairs in our new house in Columbus and come to realize that I was writing the book for the two of you. I want you to live in a world where it is all about winning, all about loving and caring and sharing and making full use of your God-given talent.

You know my air guitar, the one I pretend to play when the stereo is on real loud, pounding out a rock-and-roll tune? Daddy likes to make believe he's Eric Clapton or Jimi Hendrix, standing there strumming and picking away like crazy. I've done it for years. When I was in college at the University of Dayton in 1971 there was a big hit by Crosby, Stills, Nash and Young. I used to sing it all the time. What stuck with me was a line about how people who are on the road need a code. Not a secret code that kids can use to talk to each other without their teachers or parents understanding— though that's probably a pretty good idea. But what Graham Nash, who wrote the song, was getting at was that all of us need a code of conduct as we travel the road of life.

This book and this letter are my code. If I can pass it along to both of you, then I'll never have to write another word and never again leave a little girl chirping and babbling sweetly on the other side of a locked door or a boy bouncing a basketball all by himself in the driveway.

I didn't realize it for years, but I inherited the code from my dad and mom, from your Popey and Nana. As I get older, they both keep getting smarter and smarter—funny how that is!

As I was growing up, I'd hear what a great boss Popey was as a branch manager for Chase Manhattan Bank. People at the bank would tell me how proud I should be of him and what fun he was to work with. They also said he was pretty tough. I thought of that as I started my own career. Alle and Frankie, if people tell you that your dad is a good guy and a good boss, I have Popey to thank for setting the example. And Nana was the one who taught me to never, never, ever give up. She had to take care of Uncle Joey every day. It was so hard for her. She was always right there when he needed her. She helped Popey and was a great mom to my sister and me. Nana should write a book on courage someday.

One word I remember hearing a zillion times was "respect." It was drummed into my sister and me. We treated our parents and aunts and uncles with respect, and in turn learned that self-respect came from keeping our promises, telling the truth, working hard, and doing our best.

Popey was very strict. There used to be a TV program called "American Bandstand." It was absolutely forbidden in our house. When it was on the air and I was switching channels, your Popey would make me turn my head away so that I wouldn't see the kids dancing for even half a second. At Brooklyn Prep, where I went to high school, the other kids nicknamed him "Mr. Conservative." I rebelled against that in college. I guess it's why I'm still crazy for Bruce Springsteen and why I'd like nothing better than to play a gig with "the Boss" someday in Madison Square Garden.

I also rebelled against Popey's code. I coasted, I took shortcuts, I didn't use my full potential, I was self-centered and had all the answers. I finally woke up at about the time I married Mom, but I missed a lot of opportunities. I don't want that to happen to you.

I wish that someone had been there to set me straight. Of course, when I was really in a jam with no place to turn, there was always Popey. On my very first day at Xerox, I walked out of the cheap motel I was staying in and discovered that my beat-up old car had two flat tires. I was totally broke until payday. I had spent it all on new clothes. Popey wired me the money to fix the tires. But he was in New York and I was in Ohio; I needed to have somebody right here to say what he would have said: "Frank, what happened to your self-respect?"

That's the kind of boss I try to be. That's the kind of dad I try to be.

Even though I made a lot of mistakes and wasted too much time along the way, I was lucky. I had Popey and Nana's code to fall back on. Some people aren't so fortunate. They go to work in the morning and come home at night, and in between there's nothing to guide them. They get confused and scared and angry. I try to help them whenever I can. Frankie, you know how I'm always after you to keep practicing your foul shots? It's because I was a pretty good athlete, but I was lazy and didn't like to practice. I was never as good as I could have been. I don't want that to happen to you. I do the same thing at the office, Frankie. I bug the men and women who work for me to keep practicing their "foul shots."

The great thing about Popey and Nana's code—it's mine now too, and will be yours someday—is that when I leave home to go to the office I take it with me. Some people think they must live two lives: a work life and a family life. The reason I wrote the book was to show those who wanted to read it that one life—one code—is enough. What Dad does at the office is what he does at home. I give 100 percent all of the time. Anything less is cheating. It would cheat you, Alle and Frankie, if Mom and I didn't try to give 100 percent of our lives and care and effort to help you develop and to make home a place where you're secure and comfortable, and where you can learn the values that will carry you into the future.

In the same way, I would be cheating the people I work with if I didn't give them 100 percent support, encouragement and training. And I want 100 percent back from them. Anything less is the worst kind of cheating—they'd be cheating themselves.

Think of Uncle Joey. He was cheated by fate. There was nothing he or anybody else could do. He was never able to care for himself, go out on a date, ride a skateboard, get ready for the prom, or dream of being Michael Jordan the way you do, Frankie. How could I stand by and let you kids cheat yourselves? There's no way! How could I stand by and let my friends at the office cheat themselves? Not if I can help it!

I want you both to jump headfirst—and heartfirst—into life.

Don't hold back. Never stop dreaming and thinking wonderful thoughts about what can happen to you. Too often, adults lose sight of their dreams and then they can't figure out which way to turn. Don't be cynical. The world will have plenty of cynicism waiting for you! Make those dreams come true. Enjoy every day and every year.

Continue to be wide-eyed and curious, and please, please learn about everything you can. Be competitive in all you do, but remember you can only do your best. If that isn't enough, there's nothing to be ashamed of. You'll win and you'll lose; no matter what the outcome, it's important to keep trying and keep doing your best.

Laugh hard, play, don't be afraid to cry. That goes for you too, Frankie. It's okay for men to cry. Show your emotions. Last year, Popey got sick and I cried for the first time in many years. It felt good, and I told him that I loved him. Let's say those words to each other, "I love you," every day.

Mom and I will let you kids make your own decisions. Sure, we'll have our own opinions and you can bet that you'll hear them, but you have to live your own lives. I would only ask that you think through anything you do and understand the consequences. When you make a commitment, stick to it, make it work, or at least give it your best shot. Pacettas never quit.

Alle, they used to say, "It's a man's world." It's not anymore, and probably never was. At Xerox the women prove that every day. Many of them are moms and go home at night to kids just like you and Frankie. I don't know how they do it. I couldn't even come close. My dear baby daughter, you're fearless and spunky and make the end of the hardest days nothing but sheer delight; and I like the way you beat on your brother. I think you'll be the first female president of the United States.

Frankie, you're going to be a better athlete and student than I was. I'm so proud of what the teachers and coaches say about you, even if you do prefer Michael Jackson to Bruce Springsteen. You'll beat me at golf one day . . . and you'll have earned it fair and square because I never throw a game. I'll even keep taking you fishing— but don't ask me to bait the hook!

I can't wait to watch you kids grow up, and I'll be just like Popey one day—just as proud. When The Wall Street Journal *did its article about me, he got up at six in the morning and drove around to all the newsstands to buy a huge stack of newspapers.*

Then he delivered them to all your aunts and uncles and cousins. He was thrilled. I know someday that will also happen to me.

I want to wrap this letter up with another thought or two. Rewards, both monetary and spiritual, will come your way. While you're growing up, I'll give you a boost by being tough about your grades; you'll both have summer jobs to pay for college; and you'll do chores around the house. I'll love you, hug you, but I'll squeeze you to put the pressure on when you're not trying your best. It's worth it. Here's a saying that I want you to keep. It was written by T. C. Haliburton:

> *Suggest what is right; oppose what is wrong; what you think, speak; try to satisfy yourself, and not others; if you are not popular you will at least be respected; popularity lasts but a day, respect will descend as a heritage to your children.*

Respect—Alle. Respect—Frankie. In Italian the word is rispetto. It's all about rispetto.

All my love,
Dad